STATISTICAL TECHNIQUES FOR ANALYTICAL REVIEW IN AUDITING

Second Edition

STATISTICAL TECHNIQUES FOR ANALYTICAL REVIEW IN AUDITING

Second Edition

KENNETH W. STRINGER
TREVOR R. STEWART

Deloitte & Touche LLP

JOHN WILEY & SONS, INC.

New York • Chichester • Brisbane • Toronto • Singapore

Library of Congress Cataloging in Publication Data:
Stewart, Trevor R.
    Statistical techniques for analytical review in auditing / Trevor
R. Stewart, Kenneth W. Stringer. — 2nd ed.
        p.   cm.
    Rev. ed. of: Statistical techniques for analytical review in
auditing / Kenneth W. Stringer. c1986.
    Computer program developed by the former Deloitte Haskins & Sells,
now Deloitte Touche Tohmatsu International.
    Includes bibliographical references and index.
    ISBN 0-471-11816-8 (alk. paper)
    1. STAR (Computer file) 2. Auditing—Statistical methods—
Computer programs. 3. Auditing, Internal—Statistical methods—
Computer programs. I. Stringer, Kenneth W. II. Stringer Kenneth
W. Statistical techniques for analytical review in auditing.
III. Deloitte, Haskins & Sells. IV. Deloitte Touche Tohmatsu
International. V. Title.
HF5667.S85 1996
657'.45'02855369—dc20   95-37321

Printed in the United States of America

10 9 8 7 6 5 4 3 2 1

PREFACE

STAR (*Statistical Techniques for Analytical Review*) is a computer-based auditing technique that provides an objective basis for planning, performing, and evaluating analytical procedures. It uses regression analysis and other statistical modeling techniques in a manner that is optimized for audit applications; combines the statistics with professional audit judgments about materiality and reliability; and presents the results in terms that are easily understood and directly related to the objectives of the audit. Since 1971, when the first version of STAR was introduced into the practice of Deloitte Haskins & Sells, a predecessor of Deloitte & Touche LLP, STAR has proven itself highly effective and efficient on many thousands of applications on a wide variety of audit engagements.

This book explains the concepts and techniques that are implemented through the STAR Program and encourages their use by other auditors. Although this book has been written principally from the viewpoint of external auditors performing financial audits, the STAR Program is readily adaptable for use by internal auditors in business, government, and other organizations. It may also be adapted for use by management in making budget projections, reviewing variations between budgets and actual results, and making certain types of accounting estimates.

A secondary purpose of this book is to explain the mathematics incorporated in the STAR Program, so that most technical questions that might arise can be answered definitively. We emphasize, however, our view that an auditor does not need to understand all the mathematics to be able to use the STAR Program effectively; we think a good grasp of how the statistical techniques relate to the audit objectives is quite sufficient.

Wherever possible, the mathematical concepts are explained in a manner that is intuitively logical to auditors who are not mathematically oriented.

Customary mathematical formulas and symbols have been used for brevity and clarity, but they are supplemented with numerical examples when appropriate to make the mathematics easier to understand.

This book consists of nine chapters and is divided into four parts. Part One lays the foundation for the remainder of the book. The audit environment within which the STAR Program is used and the audit philosophy that gave rise to its development are described, analytical procedures are discussed in a general context, and the STAR Program is introduced with an illustration of its use.

Part Two presents the basic statistical concepts and formulas underlying regression analysis and the other statistical techniques that are incorporated in the STAR Program. It starts with an explanation of simple two-variable models, moves on to explain multivariate models, and closes with an explanation of the audit interface. The purpose of Part Two is to provide a basis for the auditor's understanding of the statistical concepts, so that their relevance to the audit objectives of analytical procedures will be more apparent. Some of the material that is treated superficially in Part Two to achieve this limited purpose is treated more comprehensively in Part Four.

Part Three deals with practical auditing applications and issues. Audit and statistical objectives are discussed, criteria for designing and improving audit models for analytical procedures are explained, and guidance is provided to help the auditor understand and use the results that are obtained from the STAR Program. This part is almost completely non-mathematical and focuses directly on the decisions to be made by the auditor. Although Part Three has been written from the perspective of the external auditor, much of the material also applies to internal auditors' use of STAR.

Part Four deals with more advanced mathematical and computational aspects of some of the subjects introduced in Part Two. The details of the statistical tests and transformations that are performed by the STAR Program are explained, as are the computational procedures employed by the Program to deal with multivariate models. Part Four is the most mathematically demanding part of this book and is included principally for the convenience of readers whose interest might otherwise require them to seek further references. For most readers, it will be the least important part because the parallel treatment of the topics in Part Two will be sufficient.

Readers who are interested in working through the illustrative calculations in this book should be aware that they may not be able to duplicate exactly the results that are shown. Rounded numbers are often shown in calculations (to make them more digestible), whereas the STAR Program uses numbers to the full precision allowed by the computer. In addition, to avoid the confusion that can be caused by spurious, insignificant differences, results have sometimes been rounded to make them agree exactly with the comparable results printed by the STAR Program. Readers, therefore, should interpret an equal sign as "approximately equal" when it is used in a numerical equation and should not assume that the usual rules for rounding numbers have been applied.

Where specific reference is made to the professional literature, statistical textbooks, or other publications, a number in brackets is included next to the reference (e.g., "SAS No. 47 [5]") and the source is cited at the end of the chapter.

The STAR Program has evolved over time. It started as a computer timesharing program in the early 1970s. It was transformed into a Microsoft® MS-DOS® program ten years later and was extensively overhauled for that platform in the early 1990s. The most recent version runs on Microsoft Windows® as an Excel™ spreadsheet "wizard."

This *second edition* contains many revisions and improvements. Most importantly, it has been thoroughly updated to reflect the changes required by SAS 56, and the practical guidance it provides has been significantly enhanced. Numerous other changes have been made throughout to clarify and enhance the presentation of the subject.

We are grateful to the many active and retired partners of Deloitte & Touche LLP and its predecessor, Deloitte Haskins & Sells, who have encouraged and supported the development and implementation of the STAR Program and the preparation of this book. We emphasize, however, that the views are ours alone and do not necessarily conform with the policies of the firm at the present time or as they may be in the future.

We acknowledge with appreciation the many helpful and constructive suggestions made by readers of the first edition of this book. In particular, we acknowledge the invaluable assistance of Ann Thornton and Magdalena Marriott, Director and Senior Manager, respectively, with Deloitte & Touche LLP, who assisted greatly in drafting many of the revisions included in this second edition. Finally, we are especially grateful to our wives, Catherine Stringer and Margaret Stewart, for their continued support, encouragement, and understanding.

KENNETH W. STRINGER
TREVOR R. STEWART

CONTENTS

PART ONE

OVERVIEW

1

THE AUDIT ENVIRONMENT

1.1 INTRODUCTION

In this chapter, the conceptual and practical environment in which auditing is conducted is discussed. The purpose is not to explain or expand on that environment, because this book is written for auditors who are already familiar with it. The purpose is simply to focus attention briefly on those features that will be helpful in viewing the remaining chapters in perspective against the background of the overall audit environment.

1.2 NATURE AND SCOPE OF AUDITING

A good definition of auditing, because of its conceptual clarity and completeness, is that of the American Accounting Association [1]:

Auditing is a systematic process of objectively obtaining and evaluating evidence regarding assertions about economic actions and events to ascertain the degree of correspondence between those assertions and established criteria and communicating the results to interested users.

The explanatory comments accompanying this definition emphasize the broad range of purposes and subject matter of auditing as follows [1]:

This definition is intentionally quite broad. While it conveys the basic idea that an audit is an investigative process, it is sufficiently comprehensive to encompass the many different purposes for which an audit might be conducted and the variety of subject matter that might be focused on in a specific audit engagement.

Frequently, the term audit (or auditing) is modified by a descriptive word or phrase to indicate either the particular purpose of the audit or the subject matter of the audit or both. For example, we frequently encounter such terms as financial audit, systems audit, management audit, operational audit, performance audit, and compliance audit. While all these terms convey the implication of different types of audit engagements, the above definition is broad enough to include all of them. . . .

This book has been written from the viewpoint of audits of financial statements by independent auditors. The concepts and techniques presented, however, are readily adaptable for use by internal auditors of business, nonprofit, or governmental organizations. Furthermore, they may also be useful in other management functions, such as the preparation of budgets or other operating plans, the comparison of actual results with those plans, and the preparation of certain kinds of accounting estimates.

1.3   AUDITING STANDARDS

Section 150.01 of the *Codification of Statements on Auditing Standards* (CSAS) issued by the American Institute of Certified Public Accountants (AICPA) [2] states that:

> Auditing standards differ from auditing procedures in that "procedures" relate to acts to be performed, whereas "standards" deal with measures of the quality of the performance of those acts and the objectives to be attained by the use of the procedures undertaken.

Auditing standards for independent auditors have been established by legislative, regulatory, or professional bodies in the major industrial countries throughout the world. Similar standards have also been established for internal auditors in some countries. At the present time, there is considerable commonality among the standards of different countries, but there are also some important differences. The International Federation of Accountants (IFAC) is trying to achieve greater uniformity by periodically issuing *Interna-*

tional Auditing Guidelines. These guidelines, however, are not binding on auditors in an individual country unless they are formally adopted by the professional or other body that has jurisdiction in that country.

Both the authoritative standards of the respective countries and the *International Auditing Guidelines* are stated in broad general terms, which leave latitude for differences in the underlying audit philosophy and methods of different auditors. For example, generally accepted auditing standards in the United States, which were formally adopted by the profession in 1948 and subsequently codified in CSAS Section 150.02 [3], include a standard of field work that states:

> Sufficient competent evidential matter is to be obtained through inspection, observation, inquiries, and confirmations to afford a reasonable basis for an opinion regarding the financial statements under audit.

Similarly, *International Auditing Guideline* 3 [4], which was issued in 1980, states that:

> The auditor should obtain sufficient appropriate audit evidence through the performance of compliance and substantive procedures to enable him to draw reasonable conclusions therefrom on which to base his opinion on the financial information.

A common element among auditing standards is their recognition that absolute accuracy and reliability of financial statements are not attainable at reasonable cost through the accounting and auditing processes. Accordingly, the standards acknowledge that a reasonable relationship should exist between the costs and benefits of these processes, as is necessary in other economic processes. For the auditor, this cost–benefit constraint manifests itself in two pervasive and interrelated concepts: materiality and audit risk.

CSAS Section 150.03 [2] includes the following statement, which is essentially the same as that included in the explanatory comments that accompanied the statement of generally accepted auditing standards adopted in 1948:

> "Materiality" and "relative risk" underlie the application of all of the standards, particularly the standards of field work and reporting.

These concepts have been referred to in numerous pronouncements on auditing standards since that date and were expressed more formally in the *Statement on Auditing Standards* (SAS) 47 [5], issued in 1983.

Because materiality is also an accounting concept, SAS 47 did not define it but rather referred to Financial Accounting Standards Board *Statement of Financial Accounting Concepts* No. 2 [6], which defines materiality as:

> . . . the magnitude of an omission or misstatement of accounting information that, in the light of surrounding circumstances, makes it probable that the judgment of a reasonable person relying on the information would have been changed or influenced by the omission or misstatement.

SAS 47 defines *audit risk* as "the risk that the auditor may unknowingly fail to appropriately modify his opinion on financial statements that are materially misstated."

For the purpose of this chapter, the critical concept in SAS 47 is the recognition that "Audit risk and materiality, among other matters, need to be considered together in determining the nature, timing, and extent of auditing procedures and in evaluating the results of those procedures."

1.4 AUDITING PROCEDURES

Auditing standards in the United States recognize four basic types of auditing procedures. The first two, which relate to the study and evaluation of the client's system of internal accounting control, consist of a review and preliminary evaluation of the system and tests of compliance with it. The second two, which are substantive tests, include analytical procedures and tests of details.

The nature, timing, and extent of substantive tests are influenced by the auditor's evaluation of the effectiveness of the system of internal accounting control and the implications of any special audit risks. Because of the inherent limitations on the effectiveness of internal accounting control systems, however, auditors are not permitted to rely completely on any such system but are required, in all cases, to perform some substantive procedures.

The audit objective of substantive tests is to obtain evidence concerning the validity and accuracy of transactions, balances, and other assertions in the financial statements or, conversely, to obtain evidence of any material misstatements in (including omissions from) the financial statements.

Analytical procedures are tests of financial information made by a study and comparison of relationships among data. They are a form of deductive reasoning under which the reliability of individual recorded transactions and balances is inferred from evidence of the reasonableness of the aggregate results.

Tests of details consist of examining individual transactions or account balances. Tests of details are a form of inductive reasoning under which the reasonableness of the aggregate results is inferred from the evidence of reliability of the details that have been tested.

Analytical procedures and tests of details are sometimes described as the "top down" and "bottom up" approaches, respectively. Auditing standards permit the auditor's reliance on substantive tests to be derived from analytical procedures, from tests of details, or from any combination of these procedures that the auditor considers appropriate in the circumstances.

Auditing pronouncements concerning specific areas of an audit generally focus more on the nature of the procedures to be performed than on the extent of their application and typically indicate only that extent of application is a matter of auditing judgment in the circumstances. This degree of generalization extends commonly to the level of implementation in specific audits. Instructions concerning auditing procedures to be applied to particular account balances or classes of transactions usually are provided in the form of audit programs, and such programs frequently include expressions such as "test sufficient items to satisfy yourself that . . . ," "examine a representative number of items," "review the account balances to determine their reasonableness," and other similar expressions. In such instructions, the criteria for satisfying oneself, for being representative, or for being reasonable are hardly more explicit than the general standards themselves. Although such instructions imply the existence of some criteria concerning the assurance desired by the auditor, they generally include no operational means for expressing or measuring it.

1.5 ROLE OF QUANTITATIVE TECHNIQUES

Auditors should be encouraged to use quantitative techniques to express their judgment about audit objectives and to measure the accomplishment of such objectives. Used in this way, the techniques become the focal point for implementing audit judgment. Deloitte & Touche LLP, the authors' firm, introduced statistical sampling for tests of details in 1962 and pioneered the use of regression analysis as a technique for analytical review in 1971. Both techniques have been used extensively since their introduction and are important elements in the firm's audit approach.

1.5.1   Audit Philosophy and Approach

A brief explanation of the philosophy underlying the firm's audit approach that gave rise to the use of the regression techniques described in this book will help readers understand the viewpoint of this book. It should be emphasized, however, that the techniques described in this book are not dependent on this particular approach.

The ultimate objectives of the firm's audit approach are derived from the profession's generally accepted auditing standards for field work. This approach utilizes a logical framework as a basis for exercising informed professional judgment. Where appropriate, mathematical methods are used to evaluate data that are susceptible to quantification. Analytical tools are used to enhance the auditor's understanding of the client's business and to adapt audit techniques to the client's situation. They help auditors to deal with the increasing complexities of financial systems, to control the costs of audits, to maintain quality control standards, and to provide exemplary client service.

This audit approach is quantitative in the sense that in an engagement there is an attempt to measure and evaluate in a practical manner the sufficiency of evidential matter that have been or are planned to be gathered. Such quantification is helpful in aggregating and integrating data and individual judgments related to the various parts of the audit. Specifically, the quantification process provides a useful method of integrating evaluations from internal accounting control, analytical procedures, and substantive tests of details into a composite judgment of audit reliability.

Not all aspects of information are susceptible to quantification, however, and quantification of certain information is necessarily somewhat subjective. The auditor's professional judgment is the most critical factor in an audit, and quantification is a useful tool in exercising that judgment. Moreover, a rational relationship should be maintained between the cost of quantifying evidential matter and the usefulness of the additional assurance provided by such quantification.

The firm's audit approach is structured and comprehensive in the sense that the individual steps in gathering and evaluating audit evidence are integrated and coordinated so that all aspects of the audit are considered from the viewpoint of the audit as a whole. The auditing objectives, procedures, and evaluation methods are integrated into a comprehensive structural framework that is encompassed in policy manuals, audit programs and questionnaires, computer programs, and staff training material.

The identification of common objectives, procedures, and evaluation methods that can be applied to a variety of circumstances and the incorporation of those common elements into a logically structured system promote both effectiveness and efficiency in auditing. Effectiveness is promoted through the concentrated study that precedes the adoption of particular features of the system and through the assurance that the inclusion of these features will prevent them from being overlooked in particular audits. Efficiency is promoted through the saving of time that otherwise would be required for repetitive analysis of situations that, although arising in different audits, involve essentially similar problems. Audit judgment and flexibility, of course, are required in interpreting and applying common objectives, procedures, and evaluation methods in all cases and in modifying or supplementing them in unusual cases.

1.5.2   Measures of Statistical Assurance

The unique feature of statistical techniques that distinguishes them from nonstatistical or subjective techniques in auditing is that they provide measures of the statistical assurance attributable to conclusions drawn from audit tests of details or analytical procedures. The terms used to describe these measures are not standardized in statistical literature and practice. The terms *reliability* and *precision* are used in this book as the measures of statistical assurance. In this context, reliability is the complement of detection risk, as the latter term is defined in SAS 47 [5].

Reliability and precision are dual measures that can be defined jointly at this stage as follows:

> Reliability is a measure of the mathematical probability reasonably attributable to a conclusion that an upper precision limit, properly calculated from the results of a statistical sample or statistical analytical review, will exceed the total errors in the population sampled or the data reviewed, assuming that any errors in the sample items examined or in the fluctuations investigated in the review are recognized by the auditor.

Statistical concepts and computations pertaining to these measures of assurance are discussed in later chapters.

From the definition given, it is clear that the statistical measures of reliability and precision can be related to the auditing concepts of reasonable assurance (or audit risk) and materiality, respectively. Consequently, an auditor's judgment about a reasonable level of audit assurance or risk and about materiality in financial statements can be expressed objectively by specifying the reliability level and precision limit desired from substantive audit tests. These specifications can be used first in planning the extent of audit tests and second in evaluating the results of the tests.

1.5.3   Audit Judgment and Statistical Techniques

It is important for readers to understand the relationship between audit judgment and statistical techniques in the design and evaluation of audit tests. Misunderstanding in this respect is often the cause of misguided opposition to the use of such techniques.

The relationship can be explained best by emphasizing that the auditor's judgment is really a combination of two separable decisions. The first decision relates to the audit objectives; the second relates to the extent of tests and the evaluation of the results necessary to accomplish the objectives.

An auditor's training and experience provide the best basis for judgment about the objectives of audit tests. In the absence of objective quantitative support, however, they may not provide the best basis for determining the extent of testing and for evaluating the results necessary to achieve those objectives. Decisions on these matters involve, implicitly or explicitly, consideration of the probabilities of forming correct or incorrect conclusions from the evidence obtained from audit tests. A generally accepted body of statistical concepts and techniques is available and is used widely and successfully in many other fields for dealing with similar probabilities and inferences.

The use of statistical techniques, wherever practicable, as a means of expressing and implementing audit judgment about objectives is the best way to combine the professional expertise available in the auditing and statistical disciplines. Conversely, the failure to use such techniques increases the risk that two separable decisions will be rolled into one subjective process, in which the audit objectives might not be expressed explicitly and the extent of tests and evaluation of results might be determined without reference to the probabilities that inevitably are involved.

Early research and experience in D&T and a growing body of academic research concerning decision-making processes in auditing and other fields tend to support the foregoing views. This research indicates that individuals are proficient in identifying relevant factors to be considered but generally are not proficient in integrating the effect of several interrelated factors that are relevant to their decisions. For example, Libby [7], on page 104, commented on this subject as follows:

> The limited ability of people to integrate information from different sources appears to be the most consistent finding of the literature reviewed in this book. . . . While some experimental results may overstate the magnitude of this problem, . . . [the] conclusion that "experts are much better at selecting and coding information than they are at integrating it" appears applicable to accountants and users of their information.

1.5.4   Systems and Models

It is useful to view the underlying philosophy just expressed in the broader perspective of *systems* and *models,* as these terms are used in current literature in other fields of study.

A *system* can be thought of somewhat abstractly as a set of elements that interact or are interrelated in a way that is worthy of study for some purpose. For the purpose of this discussion, systems have three general characteristics. First, they pertain to reality—real processes, events, results, conditions, and so on. For example, one may refer to the solar system, the social system, or the economic system. Second, individual systems usually are a part of larger systems and may interact with those or other systems. As a part of the economic system, for example, there are systems relating to banking, transportation, financial markets, or other sectors of economic activity. Third, the perception of a system depends on the purpose for which it is being studied. For example, an engineer might perceive the parts of an airplane as a flying system and be concerned with the laws of aerodynamics to optimize physical performance, whereas an economist might view the airplane as part of a transportation system and be concerned with payloads and flight schedules to optimize economic performance.

The principal systems with which accountants and auditors are concerned include the general economic system, the systems of business operations that generate the transactions of particular entities, and the accounting and internal control systems of those entities.

Models are simplified representations of the systems to which they relate. Models are needed when factors such as time, cost, physical conditions, or other constraints make it impractical to study systems completely.

The principal models with which accountants are concerned are the accounting model (e.g., the historical-cost or current-cost model), as defined by the applicable set of accounting principles, and financial statements of a particular entity. Such statements constitute a model of the system of business operations of the entity.

In addition to accounting models, auditors are concerned with audit models such as:

- Models of the client's accounting and internal control systems, which usually are in the form of questionnaires, flowcharts, or narrative descriptions, and the results of compliance tests
- Models of the system of business operations of the client, in the form of information obtained through substantive tests of details and analytical procedures
- An implicit or explicit materiality and audit risk model, used for combining the audit reliance on internal accounting control and on substantive tests to form an opinion on the financial statements being audited

Mathematical models highlight and clarify decisions about fundamental relationships and assumptions, the quantification of parameters, and uses of the model. This clarity invites, and often results in, criticism of the decisions by others. Such criticism may be constructive and result in improvement of the models. The imperfections present in an explicit mathematical model, however, are likely to be present, but not recognized, to an equal or greater degree in a vague subjective model.

To underscore this practical perspective that is so often ignored, this section is concluded with the following quotation from Forrester [8], which coincides with this book's point of view regarding mathematical models:

The validity and usefulness of dynamic (mathematical) models should be judged, not against an imaginary perfection, but in comparison with the mental and descriptive models which we would otherwise use. We should judge the formal models by their clarity of structure and compare this clarity to the confusion and incompleteness so often found in a verbal description. We should judge the models by whether or not the underlying assumptions are more clearly exposed than in the veiled background of our thought processes. We should judge the models by the certainty with which they show the correct time-varying consequences of the statements made in the models compared to the unreliable conclusions we often reach in extending our mental image of system structure to its behavioral implications. We should judge the models by the ease of communicating their structure compared to the difficulty in conveying a verbal description. By constructing a formal model, our mental image of the system is clearly exposed. General statements of size, magnitude, and influence are given numerical values. As soon as the model is so precisely stated, one is usually asked how he knows that the model is "right." A controversy often develops over whether or not reality is exactly as presented in the model. But such questions miss the first purpose of a model, which is to be clear and to provide concrete statements that can be easily communicated.

There is nothing in either the physical or social sciences about which we have perfect information. We can never prove that any model is an exact representation of "reality." Conversely, among those things of which we are aware, there is nothing of which we know absolutely nothing. So we always deal with information which is of intermediate quality—it is better than nothing and short of perfection. Models are then to be judged, not on an absolute scale that condemns them for failure to be perfect, but on a relative scale that approves them if they succeed in clarifying our knowledge and our insights into systems.

To summarize the views expressed in this section, statistical concepts and techniques typically are the best available means for implementing auditors' judgments about the objectives and results of audit tests and, accordingly, should be used wherever practicable. The remainder of this book is written from this perspective and is intended to encourage and facilitate the application of this philosophy in the performance of analytical procedures.

REFERENCES

1. American Accounting Association, "A Statement of Basic Auditing Concepts," *Studies in Accounting Research* No. 6, 1973.
2. American Institute of Certified Public Accountants, *Codification of Statements on Auditing Standards,* 1984.
3. American Institute of Certified Public Accountants, "Codification of Auditing Standards and Procedures." *Statement on Auditing Standards* 1, 1972.
4. International Federation of Accountants, "Basic Principles Governing an Audit." *International Auditing Guideline* No. 3, 1980.
5. American Institute of Certified Public Accountants, "Audit Risk and Materiality in Conducting an Audit." *Statement on Auditing Standards* 47, 1983.
6. Financial Accounting Standards Board, "Qualitative Characteristics of Accounting Information." *Statement of Financial Accounting Concepts* No. 2, 1980.
7. Robert Libby, *Accounting and Human Information Processing: Theory and Applications.* Englewood Cliffs, N.J.: Prentice-Hall, 1981.
8. Jay W. Forrester, *Principles of Systems.* Cambridge, Mass.: Wright Allen, 1968.

2

ANALYTICAL PROCEDURES

2.1 INTRODUCTION

The background and basic concepts underlying analytical procedures are discussed first in this chapter. Next, the advantages of performing analytical procedures versus tests of detail are presented. This is followed by a comparison of statistical and nonstatistical techniques for performing analytical procedures. The chapter is concluded with an overview of the statistical techniques that are the major topic of this book.

2.2 PROFESSIONAL PRONOUNCEMENTS

Under one name or another, analytical procedures have been performed as long as audits have been conducted. For example, a bulletin on the subject was issued for inclusion in the procedures manual of the authors' firm in the 1930s, and this bulletin undoubtedly was a formalization of already existing practices.

We believe the first use of the descriptive term *analytical review* in the authoritative professional pronouncements was in *Statement on Auditing Procedures* No. 54 [1], which was issued by the American Institute of Certified Public Accountants in 1972 and was subsequently included as CSAS Section 320 [2]. A further pronouncement dealing with the subject in more detail was issued as SAS 23 in 1978 [3] and was subsequently codified as CSAS Section 318. Paragraph 70 of that pronouncement included the following:

> The evidential matter required by the third standard is obtained through two general classes of auditing procedures: (a) tests of details of transactions and balances and (b) analytical review procedures applied to financial information. These procedures are referred to in this section as "substantive tests."

International Standards of Auditing (ISA) No. 12, "Analytical Procedures" issued by IFAC in 1994 [4], defines analytical procedures as "the analysis of significant ratios and trends including the resulting investigation of fluctuations and relationships that are inconsistent with other relevant information or which deviate from predicted amounts."

SAS 56 [5], which was issued in 1988, superseded SAS 23, dropped the term "review," and described analytical procedures as follows:

> Analytical procedures are an important part of the audit process and consist of evaluations of financial information made by a study of plausible relationships among both financial and nonfinancial data. Analytical procedures range from simple comparisons to the use of complex models involving many relationships and elements of data. A basic premise underlying the application of analytical procedures is that plausible relationships among data may reasonably be expected to exist and continue in the absence of known conditions to the contrary. Particular conditions that can cause variations in these relationships include, for example, specific unusual transactions or events, accounting changes, business changes, random fluctuations, or misstatements.

SAS 56 indicates that analytical procedures are used in three stages of an audit as follows "(a) to assist the auditor in planning the nature, timing and extent of other auditing procedures, (b) as a substantive test to obtain evidential matter about particular assertions related to account balances or classes of transactions, and (c) as an overall review of the financial information in the final review stage of the audit." SAS 56 further states that "Analytical procedures should be applied to some extent for the purposes referred to in (a) and (c) above for all audits of financial statements made in accordance with generally accepted auditing standards." SAS 56 explains the relationship of analytical procedures to tests of details as follows: "The auditor's reliance on substantive tests to achieve an audit objective related to a particular assertion may be derived from tests of details, from analytical procedures, or from a combination of both. The decision about which procedure or procedures to use to achieve a particular audit objective is based on the auditor's judgment on the expected effectiveness and efficiency of the available procedures."

We believe most auditors tend to rely relatively more on analytical review of income statement accounts and on tests of details of balance-sheet accounts. When tests of details of balances are performed as of an interim date, auditors often place substantial reliance on analytical procedures in updating their tests through the balance-sheet date.

Analytical procedures are a form of deductive reasoning in which the propriety of the individual details is inferred from evidence of the reasonableness of the aggregate results. They involve a comparison of the recorded financial results with results that may reasonably be expected in the circumstances. This comparison should either provide audit evidence of the reasonableness of the recorded amount or identify significant fluctuations from expected results that merit further investigation.

Two questions that are inherent in analytical procedures must be answered, either implicitly or explicitly, however the procedures are performed: (1) What results may reasonably be expected? (2) How much fluctuation from those results should be considered significant? SAS 56 has the following to say in this regard: "In planning the analytical procedures as a substantive test, the auditor should consider the amount of difference from the expectation that can be accepted without further investigation. This consideration is influenced primarily by materiality and should be consistent with the level of assurance desired from the procedures."

The concepts of reasonably expected results and of significant fluctuations from those results imply the existence of some system that can be studied and understood in sufficient depth to allow the development of a satisfactory model. Whether or not this task is feasible depends on factors such as the complexity of the system, its relative stability or volatility, the availability of information needed to study it, and the time and cost constraints on obtaining such information. In cases where analytical procedures are not effective or efficient the auditor's principal alternative is to obtain more reliance from tests of details than otherwise would be necessary.

2.3 ADVANTAGES OF SUBSTANTIVE ANALYTICAL PROCEDURES VERSUS TESTS OF DETAILS

Analytical review is often more efficient than tests of details of individual items as a method of obtaining support for balance-sheet or income statement accounts. The analytical approach may enable the auditor to focus on a few key factors that affect an entire account balance, rather than on details that may or may not affect a large number of individual items.

Analytical procedures also build on the auditor's knowledge of the client's business. In developing an expectation of the recorded amount, the auditor is utilizing knowledge of the company obtained during the planning process for the current year audit and during prior audits. The key factors affecting the company's business may be expected to be reflected in the relationships underlying financial data. The subsequent investigation of differences between the auditor's expectation and the recorded amount will further enhance the familiarity with the company's business. This will improve the auditor's ability to provide quality service and business advice to the client.

Substantive analytical procedures are typically more efficient than detail tests in auditing an account for understatement. For example, in a test for unrecorded sales, it may be easier to develop an expectation of sales and investigate any significant differences between the expectation and the recorded amount than to identify a reciprocal population from which to sample and then perform a large number of detail tests.

In the year of implementation, substantive analytical procedures are often more time consuming than performing detail testing of the account balance. This is caused by the time required to design the procedures, to obtain data used to develop the expectation, and to confirm the reliability of the data. The initial investment, however, should result in time savings in subsequent years. In addition, client assistance can reduce the auditor's effort in compiling the necessary data as long as such assistance is monitored to avoid undermining the independence and reliability of the data being collected.

Substantive analytical procedures may not always be practical. During periods of instability and rapid change in the company's business, it may be difficult to develop a sufficiently precise expectation of the recorded amount, and it may be more appropriate to perform detail testing.

2.4   NONSTATISTICAL TECHNIQUES

We refer to techniques that do not provide statistical measurements of the reliability and precision attributable to the results of analytical procedures as *nonstatistical techniques.* We discuss these techniques briefly here to provide a frame of reference for comparison with the statistical techniques presented later.

Nonstatistical techniques involve an intuitive modeling process that is so instinctive and automatic that it is seldom recognized as such. An intuitive modeling process is inherent even in making simple comparisons. For example, auditors often compare results for the current year with the budget for the current year or with results for the prior year. The model inherent in this process is that these amounts provide a reasonable expectation of current results. If this were not the case, the comparison would be pointless.

In making comparisons with prior years, auditors may revise the data for such years to eliminate unusual transactions or events in those years or to adjust them for the estimated effects of general inflation or specific changes in sales prices or costs. Such revisions are conscious efforts to improve the model. Similarly, the use of an average, a trend, or a growth rate based on more than one year implies that a longer period is expected to improve the model. Comparing information for corresponding months of one or more years implies that seasonality may be expected. Models used in nonstatistical procedures may also be expanded to include relationships between the accounts of interest to the auditor and other information, such as gross profit rates, turnover rates, unit costs, number of days outstanding, and similar statistics.

The preceding paragraphs describe the models that generally are used in nonstatistical analytical procedures. However, nonstatistical techniques for determining how much fluctuation from expected results is sufficient to require investigation by the auditor are more difficult to describe. The fluctuations to be investigated may be determined either completely subjectively or by judgmentally established cutoff points that are expressed as absolute amounts or as percentages of the related recorded amounts, which may or may not show a rational link to audit decisions about materiality and audit risk.

2.5   OVERVIEW OF STATISTICAL TECHNIQUES

This section presents a brief overview of the principal statistical techniques discussed in this book, of a computer program that is used to implement these techniques, and of the actions required by an auditor in a simple application of the techniques and the program. This overview is intended only as an introduction to the further discussion of these matters in later chapters. Accordingly, this section will leave many questions unanswered. Those that pertain to statistical concepts and calculations are discussed in Part Two of this book and those that relate to auditing decisions are discussed in Part Three.

The program discussed here is called STAR (an acronym for *Statistical Techniques for Analytical Review*). It has been used extensively since the early 1970s when D&T introduced it into the firm's audit practice. The STAR Program melds audit decisions about materiality, reliability, and other audit objectives with regression analysis and certain other statistical techniques into a tool that is able to produce results directly relevant to, and usable by, the auditor. The Program, originally developed for timesharing networks, now runs on Microsoft DOS- and Windows-based personal computers. It is used extensively throughout D&T and by other licensees.

The STAR Program incorporates an audit model for regression analysis, which combines the general regression model with an audit interface. The general regression model underlies the application of regression analysis for any purpose; the audit interface is an extension that adapts the general model to serve the auditing purposes of analytical review.

The steps involved in a STAR application are:

Designing the audit model

Running the STAR Program

Reviewing the Program printouts

Investigating unusual fluctuations

Evaluating audit results

These steps are discussed in the following subsections. They are illustrated in a specific example, which will reappear several times in this book.

The example relates to the analytical review of revenue for a fictitious computer software company, "Gamma Company," or Gamma for short. Gamma Company employs around 270 computer professionals who provide service to Gamma's clients for programming projects. Three categories of personnel are employed by Gamma—programmers, senior programmers, and analysts. Their latest hourly billing rates are $45, $70, and $100, respectively. The exact numbers fluctuate, but there are usually about 200 programmers, 50 senior programmers, and 20 analysts on the payroll at any one time. Gamma Company bills customers on the basis of time and expenses, although the company typically does not bill 100% of the time charged to each job. Historically, the company's realization has been around 90%. Everyone at Gamma fills out a monthly time report, which is used as the basis for the billing of customers.

The audit of revenue is clearly of central importance. The auditor has decided to review the relationship of recorded revenue to time at standard billing rates.

2.5.1 Designing the Audit Model

In the system-design phase, the auditor specifies his or her objectives and perception of the system, including the plausible relationships among elements of the system. In this phase, the auditor needs to draw on personal knowledge of the client's business and accounting practices. The information needed to develop the model is identified at this stage.

The auditor's first design decision has been indicated in the example. The audit purpose of the application is to test recorded revenue, and this becomes the *test variable,* also called the *dependent variable,* in regression terminology.

Next, the auditor needs to decide what data to use in the application. For the Gamma example, assume that the recorded revenue for a series of months is to be used. These monthly amounts are described as *observations* or *observed values* of the test variable, and the set for all of the months used is a part of the *data profile.* Because the observations cover a series of consecutive time periods, they are described as *time-series* observations, and that term is also used to describe the related data profile. The auditor might have decided to use the amount of revenue from each customer, in which case such amounts would have been known as *cross-sectional* observations and the data profile would have been described by the same term.

The auditor must also decide how many observations are to be included in the data profile. For the Gamma Company example, assume that the profile is to include the 36 months preceding the year being audited and the 12 months of that year. In this book, the observations for the preceding 36 months are referred to as the *base profile* and those for the current 12 months as the *test profile.* The remaining elements of the audit objective are established by the auditor's decisions about the primary direction of the test (i.e., for overstatement or understatement) and the reliability level and monetary precision limit desired.

Once the audit objectives are specified, the remaining step for the auditor in designing the audit model is to specify the *predicting variables* to be used; such variables are also called *independent variables* in regression terminology.

These consist of the balances, transactions, or other data that might have a relationship to the test variable and that would be useful in determining reasonably expected values for the latter.

For the Gamma Company example, assume that the auditor decides to use hourly billing rates, hours worked, and recorded revenue for each month, all of which are readily available from Gamma's records. Also assume that the auditor creates another variable that represents standard revenue based on hours worked and standard billing rates, which is called TIME AT STANDARD.

Figure 2.1 shows the data profile. This figure also shows EXPENSES charged to clients and COST OF SERVICES. These two variables are not used in this example but are included here as reference for later examples.

2.5.2   Running the STAR Program

The STAR Program comes with comprehensive instructions for running it in the applicable computer environment. Therefore, this phase of an application is not discussed further in this book.

2.5.3   Reviewing the Program Report

As will be explained in Chapter 7, the program report should be reviewed to determine whether or not it suggests any possibilities for improvements in the audit model. For this stage of the discussion, a brief description of the general content of the report is given. A complete STAR Program printout is included as Printout B.1.

To keep things simple at this stage, assume that TIME AT STANDARD was the only predicting variable specified by the auditor. EXPENSES, which also explain part of recorded REVENUE, will be considered in Chapter 4.

STAR uses regression analysis to compute the *regression function* that expresses the closest linear relationship between the test variable and the predicting variable in the base profile. A regression function with only one predicting variable is particularly easy to visualize. It is a straight line passing through a scatter of points that represent the base observations. This is illustrated in Figure 2.2. Such a function can be represented by the equation

$$\hat{Y}_t = a + bX_t$$

	Obs. No.	Rate			Hours Worked			$'000			
		Analysts R_A	Senior Prgmrs R_B	Prgmrs R_C	Analysts H_A	Senior Prgmrs H_B	Prgmrs H_C	Time at Standard (Note 1)	Expense EXP	Revenue REV	Cost of Services COS
Base profile, year 1	1	75	50	30	3,946	7,218	30,560	1,574	802	2,107	1,527
	2	75	50	30	3,499	7,760	28,427	1,503	785	1,915	1,531
	3	75	50	30	3,813	7,345	33,064	1,645	711	1,873	1,507
	4	75	50	30	2,816	6,465	28,180	1,380	844	1,978	1,681
	5	75	50	30	3,085	8,476	30,831	1,580	761	2,010	1,443
	6	75	50	30	4,486	7,426	28,951	1,576	716	1,969	1,507
	7	90	55	30	4,221	7,782	31,475	1,752	724	2,228	1,545
	8	90	55	30	3,057	5,443	32,467	1,549	753	2,152	1,376
	9	90	55	30	2,983	8,313	30,888	1,652	1,020	2,439	1,870
	10	90	55	30	3,463	7,700	30,506	1,650	878	2,318	1,744
	11	90	55	30	2,726	6,990	28,881	1,496	841	2,244	1,547
	12	90	55	30	3,741	7,287	31,124	1,671	900	2,357	1,864
Base profile, year 2	13	90	55	30	2,778	8,582	31,896	1,679	794	2,103	1,622
	14	90	55	30	3,522	8,353	33,510	1,782	873	2,457	1,699
	15	90	55	30	3,730	7,403	30,291	1,652	929	2,606	1,683
	16	90	55	30	3,176	9,325	31,909	1,756	875	2,493	1,712
	17	90	55	30	2,210	6,850	32,639	1,555	794	2,264	1,603
	18	90	55	30	3,225	8,467	28,834	1,621	813	2,058	1,550
	19	90	55	40	3,420	7,725	31,241	1,982	886	2,516	1,830
	20	90	55	40	3,930	8,186	31,153	2,050	913	2,533	2,052
	21	90	55	40	3,109	6,954	32,419	1,959	990	2,958	1,855
	22	90	55	40	2,838	6,868	30,074	1,836	963	2,564	1,759
	23	90	55	40	3,318	7,425	32,467	2,006	855	2,318	1,830
	24	90	55	40	4,158	6,325	36,060	2,164	1,058	2,928	2,333
Base profile, year 3	25	90	55	40	2,589	7,508	28,354	1,780	1,059	2,754	2,005
	26	90	55	40	2,857	7,704	34,268	2,054	966	2,678	2,000
	27	90	55	40	4,061	9,582	34,320	2,265	983	3,189	2,024
	28	90	55	40	3,796	7,814	33,633	2,117	956	3,067	2,182
	29	90	55	40	2,878	8,256	31,058	1,955	1,077	2,735	1,981
	30	90	55	40	3,708	8,428	31,541	2,059	1,108	3,029	2,073
	31	100	60	40	2,711	8,026	32,661	2,059	813	2,531	1,921
	32	100	60	40	3,405	7,740	32,333	2,096	1,101	2,765	2,110
	33	100	60	40	3,444	8,208	34,092	2,201	1,186	3,074	2,120
	34	100	60	40	3,074	6,843	32,455	2,016	1,092	2,651	2,058
	35	100	60	40	3,648	7,560	34,471	2,197	915	3,056	2,039
	36	100	60	40	2,603	9,140	31,848	2,083	1,062	3,155	2,157
Projection profile	37	100	60	40	2,018	8,085	34,712	2,075	909	2,757	1,979
	38	100	60	40	2,379	8,458	30,965	1,984	999	2,869	2,046
	39	100	60	40	3,804	9,241	35,275	2,346	1,035	3,168	2,072
	40	100	60	40	3,815	8,055	34,734	2,254	956	3,210	1,933
	41	100	60	40	3,733	7,572	33,451	2,166	1,348	2,958	2,433
	42	100	60	40	3,297	8,499	29,327	2,013	1,157	2,698	2,250
	43	100	70	45	3,642	8,548	33,947	2,490	969	3,412	2,224
	44	100	70	45	3,460	6,103	31,237	2,179	1,176	2,872	2,288
	45	100	70	45	2,765	6,572	33,515	2,245	1,331	3;263	2,421
	46	100	70	45	2,892	8,929	35,569	2,515	1,140	3,506	2,447
	47	100	70	45	3,224	8,267	33,055	2,389	1,347	3,452	2,338
	48	100	70	45	2,712	9,023	33,030	2,389	1,159	2,993	2,312

Note 1: Time at Standard = R_A*H_A + R_B*H_B + R_C*H_C

Figure 2.1 Gamma Company data profile.

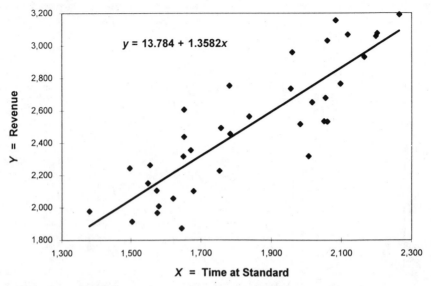

Figure 2.2 Gamma Company. Scatter diagram and line of best fit showing the base observations and the line of best fit.

where $\hat{Y}$ (pronounced "Y-hat") represents the estimate of the test variable provided by the line, and X represents the value of the predicting variable. The subscript t indicates that the values are those for observation t.

The symbols a and b represent the two parameters of the regression function: a is called the *regression constant* and b is the *regression coefficient* or simply the *coefficient* of X. The regression function for the Gamma Company example is shown in Figure 2.3 in symbols slightly different from those here, that is,

$$\hat{Y}_t = 13.78 + 1.3582 \, X_t$$

The calculation of the regression function and the other regression statistics shown on the printout, and the meaning of the statistics are explained in Chapter 3. In the equation shown on the printout, the predicting variable has been designated X_1. If there were several predicting variables, X_1, X_2, X_3, and so on would be used to represent the predicting variables, and b_1, b_2, and b_3 to represent their respective coefficients. A further subscript, t, indicates that the variables represent amounts for period t.

The regression function is used to calculate a *regression estimate* for each

Description	Input Data		Regression Function	
	Mean	Standard Error	Constant or Coefficient	Standard Error
Constant			13.78	
Predicting Variables				
X1 Time at Standard	1,832.00	246.16	1.3582	0.1359
Test Variable				
Y REVENUE	2,502.00	387.10		
Y' Expectation			2,502.00	197.9557
Coefficient of Correlation (100% = Perfect)			86%	

Expectation [Y'(t)] for observation t :
Y'(t) = 13.78 + 1.3582*X1(t)

```
================================================================================
```
AUDIT test for UNDERSTATEMENT using MP = 600, R = 3.0
```
--------------------------------------------------------------------------------
```

Obs No	Recorded Amount	Regression Estimate	Residual (Difference)	Threshold	Excess <1>	Select'n Interval	Sam ple
37	2,757	2,832	-75				
38	2,869	2,708	161	<2>			
39	3,168	3,200	-32				
40	3,210	3,075	135	<2>			
41	2,958	2,956	2				
42	2,698	2,748	-50				
43	3,412	3,396	16				
44	2,872	2,973	-101				
45	3,263	3,063	200	<2>			
46	3,506	3,430	76				
47	3,452	3,259	193	<2>			
48	2,993	3,259	-266	127	138	407	8
	37,158	36,899	259				8

<1> Significant difference in direction of test. Perform further analysis
    and inquiry to obtain and corroborate explanation. Perform optional test
    of details only if difference cannot be explained. Computed sample sizes
    less than 5 are set to the lesser of 5 and REGRESSION ESTIMATE / (MP/R).

<2> Significant difference in opposite direction to that of test. Seek an
    explanation.

Figure 2.3 Gamma Company. STAR report shows the regression function that relates REVE-
NUE as the test variable to TIME AT STANDARD as the predicting variable. The lower part
of the printout shows the result of the audit test.

observation of the test variable by simply substituting the corresponding value of the predicting variable into the equation. The differences between the actual values of the test variable and the regression estimates are known as the *residuals*.

The regression function is developed from the base profile by use of the regression module of the STAR Program. The audit interface module uses the regression function and the observations of the predicting variable in the test profile to calculate the results shown in the "audit test" section of the printout shown in Figure 2.3.

The regression estimate and residuals are calculated as just explained. The *excess to be investigated* is calculated from the reliability, precision, and direction of test specified by the auditor and from statistical calculations of the standard error of the estimates and of the most adverse possible distribution of errors among the observations of the test variable. The latter is a critical feature of the audit interface, because a material amount of error could occur in any one of the observations of the test variable or could be distributed equally or disproportionately among any number of them. The *optional sample data* are provided to assist the auditor in designing a sample for use in a test of details, if the auditor decides that such a test is needed. The audit interface calculations are explained in Chapter 5.

2.5.4   Investigating Significant Differences and Evaluating Audit Results

Having identified excess residuals that warrant investigation in the light of the auditor's specified objectives and the statistical characteristics of the data profile, the STAR Program has accomplished its purpose. Methods of investigating excesses that the Program has identified and of evaluating audit results are independent of the Program and are in the realm of audit judgment.

The differences identified for investigation could result from any of the following causes:

- An error in the recorded amount of the test variable
- An unusual transaction or event, or a change in conditions
- An error in a predicting variable, some imperfection in the audit model, or an extreme random fluctuation

Although the primary reason for investigating an excess is to determine whether it is caused by errors in the test variable, the result of the investigation may have other effects. For example, it may raise questions that need to be considered in relation to disclosures or to other phases of the audit. It may also reveal information that helps the auditor to make constructive suggestions about the client's business operations. Precautions to be taken to avoid errors in predicting variables or significant imperfections in the audit model are discussed in Chapters 6 and 7.

The investigation of an identified excess may be performed by (1) obtaining a satisfactory analytical and/or quantitative explanation of the excess or (2) performing additional tests of details of the pertinent balances or transactions. As indicated earlier, the optional sample data shown on the report are provided to assist the auditor in designing and selecting an integrated statistical sample if the latter alternative is to be followed. The investigation of excesses and the evaluation of audit results are discussed further in Chapter 7.

2.6 COMPARISON OF NONSTATISTICAL AND STATISTICAL TECHNIQUES

Although the basic concepts underlying analytical procedures are the same regardless of the techniques used, we believe that statistical techniques can offer some important advantages over nonstatistical techniques. These views on this issue are summarized in this section.

The statistical techniques described in this book can be used for making all of the types of comparisons and studies of relationships mentioned in SAS 23 and quoted in Section 2.2 of this chapter, with one general exception. That exception applies to situations in which the comparisons or studies are confined to aggregate annual data for the current audit period and for only one period or for very few other periods. In such situations, the number of observations is likely to be either insufficient to permit regression computations or inadequate to provide useful results.

In these cases, the statistical techniques tend to highlight the basic problem, which arises from the sparsity of the data being used rather than from the technique itself. The same problem, of course, is present but not highlighted when nonstatistical techniques are used. This problem can be avoided in the majority of audits by the use of data from more years or, preferably, from shorter periods (e.g., quarters or months).

The two principal advantages for using statistical techniques for analytical review relate to audit effectiveness. The first is the ability of statistical techniques to provide more objective estimates of the expected amounts of the test variables, which often comprehend complex relationships more exactly than is the case with nonstatistical estimates. The dispassionate mathematical analysis performed by the STAR Program is a safeguard against any subjective bias toward presuming that recorded amounts are correct. Furthermore, the Program is capable of assimilating and analyzing far more complex relationships than can be handled nonstatistically. The limited ability of people to handle these functions is one of the most consistent findings in research on human information processing, as noted in the quotation presented in Section 1.5.3.

The second advantage of statistical techniques lies in their ability to measure the reliability and precision that can be attributed to the audit results of a STAR application. The usefulness of these measurements and their relationship to audit objectives and judgment have already been expressed in Chapter 1.

The efficiency of statistical techniques should be assessed by weighing the costs against the benefits. The costs relate principally to development of the data profile. However, those costs are not prohibitive initially and subsequent costs tend to be insignificant.

REFERENCES

1. American Institute of Certified Public Accountants, "The Auditor's Study and Evaluation of Internal Control." *Statement on Auditing Procedures* No. 54, 1972.
2. American Institute of Certified Public Accountants. *Codification of Statements on Auditing Standards* No. 1 to No. 47, 1984.
3. American Institute of Certified Public Accountants, "Analytical Review Procedures." *Statement on Auditing Standards* No. 23, 1978.
4. International Federation of Accountants, "Analytical Procedures." *International Standards of Auditing* No. 12, 1994.
5. American Institute of Certified Public Accountants, "Analytical Procedures." *Statement on Auditing Standards* No. 56, 1988.

PART TWO

BASIC CONCEPTS OF REGRESSION ANALYSIS

3

THE SIMPLE REGRESSION MODEL

3.1 INTRODUCTION

The simplest type of regression model is one that relates a test variable to only one predicting variable as a linear function. Not only is this two-variable function relatively easy to calculate, it is also easy to visualize because it can be depicted as a straight-line graph. By contrast, a multiple or multivariate regression function that relates a test variable to two or more predicting variables is difficult to graph and is considerably more complex to calculate.

In this chapter, the calculation of a simple regression function and other regression statistics and the nature and purpose of the latter will be explained. Spending the time needed to understand the properties of simple regression functions is worthwhile, because many of these properties apply with little change to the multivariate functions that are discussed in subsequent chapters.

Before dealing with regression functions, some basic statistical concepts and notations are introduced.

3.2 BASIC STATISTICAL CONCEPTS AND NOTATION

In mathematics, it is traditional to use the symbol Σ, the Greek capital letter sigma, to indicate the process of summing a sequence of numbers. For example, if Y_t represents sales in period t, the sum of sales in periods 1 through 4 (namely, $Y_1 + Y_2 + Y_3 + Y_4$) can be written as

$$\sum_{t=1}^{4} Y_t$$

In a more general context,

$$\sum_{t=m}^{n} Y_t$$

is the sum of the quantities Y_m through Y_n. The variable t is the *index* of the summation, and m through n is its *range*. When the range of the index is obvious from the context, the sum may be written more closely and simply as $\sum Y_t$ or as $\sum Y$.

The most used and simplest type of statistical estimate is the *mean estimate*. It may also be the best estimate in situations in which there is no significant predicting variable. This type of estimate is used here as a prelude to regression estimates, because many of the concepts carry over to the latter, more complex case.

A mean estimate is made by calculating the mean of a set of sample observations and using that mean to estimate future results. For example, Figure 3.1 shows the six most recent monthly payroll totals for Company A. In the absence of any further information, it might be reasonable to use the mean of those results to estimate payroll costs for period 7. Doing this, of course, implies a model of some underlying process that, in the short term at least, tends to cause payroll costs to fluctuate around the same mean.

The mean of n observations $Y_1, Y_2, \ldots, Y_n$ of a variable Y is

$$\bar{Y} = \frac{\sum_{t=1}^{n} Y_t}{n}$$

The symbol $\bar{Y}$ is pronounced "Y bar." In the previous example

$$\bar{Y} = \frac{\sum_{t=1}^{6} Y_t}{6} = \frac{600}{6} = 100$$

In the audit applications, a mean estimate can be useful, provided that the assumption is fair that the same process that generated the base results will

Period	$ '000
1	97
2	103
3	98
4	105
5	96
6	101
Total	600
Mean	100

Figure 3.1 Company A payroll.

also generate the audit period results, more particularly, that the audit period results will tend to fluctuate around the same mean. A mean estimate is said to be *unbiased* if, on average, it will yield the true value of the underlying process, even though individual estimates might deviate.

How accurate a mean estimate is likely to be depends, in part, on how much deviation from the mean is expected. In the case of Company A, the payrolls for periods 1 through 6 cluster quite closely around their mean. If these observations are typical, then an estimate of 100 for period 7 is likely to be reasonably accurate.

By contrast with the amounts for Company A, the amounts for Company B, shown in Figure 3.2, are much more widely dispersed about their mean, although the mean is the same as that for Company A. All other things being equal, and assuming that the observed degrees of dispersion are representative of the actual variability of the underlying processes, a mean estimate for Company A is likely to be more accurate than a mean estimate for Company B.

These examples illustrate the well-known point that averages can be misleading unless it is known how well they represent the data. A facetious example is that of someone with feet in the freezer and head in the oven who is "comfortable on average." Clearly, there is a need to measure the variability in data.

Several statistics are used to measure the variability of data. Their com-

Period	$ '000
1	73
2	109
3	101
4	110
5	80
6	127
Total	600
Mean	100

Figure 3.2　Company B payroll.

mon starting point is the sum of the squares of the deviations from the mean.
These squared differences for Company A and Company B are shown in
Figure 3.3 with several other statistics to be explained now.

A useful convention, which is observed in this book, is that original variables are represented by uppercase letters and deviations from means are
represented by the corresponding lowercase letters. Thus, if Y_t is used to
designate payroll cost for period t and $\bar{Y}$ is the mean, then the deviations
$Y_t - \bar{Y}$ are designated by y_t. The sum of the squares of the deviations is

$$\Sigma y_t^2 = \Sigma (Y_t - \bar{Y})^2$$

If there are n items, their *variance* is defined as

$$s_y^2 = \frac{\Sigma y_t^2}{n - 1}$$

This statistic measures the "average" squared variability in n items and is also
known as the *mean square error.* (It is not quite an average because the divisor
is $n - 1$ rather than n.) For Company A, the variance is

$$s_y^2 = \frac{64}{5} = 12.8$$

Period	Company A			Company B		
	Y	y	y^2	Y	y	y^2
1	97	(3)	9	73	(27)	729
2	103	3	9	109	9	81
3	98	(2)	4	101	1	1
4	105	5	25	110	10	100
5	96	(4)	16	80	(20)	400
6	101	1	1	127	27	729
Totals	600	-	64	600	-	2,040

Variance	12.8	408.0
Standard Deviation	3.6	20.2

Figure 3.3   Measures of variation for sample data.

Figure 3.3 shows the payroll amounts (Y) for Companies A and B, the deviations of those amounts from their respective means (y), and the squares of those deviations (y^2). The derived statistics are explained in the text for Company A.

Just as the calculated mean is an estimate of the mean of the underlying process, the calculated variance is an estimate of the variance of that process. It might seem odd to divide by $n - 1$ rather than by n in the formula just given. The reason (stated here without proof) is to ensure that the calculated variance is an *unbiased* estimate of the variance of the underlying process. (This means that, on average, the variance based on the sample observations can be expected to equal the variance of the underlying process.) The divisor, $n - 1$, has a special name. It is called the number of *degrees of freedom*. As will be explained in Section 3.4.2, the general formula for the number of degrees of freedom in regression analysis is $n - k - 1$, where k is the number of predicting variables used. In the case of a mean estimate, there are no predicting variables.

The variance is difficult to interpret, because it is expressed in squared units rather than in the original units of the variable. A statistic that relates better to the original variable is the *standard deviation,* or *standard error.* It is the square root of the variance

$$s_y = \sqrt{s_y^2}$$

The variance and standard error are statistics that are estimates of the equivalent parameters of the assumed underlying process. The symbol σ_y^2 (σ is the Greek lowercase letter sigma) is used to denote the variance of the underlying process to distinguish it from s_y^2, the statistic that is an estimate of it. Similarly, σ_y is the standard error of the underlying process that is estimated by s_y.

In this book, the terms *variance* and *standard error* are used strictly as defined here. *Variance* should not be confused with its accounting usage in relation to standard cost or budget systems or with the general concepts of variability or variation in the broader statistical sense. The term *error* should not be confused with error in the accounting or auditing context. The use of that term originated from the application of statistics to the analysis of errors that are inherent in methods of scientific measurement.

3.3   REGRESSION FUNCTION

If the relationship between a test variable and a predicting variable is exactly linear, it can be depicted as a straight line on a graph and expressed by an equation of the form

$$Y = \alpha + \beta X$$

where α is the *constant* and β is the *coefficient* of X. For example, if the rates for a rental car are $15 per day plus 20¢ per mile, the rental for one day is expressed by the function

$$Y = 15.00 + 0.20X$$

where X is miles driven and Y is the daily rental cost. The relationship can be depicted by the line shown in Figure 3.4. This line intercepts the Y axis at $15 (the rental if X is zero) and has a slope of 0.2. The slope indicates that the line rises by 20¢ with each additional mile. Accordingly, the constant and the regression coefficient are often referred to as the *intercept* and the *slope,* respectively.

In this example, the linear function can be used to compute an exact value for Y given any value of X. Auditors are seldom able to work with relationships that are such exact predictors. They nearly always have to deal with an element of variability that, for all intents and purposes, is random. This variability can be dealt with by assuming that the relationship between X and Y can be represented by some *underlying linear relationship* (ULR) (as in the

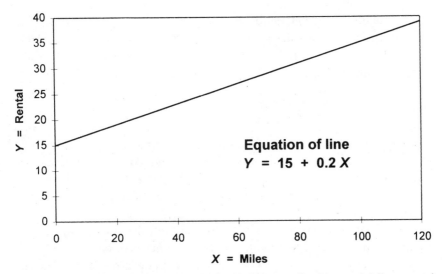

Figure 3.4 Linear function depicts the relationship between miles driven and daily car-rental cost assuming a rate of $15 per day plus 20¢ per mile. Note that the line intercepts the Y axis at 15 and that the slope of the line is 0.2.

car rental example) plus a factor to account for the random variability from the ULR. Such a model can be expressed as

$$Y_t = \alpha + \beta X_t + u_t$$

where $\alpha + \beta X_t$ is the part that represents the ULR and u_t is the part that represents the random variability. The variable u_t is also known as the *disturbance term* because it represents the disturbance from an otherwise exact relationship in period t. In statistics, a variable such as u_t that represents unpredictable and essentially random events is called a *random variable*. It is because the u_t's can be regarded as random variables that the powerful analytical tools of modern statistics can be used.

One of the most important parameters of the ULR is the *standard error of the disturbance*. It measures the expected size of the disturbances, which in auditing terms is the expected variability from the ULR. The standard error of the disturbance is denoted by σ_u.

Another important difference between the car rental example and most audit applications is that, in the car rental example, the coefficient and the constant are fixed by a rental agreement; in most audit applications, the coefficient and the constant must be estimated from empirical observations. Regression analysis provides a means of estimating the parameters α and β of the ULR from a sample of base observations. These estimates are usually denoted by a and b, respectively. The resulting regression function is written as

$$Y_t = a + bX_t + e_t$$

where $a + bX_t$ is an estimate of the ULR and e_t is the *residual* that approximates the disturbance u_t. The residuals can be used to calculate the *standard error of the regression function*. This is denoted by s_u and is an estimate of σ_u, the standard error of the disturbance. Its calculation will be explained in Section 3.4.

It is important to remember that the constant, the coefficient, and the standard error of the regression function are estimates of the parameters of the ULR and as such are subject to a certain amount of error. Had the underlying processes of the business yielded a different sample of base observations, the resulting regression function would have been slightly different. This is one of the factors that is taken into account in the audit interface.

The *method of least squares* is used to calculate a "line of best fit" for the observed data, such as the one shown in Figure 2.2 in Chapter 2. This method, first suggested in the early nineteenth century by the French mathematician Adrien Legendre, results in a line that is "best" in the sense that it minimizes the sum of the squared deviations from the line.

By following the method of least squares, the coefficient and constant for the regression function are calculated using the following steps.

1.   Calculate the means of the X's and the Y's.

$$\bar{X} = \frac{\sum X_t}{n} \qquad \bar{Y} = \frac{\sum Y_t}{n}$$

2.   Calculate the deviation of each observation from the related mean.

$$x_t = (X_t - \bar{X})$$
$$y_t = (Y_t - \bar{Y})$$

3.   Calculate the *sum of the squares* of the deviations x_t.

$$\sum x_t^2$$

4.   Calculate the *sum of the cross products* of the deviations.

$$\sum x_t y_t$$

5.   Calculate the regression coefficient.

$$b = \frac{\sum x_t y_t}{\sum x_t^2}$$

6.   Calculate the regression constant.

$$a = \bar{Y} - b\bar{X}$$

The deviations from the mean, the squared deviations, and the cross products of the deviations for the Gamma Company data of Figure 2.1 are shown in Figure 3.5. Although not needed for computing the regression function, the squared deviations of the Y values are shown because they will be used later.

The calculations for the Gamma Company are

$$b = \frac{\sum x_t y_t}{\sum x_t^2} = \frac{2,880,436}{2,120,780} = 1.3582$$

$$a = \bar{Y} - b\bar{X} = 2502 - 1.3582 \times 1832 = 13.78$$

Therefore, the Gamma Company regression function is

$$\hat{Y}_t = 13.78 + 1.3582X_t$$

The regression line for this function is illustrated in Figure 2.2 in Chapter 2.

To distinguish it from certain more exotic functions (which will be referred to in later chapters), a regression function that is calculated according to the method just given is often referred to as an *ordinary least squares* (OLS) function. A feature of an OLS function is that it always passes through the center of the points in the scatter diagram—the point that represents the mean of the variables (1832, 2502) in the example. This guarantees that the residuals

Obs. #	Original Variables X	Original Variables Y	Deviations from Means x	Deviations from Means y	Squares and Cross Products x^2	Squares and Cross Products xy	Squares and Cross Products y^2
1	1,574	2,107	(258)	(395)	66,564	101,910	156,025
2	1,503	1,915	(329)	(587)	108,241	193,123	344,569
3	1,645	1,873	(187)	(629)	34,969	117,623	395,641
4	1,380	1,978	(452)	(524)	204,304	236,848	274,576
5	1,580	2,010	(252)	(492)	63,504	123,984	242,064
6	1,576	1,969	(256)	(533)	65,536	136,448	284,089
7	1,752	2,228	(80)	(274)	6,400	21,920	75,076
8	1,549	2,152	(283)	(350)	80,089	99,050	122,500
9	1,652	2,439	(180)	(63)	32,400	11,340	3,969
10	1,650	2,318	(182)	(184)	33,124	33,488	33,856
11	1,496	2,244	(336)	(258)	112,896	86,688	66,564
12	1,671	2,357	(161)	(145)	25,921	23,345	21,025
13	1,679	2,103	(153)	(399)	23,409	61,047	159,201
14	1,782	2,457	(50)	(45)	2,500	2,250	2,025
15	1,652	2,606	(180)	104	32,400	(18,720)	10,816
16	1,756	2,493	(76)	(9)	5,776	684	81
17	1,555	2,264	(277)	(238)	76,729	65,926	56,644
18	1,621	2,058	(211)	(444)	44,521	93,684	197,136
19	1,982	2,516	150	14	22,500	2,100	196
20	2,050	2,533	218	31	47,524	6,758	961
21	1,959	2,958	127	456	16,129	57,912	207,936
22	1,836	2,564	4	62	16	248	3,844
23	2,006	2,318	174	(184)	30,276	(32,016)	33,856
24	2,164	2,928	332	426	110,224	141,432	181,476
25	1,780	2,754	(52)	252	2,704	(13,104)	63,504
26	2,054	2,678	222	176	49,284	39,072	30,976
27	2,265	3,189	433	687	187,489	297,471	471,969
28	2,117	3,067	285	565	81,225	161,025	319,225
29	1,955	2,735	123	233	15,129	28,659	54,289
30	2,059	3,029	227	527	51,529	119,629	277,729
31	2,059	2,531	227	29	51,529	6,583	841
32	2,096	2,765	264	263	69,696	69,432	69,169
33	2,201	3,074	369	572	136,161	211,068	327,184
34	2,016	2,651	184	149	33,856	27,416	22,201
35	2,197	3,056	365	554	133,225	202,210	306,916
36	2,083	3,155	251	653	63,001	163,903	426,409
	65,952	90,072	-	-	2,120,780	2,880,436	5,244,538

Mean   1,832   2,502

Figure 3.5   Gamma Company basic calculations required for regression.

related to the observations used to develop the OLS regression function will net to zero.

Once computed, the regression function can be used to calculate the estimated Y value and the residual for each observation. These amounts and the squares of the residuals for the Gamma Company are shown in Figure 3.6.

3.3.1   Mathematical Note on the Method of Least Squares

The least squares method determines the values of a and b that minimize the sum of the squared residuals in the equation

$$Y_t = a + bX_t + e_t$$

To show how this is done, first rewrite the basic equation as

$$e_t = Y_t - a - bX_t$$

For the n base profile observations, we have

$$e_1 = Y_1 - a - bX_1$$
$$e_2 = Y_2 - a - bX_2$$
$$\cdot$$
$$\cdot$$
$$\cdot$$
$$e_n = Y_n - a - bX_n$$

Squaring each side of each equation and summing the results produces

$$\sum e_t^2 = \sum (Y_t - a - bX_t)^2$$

Because $\sum e_t^2$ is a function of a and b, we can write

$$f(a, b) = \sum (Y_t - a - bX_t)^2$$

where f is the function whose value is to be minimized.

Differential calculus provides a technique for just this kind of minimization problem. The technique is to differentiate f with respect to a and to b, to set both derivatives equal to zero, and to solve simultaneously for a and b.

Obs. #	Original Variables		Regression Estimate	Residual	Squared Residual
	X	Y	Y'	e	e^2
1	1,574	2,107	2,152	(45)	1,988
2	1,503	1,915	2,055	(140)	19,643
3	1,645	1,873	2,248	(375)	140,638
4	1,380	1,978	1,888	90	8,083
5	1,580	2,010	2,160	(150)	22,420
6	1,576	1,969	2,154	(185)	34,337
7	1,752	2,228	2,393	(165)	27,339
8	1,549	2,152	2,118	34	1,181
9	1,652	2,439	2,258	181	32,933
10	1,650	2,318	2,255	63	3,993
11	1,496	2,244	2,046	198	39,344
12	1,671	2,357	2,283	74	5,427
13	1,679	2,103	2,294	(191)	36,556
14	1,782	2,457	2,434	23	525
15	1,652	2,606	2,258	348	121,435
16	1,756	2,493	2,399	94	8,878
17	1,555	2,264	2,126	138	19,105
18	1,621	2,058	2,215	(157)	24,781
19	1,982	2,516	2,706	(190)	35,997
20	2,050	2,533	2,798	(265)	70,271
21	1,959	2,958	2,674	284	80,377
22	1,836	2,564	2,507	57	3,200
23	2,006	2,318	2,738	(420)	176,674
24	2,164	2,928	2,953	(25)	621
25	1,780	2,754	2,431	323	104,088
26	2,054	2,678	2,804	(126)	15,755
27	2,265	3,189	3,090	99	9,781
28	2,117	3,067	2,889	178	31,653
29	1,955	2,735	2,669	66	4,348
30	2,059	3,029	2,810	219	47,825
31	2,059	2,531	2,810	(279)	78,014
32	2,096	2,765	2,861	(96)	9,132
33	2,201	3,074	3,003	71	5,016
34	2,016	2,651	2,752	(101)	10,182
35	2,197	3,056	2,998	58	3,394
36	2,083	3,155	2,843	312	97,402
	65,952	90,072	90,072	-	1,332,340

Figure 3.6 Gamma Company calculation of residuals and squared residuals. The regression estimate is 13.78 + 1.3582X. The residual is Y minus the regression estimate.

The function $f(a, b)$ will be a minimum for these values of a and b. Differentiating yields

$$\frac{df}{da} = -2\Sigma(Y_t - a - bX_t)$$

$$\frac{df}{db} = -2\Sigma X_t(Y_t - a - bX_t)$$

Setting these two equations equal to zero produces

$$\Sigma(Y_t - a - bX_t) = 0$$

$$\Sigma X_t(Y_t - a - bX_t) = 0$$

which may be written in what is known as the "normal form"

$$an + b\Sigma X_t = \Sigma Y_t$$

$$a\Sigma X_t + b\Sigma X_t^2 = \Sigma X_t Y_t$$

Solving these simultaneous equations for b produces

$$b = \frac{\Sigma X_t Y_t - (\Sigma X_t)(\Sigma Y_t)/n}{\Sigma X_t^2 - (\Sigma X_t)^2/n}$$

This formula for b can be written in terms of deviations from the means $\bar{X}$ and $\bar{Y}$ as

$$b = \frac{\Sigma(X_t - \bar{X})(Y_t - \bar{Y})}{\Sigma(X_t - \bar{X})^2} = \frac{\Sigma x_t y_t}{\Sigma x_t^2}$$

The constant a can be obtained by solving the first of the two normal equations

$$a = \frac{\Sigma Y_t}{n} - b\frac{\Sigma X_t}{n}$$

$$= \bar{Y} - \bar{X}$$

The method of least squares results in estimates of α and β that are known as *best linear unbiased* (or BLU) estimates. Although other methods of estimation are possible, it is the BLU property of the least squares estimators that has ensured their enduring popularity. The fact that a and b are BLU can be proved mathematically (see, e.g., Johnston [1], pp. 18–24).

The fact that a and b are "linear" estimators means that they can be expressed as linear functions of the observed Y values. That they are "unbiased" means that, if the regression procedure were to be repeated again and again with different sets of observations on X and Y, the estimates a and b would, on average, equal the parameters α and β. A biased estimate is one that, on average, does not equal the true value. That a and b are "best" linear unbiased estimators means that, of all possible linear unbiased estimators of α and β, a and b have the smallest variance. That is, they will have values that, on average, are closer to those of α and β than any other linear unbiased estimators.

3.4   OTHER REGRESSION STATISTICS

In addition to the regression function, several interesting statistics are computed by the STAR Program. Their purpose and computation are discussed in the remainder of this section.

3.4.1   Measures of Variation in Regression Analysis

If the observations of a test variable are viewed by themselves, simply as an isolated set of data without reference to the values of any predicting variables, then, as explained in Section 3.2, the fluctuations that are measured are those of the variable about its mean. Regression analysis seeks to improve on the mean estimate by "explaining" the fluctuation of the test variable from its mean. Several statistics are used to measure the extent to which this objective has been achieved. The starting point in the calculation of these statistics is the analysis of total variation.

$$Y_t - \bar{Y} = (\hat{Y}_t - \bar{Y}) + (Y_t - \hat{Y}_t)$$

or, in terms of the lower case convention

$$y_t = \hat{y}_t + e_t$$

The first component, $\hat{y}_t$, measures the difference between the regression estimate and the mean estimate—the amount of variation that has been "explained by" the regression. The second component, e_t, is the "unexplained" or residual variation arising from the deviation of the recorded value from the regression estimate. The sum of the two components is the total variation.

Because of the way in which the regression line is calculated, it turns out that the analysis of total variation as applied to each observation also holds true for the total squared variation for all observations. Therefore,

$$\sum y_t^2 = \sum \hat{y}_t^2 + \sum e_t^2$$

In other words

$$\frac{\text{Total sum}}{\text{of squares}} = \frac{\text{Explained sum}}{\text{of squares}} + \frac{\text{Residual sum}}{\text{of squares}}$$

Rearranging the terms produces

$$\sum \hat{y}_t^2 = \sum y_t^2 - \sum e_t^2$$

which highlights the fact that the variation explained by the regression analysis is simply the total variation less the variation that remains unexplained after the regression analysis.

For the Gamma Company example, the total squared variation, 5,244,538, is shown in the y^2 column in Figure 3.5. The squared unexplained variation, 1,332,340, is shown in the e^2 column in Figure 3.6. The explained variation is the difference, 3,912,198.

3.4.2 Measures of "Goodness of Fit"

From this point forward, a regression function's relative success in minimizing the unexplained variation, and thus maximizing the explained variation, will be referred to as its *goodness of fit*. Although this is not an elegant term, it is nevertheless commonly used and is concisely descriptive of the concepts that need to be communicated.

The goodness of fit of a regression function is measured using various statistics that analyze, from somewhat different perspectives, the improvement in the estimate that is brought about by regression analysis. Some of these statistics focus on the explained portion of the variation, whereas others focus on the unexplained portion. They are of interest to the user for general descriptive purposes and for comparisons among different applications.

The basic measure of unexplained variation in regression analysis is the *standard error of the regression function,* denoted by s_u. (Some authors describe this measure as the *standard error of the estimate.* In this book, it is used to describe another measure in Section 3.5.) The standard error of the regression function is essential to the analysis that is performed by STAR, because it is used in the process of identifying fluctuations that are statistically significant. The formula for the standard error of the regression function is

$$s_u = \sqrt{\frac{\sum e_t^2}{n-2}}$$

The divisor, $n-2$, is the degrees of freedom; it "averages" the residual sum of squares to produce a *mean square error.* Thus, in a sense the standard error measures the "average" of the variability represented by the residuals. In general, if there are k predicting variables in the regression, then the number of degrees of freedom is $n-k-1$. When a mean estimate rather than a regression estimate is used and there are therefore no predicting variables, $k = 0$ and the number of degrees of freedom is $n-1$ (see Section 3.2). When one predicting variable has been used, $k = 1$. Taking the square root of the mean square error reduces the latter to original units.

The standard error of the regression function is an estimate of the standard error of the disturbances from the underlying linear model. Dividing by the degrees of freedom, $n-k-1$, rather than by the number of observations, n, yields an unbiased estimate of σ_u, the standard error of the ULR.

In the Gamma Company example, the standard error of the regression function is

$$s_u = \sqrt{\frac{1,332,340}{36-2}} = 197.9557$$

as shown on the STAR printout in Figure 2.3. Thus, 197.9557 is the best estimate that can be made of σ_u, the standard error of the disturbances from the ULR.

A measure of goodness of fit that is based on explained rather than unexplained variation is the *coefficient of determination*. This coefficient, denoted by R^2, is the ratio of the explained sum of squares to the total sum of squares. Thus,

$$R^2 = \frac{\sum \hat{y}_t^2}{\sum y_t^2}$$

Because the coefficient of determination is derived from squared deviations, many people prefer to use its square root, which is called the *coefficient of correlation*

$$R = \sqrt{R^2}$$

For the Gamma Company application,

$$R^2 = \frac{3,912,198}{5,244,538} = 0.74596$$

$$R = \sqrt{0.74596} = 0.86$$

An alternative formula for the coefficient of correlation that is often used in practice is

$$R = \frac{\sum x_t y_t}{\sqrt{\sum x_t^2} \sqrt{\sum y_t^2}}$$

The formula expressed in this way is quite illuminating, because it shows how correlation depends on the interaction of the test and predicting variables. As an illustration, the scatter diagram for Y and X is divided into quadrants in Figure 3.7. Because the center of the quadrants is exactly in the middle of the scatter (at the mean of Y and X), the deviations from the means (y and x) determine into which quadrants the points fall.

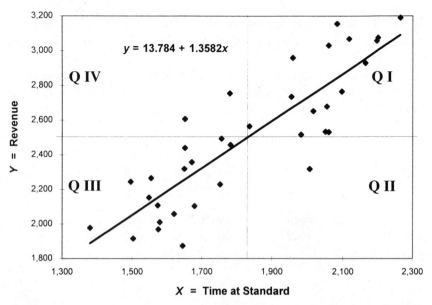

Figure 3.7   Gamma Company. Scatter diagram shows division of observation into quadrants. The predominance of points in quadrants I and III is indicative of positive correlation. In these quadrants, xy is positive. In quadrants II and IV, xy is negative.

If most of the points fall into quadrants I and III (as they do in Figure 3.7), then positive y's tend to be accompanied by positive x's and negative y's tend to be accompanied by negative x's. In both cases, the *cross product* $x_t y_t$ is positive. This indicates a positive correlation between them. Positive y's accompanied by negative x's and negative y's accompanied by positive x's (negative cross products) are indications of negative correlation. The sum of the cross products, $\sum x_t y_t$, measures the total interaction between x and y. It is divided by $\sqrt{\sum x_t^2}$ and $\sqrt{\sum y_t^2}$ to reduce it to standard units that measure the relative strength of the correlation.

In the Gamma Company example, the coefficient of correlation can be recalculated as

$$R = \frac{2,880,436}{\sqrt{2,120,780}\,\sqrt{5,244,538}} = 0.86$$

which is the same as the square root of the coefficient of determination.

3.4.3   Standard Error of the Regression Coefficient

In many applications of regression analysis, the main purpose of the application is calculation of the slope of the regression line. For instance, in an economic model that relates consumption to income, the coefficient (i.e., the slope) of the line represents the estimated marginal propensity to consume. In such applications the regression coefficient is an estimate of the coefficient of the ULR, and it is often important to know how accurate the estimate is. Because the regression function is computed from a sample of data, the regression coefficient is affected by the random variability in the sample data. If the regression function were to be computed repeatedly, each time from a different set of sample data, a degree of variability would be observed in the regression coefficient. The *standard error of the regression coefficient* measures the average of that variability.

One factor that affects the standard error of the regression coefficient is the standard error of the regression function. If the observations were all very close to the regression function, the standard error of regression would be small and it would be reasonable to suppose that, if the regression line were to be recalculated based on another set of observations, the new line would be very similar to the original one.

A second factor that affects the standard error of the regression coefficient is the total spread of values of the predicting variable as measured by the sum of the squared deviations from its mean. This, in turn, depends on the number of observations (the more, the better) and the sizes of the individual deviations (the larger, the better). A function based on a large number of widely spread observations on the predicting variable will have a coefficient with a lower standard error than one based on fewer observations or a narrower spread.

The formula for the standard error of the coefficient reflects all three of these factors.

$$s_b = \frac{s_u}{\sqrt{\sum x^2}}$$

In the Gamma Company example, the calculation is

$$s_b = \frac{197.9557}{\sqrt{2,120,780}} = 0.1359$$

3.5   STANDARD ERROR OF INDIVIDUAL RESIDUALS

In Section 3.3, it was explained that the disturbance u_t represents the amount by which the test variable fluctuates from the ULR in period t. It was explained further that the expected size of the fluctuation is represented by σ_u, the standard error of the disturbance, and that the standard error of the regression function, s_u, is an estimate of σ_u. In practice, of course, the exact formula for the ULR is not known; neither are the exact sizes of the disturbances. Instead, interest is focused on the regression function and on the residuals from that function. For reasons that are explained in Chapter 5, it is important to estimate the standard error of each residual in the audit period. This section explains the calculation.

There are two elements of variability that explain why the recorded value of a test variable differs from its regression estimate. First, the test variable might differ from the ULR (it differs by the amount of the disturbance). Second, the regression function, being an estimate of the ULR, might differ from the ULR. These elements of variability can be seen more clearly if the residual is expressed as

$$e_t = Y_t - \hat{Y}_t = (Y_t - \text{ULR}_t) + (\text{ULR}_t - \hat{Y}_t)$$

This difference is illustrated in Figure 3.8. Because the residual can be expressed in this manner, its standard error can be expressed as a combination of the standard errors of the two terms on the right-hand side of the equation. The easy part is the standard error of $Y_t - \text{ULR}_t$. In terms of the linear model, the standard error is σ_u. It is approximated by s_u.

The term $\text{ULR}_t - \hat{Y}_t$ represents the difference between the regression estimate for observation t and the estimate that would be obtained if the formula for the ULR were known. Naturally, this difference will vary depending on the particular observations that were used to generate the regression function. Its standard error is called the *standard error of the regression estimate*.

The standard error of the regression estimate depends on a number of factors.

1.   On σ_u, the inherent variability of the disturbances from the ULR. The greater this variability, the greater the variability in the various regression functions that could be generated.

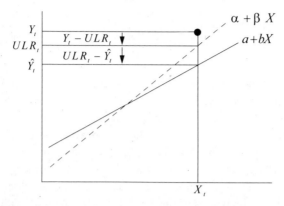

Figure 3.8 Elements of variability. This diagram shows that the variation of the recorded amount from the regression estimate can be analyzed into two parts: the part that represents the variation from the ULR, and the part that represents the difference between the ULR and the regression estimate.

2. On n, the number of base observations. The more observations that are used, the less variation is likely between the various functions that could be generated.

3. On the total spread of the X values on which the function has been based. If this spread is wide, the function is more likely to be a good estimate of the ULR over a broader range of X values than if the function were more narrowly based. This total spread is measured by $\sum x^2$, the sum of the squared differences of the base X values from their mean.

4. On the position of the X value being used for the estimate. For X values near the center of those used to generate the function, estimates should be closer to the ULR than for X values toward and beyond the fringe of the base values. This is simply because, at the center of the scatter, all the points will tend to confirm and corroborate the position of the regression function. At the fringe of the scatter, the position of the regression function is based on more tenuous information.

All these factors are brought together in the formula for the standard error of the regression estimate

$$\sigma(\text{ULR}_t - \hat{Y}_t) = \sqrt{\frac{\sigma_u^2}{n} + \frac{(X_t - \bar{X})^2}{\sum x^2}\,\sigma_u^2}$$

It is readily apparent that the value of the first term on the right-hand side of the equation varies directly with σ_u, the standard error of the ULR, and inversely with n, the number of base-period observations. The second term also varies directly with σ_u and with the distance between the particular X value and the mean of the X's. This illustrates that the standard error is smallest when X_t equals the mean of the X's and becomes larger the further X_t is from the center. In addition, the second term varies inversely with the sum of the squared deviations of the X's from their mean. This illustrates that the greater the total spread of X values, the smaller will be the standard error.

Under certain conditions, the standard error of the sum of two random variables is the square root of the sum of the squared standard errors of the variables. The conditions are met in this case, and therefore the *standard error of the individual residual* is

$$\sigma(e_t) = \sqrt{\sigma_u^2 + \frac{\sigma_u^2}{n} + \frac{(X_t - \bar{X})^2}{\sum x^2}\,\sigma_u^2}$$

which simplifies to

$$\sigma(e_t) = \sigma_u \sqrt{1 + \frac{1}{n} + \frac{(X_t - \bar{X})^2}{\sum x^2}}$$

One remaining problem is that this formula depends on σ_u, the true standard error of the disturbances, which is unknown. Thus, σ_u must be replaced by its estimator s_u, which, like the residuals on which it is based, is subject to a certain amount of random variability. The formula therefore becomes

$$s(e_t) = s_u \sqrt{1 + \frac{1}{n} + \frac{(X_t - \bar{X})^2}{\sum x^2}}$$

As we shall show in the next section, this adjustment has a subtle effect on the distribution of the residual.

3.6 DISTRIBUTION OF RESIDUALS

When the disturbance u_t is viewed as a *random variable,* it becomes meaningful to talk about the *probability* that its value will be greater than some amount, less than some amount, or between two amounts. The probabilistic behavior of random variables is the subject of a highly developed branch of mathematics known as *probability theory.* The foundations of probability theory were laid largely in the eighteenth century by French mathematicians who were hired for the highly practical job of calculating gambling odds.

As an example of how random variables occur, let us consider what might happen in 100 fair tosses of a balanced coin. Let H denote the number of heads observed in a set of 100 tosses. No formal knowledge about probability theory is needed to understand certain things about the behavior of the random variable H. Here are some examples.

- Although it is impossible to determine in advance how many heads will be observed, the most likely number is $H = 50$.
- The probability of observing exactly 50 heads in any given set of 100 tosses is fairly low because of the variability that is inherent in the underlying process.
- The probability that H will be greater than 50 is the same as the probability that it will be less than 50.
- The probability that H will be between, say, 35 and 45 is the same as the probability that it will be between 55 and 65. In other words, the probability distribution of H is symmetrical.
- The probability that H will be between 35 and 45 is greater than the probability that H will be between 25 and 35. In other words, extreme values of H are less probable than values closer to 50.

The probabilistic behavior of H can be described precisely by the so-called *binomial probability distribution.* This distribution is based on a mathematical function that can be used to determine the probability that H will lie within any range of values. Although the binomial distribution is the exact distribution of H, the behavior of H can be very well approximated by the so-called *normal probability distribution.* The graph of the normal approximation to the probability distribution of H is shown in Figure 3.9. The probability that H will lie between any two values is represented by the relative area under

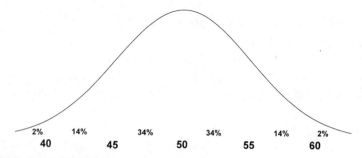

Figure 3.9 Approximate probability distribution of *H*, the number of heads in 100 fair tosses of a balanced coin. Although the binomial distribution is the exact distribution of *H*, the normal distribution shown is a good approximation. The probability that *H* will be within any range of values is represented by the area under the curve within that range. The total area is 1. For example, the area under the curve between 50 and 55 is 0.34, and therefore, the probability of 50 to 55 heads is 34%.

the curve between those two values. For example, the probability that *H* will be between 50 and 55, inclusive, is 34%. The probability that *H* will be greater than 60 is only 2%.

It can be shown that the standard error of *H* is 5. That is, if the experiment (tossing the coin 100 times) were to be repeated again and again ad infinitum, the "average" variation that would be observed is 5. A property of the normal distribution, shown in Figure 3.9, is that about 68% of the observed values of *H* will fall within 1 standard error of the mean (i.e., 45 to 55 heads) and about 95% will fall within 2 standard errors (i.e., 40 to 60 heads). In fact, the probability of *H* being greater or less than any specified amount or between any two specified amounts can be approximated from the normal distribution.

In the example, it so happens that *H* can only take on integer values between 0 and 100. The random variables that are ordinarily dealt with in analytical review can take on any value, not just whole numbers. The normal distribution is specifically applicable to such variables. If *H* is simply redefined as a random variable that is normally distributed with a mean of 50 and a standard error of 5 and the condition that it can only take on integer values is dropped, then the distribution of *H* as illustrated in Figure 3.9 is exact.

The normal probability distribution was derived in 1738 by De Moivre, an English mathematician of French origin, after he had done considerable work on the theory of games of chance. This distribution is of central importance in modern statistics, not so much because of its applicability to games of chance but because the behavior of a surprising number of things can be measured and described by statistics with probability distributions that are normal, approximately normal, or closely related to the normal. Besides the empirical evidence that supports the use of the normal distribution, there is a strong case for its use that is proved by the so-called *central limit theorem* of statistics.

The gist of the central limit theorem is that, under remarkably general conditions, the distribution of a random variable that is the net effect of a number of independent random events will tend to normality. An assumption in regression analysis, ordinarily very reasonable in practice, is that each disturbance from the ULR is the net effect of many minor unpredictable factors, or random events. Under such conditions, the central limit theorem provides strong theoretical grounds for belief that the disturbance will behave normally. In other words, if it were possible to keep the predicting variable constant and to make many observations of the related Y value, the disturbance term would be seen to follow an approximately normal distribution.

The significance of this is that an observed Y value that is significantly improbable according to the normal probability distribution provides prima facie evidence that some unusual factor (possibly an error or irregularity) has induced the disturbance. An analogous situation would occur in the coin-tossing experiment if, say, a total of 90 heads was observed in 100 tosses. Although this event can occur, the probability of its occurring if the coin is balanced and the tosses are fair is so remote that its actual occurrence would be prima facie evidence to the contrary.

The "shape" of a particular normal distribution depends on the standard error of the random variable. A random variable with a large standard error will have a flatter distribution than one with a small standard error. To avoid dealing with different-shaped distributions, statisticians frequently divide the random variable by the amount of its standard error. This yields a random variable with a standard error of 1. Therefore, if the disturbance term u_t is normally distributed with mean 0 and standard error σ_u, then u_t/σ_u has a normal distribution with a mean of 0 and a standard error of 1. Similarly, the *standardized residual*

$$\frac{e_t}{\sigma(e_t)}$$

has a normal distribution with a mean of 0 and a standard error of 1. Because the normal distribution with a mean of 0 and a standard error of 1 is used so frequently, it is given a special name, *the standard normal distribution.*

As we indicated at the end of the previous section, one problem with the formula just given for the standardized residual is that the denominator $\sigma(e_t)$ uses the true standard error of the disturbances σ_u, which is unknown. Therefore σ_u must be replaced by its estimator, s_u. The standardized residual thus becomes

$$\frac{e_t}{s(e_t)}$$

The difference between $s(e_t)$ and $\sigma(e_t)$ is that $\sigma(e_t)$ is the true (albeit un-known) standard error of e_t and therefore is a constant value; $s(e_t)$ is an estimate of $\sigma(e_t)$ and as such is susceptible to a certain amount of random variability. In other words, $s(e_t)$ is a random variable with its own probability distribution. Thus, the ratio $e_t/s(e_t)$ is the ratio of two random variables, each with its own probability distribution. The distribution of the ratio is the so-called *Student's t distribution,* or just *t distribution.*

When the regression function is based on a large number of degrees of freedom, the variability in $s(e_t)$ is very small, and the use of $s(e_t)$ instead of $\sigma(e_t)$ makes practically no difference. The distribution of the standardized residual will, for all intents and purposes, be well approximated by the standard normal distribution. However, when the degrees of freedom are few, as they often are, the use of $s(e_t)$ makes the standard normal distribution inappropriate. In fact, the derivation of the t distribution in 1908 by W. S. Gosset was motivated by a need to deal correctly with small samples. Gosset worked for Messrs. Guinness, the Irish brewing company, and needed the t distribution to deal statistically with the variety of small sample experiments required to operate the brewery properly. He published his works under the pen name "A Student": hence Student's t distribution. From a computational point of view, there is little difference between working with a normal distri-bution or a t distribution. Therefore, STAR always uses the t distribution.

Although there is only one standard normal distribution, there is a differ-ent t distribution for every number of degrees of freedom. Therefore, a ran-dom variable is often described as being "distributed as t with v degrees of freedom" to identify the appropriate t distribution. The degrees of freedom, v, is the same as the degrees of freedom associated with the standard error used to standardize the random variable. Because the estimated standard error of the residual has $n - k - 1$ degrees of freedom (k is the number of predicting variables used), the standardized residual $e_i/s(e_i)$ is distributed as t with $n - k - 1$ degrees of freedom.

In the Gamma Company example, the t distribution has 34 degrees of freedom because there are 36 base observations and 1 predicting variable (36 $- 1 - 1 = 34$). A graph of the t distribution with 34 degrees of freedom is shown in Figure 3.10.

3.6.1   Illustrative Calculation of Standardized Residual

How the calculations are made for period 48 for the Gamma Company example will be shown here. Because period 48 is the one period in which an excess to be investigated was identified (see Figure 2.3), these results will be used again when discussing the audit interface in Chapter 5.

The estimated standard error of e_{48} (the residual in period 48) can be calculated from the formula

$$s(e_{48}) = s_u \sqrt{1 + \frac{1}{n} + \frac{(X_{48} - \bar{X})^2}{\sum x^2}}$$

and the standardized residual is

$$\frac{e_{48}}{s(e_{48})}$$

All the factors that are needed for this calculation have been derived in this chapter. Some of them also appear on the STAR printout shown as Figure 2.3. They are

s_u	197.9557	Figure 2.3
n	36	Figure 3.5
X_{48}	2,389	Figure 2.1
$\bar{X}$	1,832	Figure 3.5
$\sum x^2$	2,120,780	Figure 3.5

Therefore,

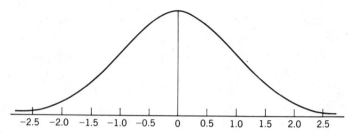

Figure 3.10   *t* Distribution with 34 degrees of freedom. The probability that *t* will fall between any two values on the horizontal axis is equal to the relative area under the curve.

$$s(e_{48}) = 197.9557 \sqrt{1 + \frac{1}{36} + \frac{(2,389 - 1,832)^2}{2,120,780}} = 214.4938$$

The degrees of freedom associated with this standard error are $36 - 1 - 1 = 34$. Therefore,

$$\frac{e_{48}}{214.4938}$$

is a point on the *t* distribution with 34 degrees of freedom.

Because the actual observed residual for period 48 shown in the STAR printout of Figure 2.3 is −266, the standardized residual is

$$\frac{-266}{214.4938} = -1.24$$

standard errors.

The *t* distribution can be used to make some statements about how the residual is expected to behave, assuming that it does not contain any error. For example, there is a 95% probability that the residual will be less than 1.69 standard errors (see Figure A.2 in Appendix A or Figure 3.8). Because 1 standard error equals 214.4938, there is a 95% probability that the residual will be less than 362 (i.e., 1.69×214.4938). It is also possible to work backward from the observed residual and make statements about the probability that a residual of that size could occur. If the residual is so large as to be significantly improbable, a reasonable conclusion is that it might have been affected by an error or some other factor not comprehended by the model.

How the standard error, the probability distribution, and the audit parameters relating to reliability and materiality are combined to provide results that are meaningful in an audit context will be shown in Chapter 5.

3.7 NONLINEAR RELATIONSHIPS

The discussion to this point has been confined to linear relationships, for which the regression function has been expressed as

$$Y = a + bX + e$$

A function in this form is described as a *linear function* because all of its parameters are linear. Aside from extensions to include more predicting variables, as will be discussed in the next chapter, a regression function in any other form is described as a *nonlinear function*. For example,

$$Y = a + bX^2 + e$$

is a nonlinear function because X^2 is a nonlinear term. In the remainder of this section, only $\hat{Y}$ (the estimate of Y) is considered and therefore the residual e is omitted from the formulas given.

Linear functions are ordinarily satisfactory for auditing purposes. For some auditing and nonauditing applications, however, the regression model may be improved by specifying a nonlinear function. Possibilities for such improvement may be indicated by (1) knowledge of underlying conditions that cause a nonlinear relationship to be expected or (2) observation of a nonlinear pattern in a graph of the variables. The remainder of this section deals with certain mathematical aspects of nonlinear functions. The discussion in Chapter 6 relating to auditing matters to be considered in designing models applies to both linear and nonlinear functions.

3.7.1 Classification and General Approach

Nonlinear regression functions can be classified broadly as (1) those that are *intrinsically nonlinear* or (2) those that are *intrinsically linear* but have nonlinear parameters. The basic distinction is that a function of the second type can be transformed into a linear form by transformation of its parameters so that the method of least squares can be applied, whereas a function of the first type cannot. Intrinsically nonlinear functions require the use of more complicated mathematics; they are not dealt with in this book nor can they be handled by the present version of the STAR Program.

Intrinsically linear functions can be classified further as those in which the transformation involves (1) only the predicting variables or (2) the test variable, either alone or in addition to the predicting variables. In the remainder of this section, it is assumed that the model includes only one predicting variable, but the general approach can be extended to models that include more predicting variables.

The number of possible curves that can be described by nonlinear functions is unlimited, but only a few types of curves are commonly used for statistical analysis. A judicious selection from the commonly used functions is generally considered adequate for most applications of regression analysis and should be adequate for auditing applications. A few of the commonly used functions and their general characteristics are discussed in the next two subsections, and numerical illustrations are included in Section 3.7.4. The purpose of this discussion and the illustrations is to assist readers in identifying nonlinear functions that may improve regression models and in making the necessary transformations.

3.7.2   Transformations of the Predicting Variable Only

If the transformation involves the predicting variable only, then the transformed variable can simply be substituted for the original variable, and the results from the STAR Program can be used in the usual way for typical analytical review applications. The only change that affects the use of the results in this case is that the coefficient b of the predicting variable relates to the transformed variable. This is important only if the coefficient is a feature of interest, which ordinarily is not the case in STAR applications.

The following three transformations are examples of transformations that involve only the predicting variable:

Type	Nonlinear function	Transformation	Linear function
Log	$\hat{Y} = a + b \ln X$	$X' = \ln X$	$\hat{Y} = a + bX'$
Reciprocal	$\hat{Y} = a + b\,(1/X)$	$X' = 1/X$	$\hat{Y} = a + bX'$
Power	$\hat{Y} = a + bX^p$	$X' = X^p$	$\hat{Y} = a + bX'$

In these examples, $\hat{Y}$ is the estimate of the test variable, X is the original predicting variable, X' is the transformed predicting variable, ln is the natural logarithm, and p is a power of X.

Each of these transformations is discussed briefly in regard to the general characteristics of the related functions and graphs are presented illustrating segments of the curves generated by them. The graphs on the left sides of the figures are for positive correlation between $\hat{Y}$ and X' and those on the right are for negative correlation, as indicated by the respective signs of the coefficient b. The sign of the coefficient, of course, depends on the data and thus is not a matter of choice. However, the type of transformation, if any, to be used is a matter to be specified in designing the model. The material to be presented shows that a discerning choice among these transformations can accommodate a variety of nonlinear relationships.

Independent log transformation. For positive coefficients in the function generated by this transformation, the value of $\hat{Y}$ increases, but at a decreasing rate, as X increases; for negative coefficients, $\hat{Y}$ decreases at a decreasing rate. This is illustrated in Figure 3.11. The curve can be inverted by using the following modified transformation, in which X_{max} is the largest value of X in the data being used:

$$X' = \ln X_{max} - \ln X$$

Independent reciprocal transformation. For positive coefficients in the function resulting from this transformation, the value of $\hat{Y}$ decreases at a decreasing rate as X increases, and the curve is concave from above; for negative coefficients, $\hat{Y}$ increases at a decreasing rate, and the curve is convex. In both cases, the curve becomes asymptotic to the X axis when X is very large. This is illustrated in Figure 3.12. This curve can be inverted so that the characteristics just described are reversed by using the following modified transformation:

$$X' = 1 - 1/X$$

Independent power transformation. The shape of the power curve that results from this transformation depends on both the sign of the coefficient b and the value of the power p. If b is positive and p is greater than 1, the value of $\hat{Y}$ increases at an increasing rate as X increases. If b is positive and p is

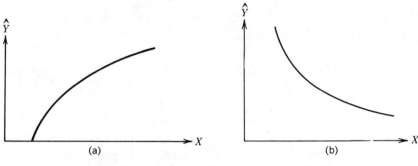

Figure 3.11   (a) $\hat{y} = a + b\ln X$;   (b) $\hat{y} = a - b\ln X$

between 0 and 1, $\hat{Y}$ increases but at a decreasing rate. These curves are illustrated in Figure 3.13a. If b is negative, the characteristics just described are reversed, as illustrated in Figure 3.13b.

The square root transformation, which is equivalent to a power of 0.5, is a common example of this type of transformation. Because the auditor can specify any value for the power p, this transformation is potentially more useful for STAR applications than the two described previously. However, the value to be specified is not likely to be intuitively apparent. If the auditor has any knowledge of underlying conditions or previous experience that is relevant for this purpose, such information obviously should be used for guidance. Otherwise, the power to be specified can be determined by an examination of a scatter diagram of the variables and some experimentation.

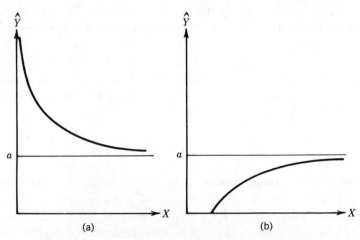

Figure 3.12   (a) $\hat{y} = a + b(1/X)$;   (b) $\hat{y} = a - b(1/X)$

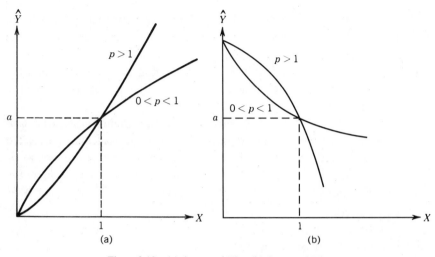

Figure 3.13   (a) $\hat{y} = a + bX^p$;   (b) $\hat{y} = a - bX^p$

Figure 3.13a may be helpful in choosing an appropriate power. The concave curve results from the equation

$$Y = a + bX^{1.5}$$

A more concave curve would indicate a power higher than 1.5. Less concavity would indicate a power lower than 1.5. The convex curve in Figure 3.13a results from the equation

$$Y = a + bX^{0.5}$$

A more convex curve would indicate a power lower than 0.5. Less convexity would indicate a power greater than 0.5. Some experimentation with different powers of X in the region of that suggested by an examination of the scatter diagram should produce a regression function with an approximately maximal coefficient of correlation. A numerical example of such an experimental approach is given in Section 3.7.4.

3.7.3   Transformations of the Test Variable

Several common types of transformation involve the test variable, either alone or in addition to the predicting variable. For all of these, the regression estimates and the related residuals and standard errors will be expressed in terms of the transformed test variable. If, for example, that variable is the logarithm of Y, then all of the results will be expressed as logarithms and the residuals cannot be used in the audit interface in the usual way. Consequently, the statistical properties of the regression function, including the best least squares fit, apply to the transformed variables but not necessarily to the original variables.

If regression results are needed in terms of the original test variable, it becomes necessary to retransform the estimates and to recalculate the related residuals and standard errors. This makes the calculation of excesses to be investigated (see Chapter 5) more complicated. For this reason, the direct use of transformations that affect the test variable in typical STAR applications is discouraged.

3.7.4   Numerical Illustrations

In this section, a few illustrations are included to demonstrate the concepts and computations just discussed and to give some general indication of the numerical effects of the transformations. For this purpose, the information shown in these illustrations is taken only from relevant portions of the STAR printouts. Where necessary, a scaling factor has been used in making the transformations so that the transformed variable will be expressed in whole numbers.

Independent log transformation.   Figure 3.14 lists three variables. The variable labeled Y_{log} was derived exactly from the X variable through the formula

$$Y = -4028 + 1749.8 \ln X$$

The variable labeled Y_{exp} was derived through the formula

$$Y_{exp} = X^{1.5}$$

The STAR printout in Figure 3.15 shows what happens when Y is regressed against $1,000 \ln X$ (denoted by $1,000 * \log(X)$ by STAR). Not surprisingly, the fit is exact apart from minor aberrations caused by rounding. Notice that the coefficient is 1.7498 rather than 1749.8. This reflects the fact that the Y is regressed against $1,000 \ln X$ rather than against $\ln X$.

	X	Y$_{log}$	Y$_{exp}$
1	100	4,030	1,000
2	200	5,243	2,828
3	300	5,952	5,196
4	400	6,456	8,000
5	500	6,846	11,180
6	600	7,165	14,697
7	700	7,435	18,520
8	800	7,669	22,627
9	900	7,875	27,000
10	1,000	8,059	31,623
11	1,100	8,226	36,483
12	1,200	8,378	41,569
13	1,300	8,518	46,872
14	1,400	8,648	52,383
15	1,500	8,769	58,095
16	1,600	8,882	64,000
17	1,700	8,988	70,093
18	1,800	9,088	76,368
19	1,900	9,182	82,819
20	2,000	9,272	89,443
	21,000	154,681	760,796

Figure 3.14   Data for independent log and power functions.

```
Stepwise Multiple Regression Model
                          Input Data              Regression Function
                  ---------------------------  -------------------------
                                   Standard    Constant or    Standard
    Description       Mean          Error      Coefficient     Error
-----------------  -----------   -----------   -----------   -----------
Constant                                        -4,027.78

Predicting Variables
X1  LOG(X)*1000    6,721.95       812.78         1.7498       0.0002

Test Variable
Y                  7,734.05      1,422.17
Y'  Expectation                                 7,734.05      0.6452

Coefficient of Correlation (100% = Perfect) Exceeds        99%


Expectation [Y'(t)] for observation t :
Y'(t) = -4,027.78 + 1.7498*X1(t)
```

Figure 3.15   Model for independent log function.

For comparative purposes, Figure 3.16 shows the STAR printout that results when Y is regressed against the original X. The residual plot in Figure
3.17 reveals a curve that is characteristic of an underlying logarithmic relationship. This clear pattern, however, results from the fact that the observations of the predicting variable are in ascending order in these illustrations,
which ordinarily would not be the case in either time-series or cross-
sectional applications.

Independent power transformation.   The STAR printout in Figure 3.18 shows
what happens when Y is regressed against $X^{1.5}$ (denoted as $X^{\wedge}1.5$ by STAR).
Not surprisingly, the fit is exact apart from minor aberrations caused by
rounding.

For comparative purposes, Figure 3.19 shows the STAR printout that results when Y is regressed against the original X. The residual plot in Figure
3.20 reveals a curve that is characteristic of an underlying power ($p > 1$)
relationship. This clear pattern, however, results from the fact that the observations of the predicting variable are in ascending order in these illustrations,
which ordinarily would not be the case in either time-series or cross-
sectional applications.

Experimental determination of a power.   Figure 3.21 shows two variables. A
scatter diagram depicting their relationship is shown in Figure 3.22.

The first step in the experimental procedure is to compare the scatter dia-

	Input Data		Regression Function	
Description	Mean	Standard Error	Constant or Coefficient	Standard Error
Constant			5,383.31	
Predicting Variables				
X1 X	1,050.00	591.61	2.2388	0.2064
Test Variable				
Y Y	7,734.05	1,422.17		
Y' Expectation			7,734.05	532.1586
Coefficient of Correlation (100% = Perfect)			93%	

Expectation [Y'(t)] for observation t :
Y'(t) = 5,383.31 + 2.2388*X1(t)

Figure 3.16   Linear model for comparison with model in Figure 3.15.

Plot of Residuals

Obs No	Recorded Amount	Regression Estimate	Residual (Difference)	Residuals Graphed in Units of One Standard Error
				-4 -3 -2 -1 0 1 2 3 4
				- --+--+--+-- --+--+--+-- -
1	4,030	5,607	-1,577	- *·
2	5,243	5,831	-588	- · *
3	5,952	6,055	-103	- *
4	6,456	6,279	177	- *
5	6,846	6,503	343	- *
6	7,165	6,727	438	- *
7	7,435	6,950	485	- *
8	7,669	7,174	495	- *
9	7,875	7,398	477	- *
10	8,059	7,622	437	- *
11	8,226	7,846	380	- *
12	8,378	8,070	308	- *
				- --+--+--+-- --+--+--+-- -
13	8,518	8,294	224	- *
14	8,648	8,518	130	- *
15	8,769	8,742	27	- *
16	8,882	8,965	-83	- *
17	8,988	9,189	-201	- *	
18	9,088	9,413	-325	- *
19	9,182	9,637	-455	- *
20	9,272	9,861	-589	- *
				- --+--+--+-- --+--+--+-- -

Figure 3.17 Regression results for the linear model in Figure 3.16.

Stepwise Multiple Regression Model

	Input Data		Regression Function	
Description	Mean	Standard Error	Constant or Coefficient	Standard Error
Constant			0.00	
Predicting Variables				
X1 X^1.5	38,039.80	28,246.63	1.0000	0.0000
Test Variable				
Y	38,039.80	28,246.63		
Y' Expectation			38,039.80	0.0004

Coefficient of Correlation (100% = Perfect) Exceeds   99%

Expectation [Y'(t)] for observation t :
Y'(t) = 0.00 + 1.0000*X1(t)

Figure 3.18 Model for independent power function.

```
Stepwise Multiple Regression Model
                             Input Data              Regression Function
                        ------------------------    ------------------------
                                     Standard        Constant or   Standard
           Description     Mean      Error           Coefficient   Error
        ------------------ --------- ------------    ----------- ------------
Constant                                             -11,645.63

Predicting Variables
X1                       1,050.00    591.61          47.3195       1.5001

Test Variable
Y                       38,039.80  28,246.63
Y'  Expectation                                      38,039.80   3,868.2910

Coefficient of Correlation (100% = Perfect)                 99%
```

Expectation [Y'(t)] for observation t :
Y'(t) = -11,645.63 + 47.3195*X1(t)

Figure 3.19   Linear model for comparison with model in Figure 3.18.

Plot of Residuals

Obs No	Recorded Amount	Regression Estimate	Residual (Difference)	Residuals Graphed in Units of One Standard Error
				-4 -3 -2 -1 0 1 2 3 4
				- | --+--+--+-- | --+--+--+-- | -
1	1,000	-6,914	7,914	- * -
2	2,828	-2,182	5,010	- . * -
3	5,196	2,550	2,646	- * -
4	8,000	7,282	718	- * -
5	11,180	12,014	-834	- * -
6	14,697	16,746	-2,049	- * -
7	18,520	21,478	-2,958	- * -
8	22,627	26,210	-3,583	- * -
9	27,000	30,942	-3,942	- * -
10	31,623	35,674	-4,051	- * -
11	36,483	40,406	-3,923	- * -
12	41,569	45,138	-3,569	- * -
				- --+--+--+-- | --+--+--+-- -
13	46,872	49,870	-2,998	- * -
14	52,383	54,602	-2,219	- * -
15	58,095	59,334	-1,239	- * -
16	64,000	64,066	-66	- * -
17	70,093	68,797	1,296	- * -
18	76,368	73,529	2,839	- * -
19	82,819	78,261	4,558	- * -
20	89,443	82,993	6,450	- * -
				- | --+--+--+-- | --+--+--+-- | -

Figure 3.20   Regression results for the linear model in Figure 3.19.

	X	Y
1	100	382
2	200	2,686
3	300	4,599
4	400	8,593
5	500	12,482
6	600	13,787
7	700	18,249
8	800	21,180
9	900	26,607
10	1,000	32,246
11	1,100	35,276
12	1,200	40,949
13	1,300	46,949
14	1,400	51,745
15	1,500	57,222
16	1,600	65,723
17	1,700	70,106
18	1,800	76,023
19	1,900	81,759
20	2,000	90,647
	21,000	757,210

Figure 3.21   Variables related by power function.

gram with Figure 3.13a. This comparison reveals that a concave function would be appropriate. A first approximation using a value of 1.5 for p seems reasonable. This value of p is used to transform the X values into values of $X' = X^{1.5}$. Then Y is regressed against X'. The STAR printout for this model is shown in Figure 3.23, and the result is summarized as iteration 1 in Figure 3.24.

A better value than 1.50 might lie on either side of 1.50. We start by choosing a value a little greater, say 1.51. This value is used to transform X into X' and Y is regressed against X'. The result for this model is shown as iteration 2 in Figure 3.24. Clearly, we are moving in the right direction from 1.50, because otherwise the coefficients of residual variation would have increased rather than decreased.

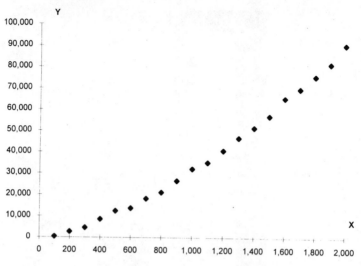

Figure 3.22   Scatter diagram relating variables shown in Figure 3.21.

We continue in the same direction and try $p = 1.52$ and then $p = 1.53$. For the latter value, the residual variation increases as shown in Figure 3.24. Therefore, $p = 1.52$ is the best value of p.

At this point, one could try to determine whether the actual "best" p is between 1.51 and 1.52 or between 1.52 and 1.53. For practical purposes, however, $p = 1.52$ will be quite accurate enough. A STAR printout for the

```
Stepwise Multiple Regression Model
                              Input Data              Regression Function
                         -------------------------    -------------------------
                                       Standard       Constant or    Standard
        Description        Mean          Error        Coefficient      Error
   ---------------------  ----------   ----------     -----------    ----------
   Constant                                              -339.76

   Predicting Variables
   X1    X^1.5            38,039.80    28,246.63          1.0042         0.0072

   Test Variable
   Y                      37,860.50    28,378.87
   Y'   Expectation                                      37,860.50      885.3140

   Coefficient of Correlation (100% = Perfect) Exceeds       99%


   Expectation [Y'(t)] for observation t :
   Y'(t) = -339.76 + 1.0042*X1(t)
```

Figure 3.23   Regression function obtained after relating Y to $X^{1.5}$.

Iteration	Trial Value	Regression Model Constant	Coefficient	Correlation
1	1.50	-339.7773	1.0042	0.9995
2	1.51	-175.1328	0.9302	0.9995
3	1.52	-12.1992	0.8616	0.9996
4	1.53	149.0625	0.7981	0.9996

Figure 3.24 Summarized results for experimental determination of a power.

```
Stepwise Multiple Regression Model
                              Input Data            Regression Function
                         ------------------------   ---------------------

                                        Standard    Constant or  Standard
      Description         Mean          Error       Coefficient  Error
-------------------      ----------    ----------   ----------   ----------
Constant                                            -12.14

Predicting Variables
X1   X^1.52             43,955.40      32,922.08     0.8616       0.0061

Test Variable
Y                       37,860.50      28,378.87
Y' Expectation                                      37,860.50    872.1523

Coefficient of Correlation (100% = Perfect) Exceeds      99%


Expectation [Y'(t)] for observation t :
Y'(t) = -12.14 + 0.8616*X1(t)

================================================================================
Plot of Residuals

Obs   Recorded    Regression   Residual       Residuals Graphed in Units
No    Amount      Estimate     (Difference)      of One Standard Error
----  ---------   ----------   -----------    -------------------------
                                              -4 -3 -2 -1  0  1  2  3  4
                                             -|--+--+--+--|--+--+--+--|-
  1        382          932       -550       -            *  |            -
  2      2,686        2,698        -12       -               *            -
  3      4,599        5,006       -407       -            *  |            -
  4      8,593        7,758        835       -               |  *         -
  5     12,482       10,896      1,586       -               |    *       -
  6     13,787       14,379       -592       -            *  |            -
  7     18,249       18,179         70       -               |*           -
  8     21,180       22,273     -1,093       -         *     |            -
  9     26,607       26,642        -35       -               |*           -
 10     32,246       31,271        975       -               |  *         -
 11     35,276       36,148       -872       -         *     |            -
 12     40,949       41,261       -312       -             * |            -
                                             -|--+--+--+--|--+--+--+--|-
 13     46,949       46,601        348       -               |*           -
 14     51,745       52,159       -414       -            *  |            -
 15     57,222       57,927       -705       -          *    |            -
 16     65,723       63,899      1,824       -               |    *       -
 17     70,106       70,068         38       -               *            -
 18     76,023       76,429       -406       -            *  |            -
 19     81,759       82,977     -1,218       -        *      |            -
 20     90,647       89,706        941       -               |  *         -
                                             -|--+--+--+--|--+--+--+--|-
```

Figure 3.25 Regression function obtained after relating Y to $X^{1.52}$.

value $p = 1.52$ is shown in Figure 3.25. The residuals from the regression function are also shown in Figure 3.25.

REFERENCES

1. J. Johnston, *Econometric Methods,* 3rd ed. New York: McGraw-Hill, 1984.

GENERAL REFERENCES

S. Chaterjee, *Regression Analysis by Example,* 2nd ed. New York: Wiley, 1991.

N. R. Draper and H. Smith, *Applied Regression Analysis,* 2nd ed. New York: Wiley, 1981.

M. Ezekiel and K. A. Fox, *Methods of Correlation and Regression Analysis,* 3rd ed. New York: Wiley, 1959.

A. Koutsoyiannis, *Theory of Econometrics,* 2nd ed. London: Macmillan, 1977.

M. S. Lewis-Beck, *Applied Regression: An Introduction.* Beverly Hills, CA: Sage Publications, 1980.

J. Neper, *Applied Linear Regression Models.* Homewood, IL: R. D. Irwin, 1983.

K. W. Smillie, *An Introduction to Regression and Correlation.* New York: Academic Press, 1966.

4

THE GENERAL REGRESSION MODEL

4.1 INTRODUCTION

The simple regression model (with one predicting variable) described in Chapter 3 is important as the starting point for understanding regression analysis, and it is adequate for many applications. There is no need, however, to limit applications to only one predicting variable, and in some cases the regression function can be improved significantly by the inclusion of several predicting variables.

In some fields, such as econometrics, it is sometimes necessary to study the simultaneous effect of dozens of predicting variables. Auditors, however, seldom need to focus on the fundamental social and economic factors that ultimately determine test variables. Instead, they are normally more concerned with the relationships between a few key variables. In practice, the ability of the STAR Program to handle up to 25 variables simultaneously is more than adequate for audit applications.

In this chapter, the extension of the simple two-variable model (one test and one predicting variable) to the three-variable model (one test and two predicting variables) is illustrated. The Gamma Company example from Chapter 3 is used to illustrate the concepts and computations.

When several predicting variables are specified by the auditor, it often happens that some do not contribute significantly to the explanatory power of the model. The STAR Program and many other regression programs incorporate a procedure that is designed to ensure that only the significant variables are included. A brief overview of this procedure is given in this chapter. Some of the statistical aspects are explained in Chapter 8, and a detailed analysis of the computational methods used in the STAR Program is provided in Chapter 9.

The final section of this chapter contains an introductory discussion of the statistical assumptions that underlie the use of regression analysis, their audit implications, and what the STAR Program does about them. A more detailed analysis is provided in Chapter 8.

4.2 REGRESSION WITH TWO PREDICTING VARIABLES

Just as two variables can be represented in a two-dimensional scatter diagram, three variables can be displayed in three dimensions. The three-dimensional equivalent of graph paper can be visualized as a box divided into small cubes. The predicting variables are graded along two horizontal edges of the box, and the test variable is graded along a vertical edge. First, every combination of the two predicting variables is marked as a dot on the floor of the box. Second, each dot is raised vertically by the amount of the test variable. The result is a swarm of dots in the box.

The relationship between the three variables can be represented by a flat plane that passes through the swarm of dots. The *plane of best fit* is the one that best fits the scatter in the sense of minimizing the sum of the squared deviations from the plane. It is the three-dimensional equivalent of a line of best fit (see Figure 2.2). A three-dimensional scatter diagram and plane of best fit are shown in Figure 4.1. A residual in this case is the vertical difference between the height of a dot and the height of the plane of best fit at the point of the plane lying directly above or below the dot. The method of least squares is used to calculate the plane that minimizes the sum of the squared residuals.

4.2.1 Regression Function

The formulas for calculating the regression function for the model with two predicting variables are similar to those for the model with one predicting variable in that they involve the squares and cross products of deviations

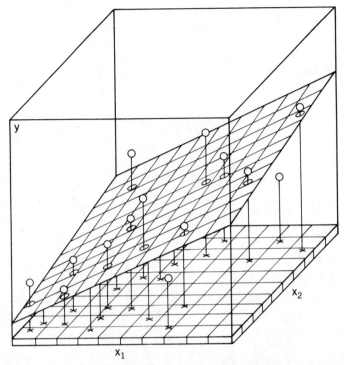

Figure 4.1 Three-dimensional scatter diagram. The points are depicted in a box. The floor of the box contains the X_1, X_2 coordinates. Each point lies directly above its X_1, X_2 coordinate. The Y coordinate is measured along a vertical edge as shown. A plane of best fit is also shown. The coefficient of X_1 is the slope of the plane in the X_1 direction; the coefficient of X_2 is the slope of the plane in the X_2 direction; and the constant is the point on the Y axis that is intercepted by the plane.

from the means of the variables; but they are more complex in that they require more combinations of these results. The data required for the Gamma Company calculations are shown in Figure 4.2. (Of course, to a computer program, the extra calculations just involve manipulation of more columns of data, and there is very little difference between calculating a regression with one predicting variable and calculating a function with several variables. A STAR report that shows the effect of including EXPENSES as a variable in the Gamma Company case is shown in Figure 4.5.)

The formulas for the regression function and the illustrative calculations for the Gamma Company are

Obs. #	Observations			Deviations			Squared Deviations			Cross Products		
	X_1	X_2	Y	x_1	x_2	y	x_1^2	x_2^2	y^2	x_1x_2	x_1y	x_2y
1	1,574	802	2,107	(258)	(109)	(395)	66,564	11,881	156,025	28,122	101,910	43,055
2	1,503	785	1,915	(329)	(126)	(587)	108,241	15,876	344,569	41,454	193,123	73,962
3	1,645	711	1,873	(187)	(200)	(629)	34,969	40,000	395,641	37,400	117,623	125,800
4	1,380	844	1,978	(452)	(67)	(524)	204,304	4,489	274,576	30,284	236,848	35,108
5	1,580	761	2,010	(252)	(150)	(492)	63,504	22,500	242,064	37,800	123,984	73,800
6	1,576	716	1,969	(256)	(195)	(533)	65,536	38,025	284,089	49,920	136,448	103,935
7	1,752	724	2,228	(80)	(187)	(274)	6,400	34,969	75,076	14,960	21,920	51,238
8	1,549	753	2,152	(283)	(158)	(350)	80,089	24,964	122,500	44,714	99,050	55,300
9	1,652	1,020	2,439	(180)	109	(63)	32,400	11,881	3,969	(19,620)	11,340	(6,867)
10	1,650	878	2,318	(182)	(33)	(184)	33,124	1,089	33,856	6,006	33,488	6,072
11	1,496	841	2,244	(336)	(70)	(258)	112,896	4,900	66,564	23,520	86,688	18,060
12	1,671	900	2,357	(161)	(11)	(145)	25,921	121	21,025	1,771	23,345	1,595
13	1,679	794	2,103	(153)	(117)	(399)	23,409	13,689	159,201	17,901	61,047	46,683
14	1,782	873	2,457	(50)	(38)	(45)	2,500	1,444	2,025	1,900	2,250	1,710
15	1,652	929	2,606	(180)	18	104	32,400	324	10,816	(3,240)	(18,720)	1,872
16	1,756	875	2,493	(76)	(36)	(9)	5,776	1,296	81	2,736	684	324
17	1,555	794	2,264	(277)	(117)	(238)	76,729	13,689	56,644	32,409	65,926	27,846
18	1,621	813	2,058	(211)	(98)	(444)	44,521	9,604	197,136	20,678	93,684	43,512
19	1,982	886	2,516	150	(25)	14	22,500	625	196	(3,750)	2,100	(350)
20	2,050	913	2,533	218	2	31	47,524	4	961	436	6,758	62
21	1,959	990	2,958	127	79	456	16,129	6,241	207,936	10,033	57,912	36,024
22	1,836	963	2,564	4	52	62	16	2,704	3,844	208	248	3,224
23	2,006	855	2,318	174	(56)	(184)	30,276	3,136	33,856	(9,744)	(32,016)	10,304
24	2,164	1,058	2,928	332	147	426	110,224	21,609	181,476	48,804	141,432	62,622
25	1,780	1,059	2,754	(52)	148	252	2,704	21,904	63,504	(7,696)	(13,104)	37,296
26	2,054	966	2,678	222	55	176	49,284	3,025	30,976	12,210	39,072	9,680
27	2,265	983	3,189	433	72	687	187,489	5,184	471,969	31,176	297,471	49,464
28	2,117	956	3,067	285	45	565	81,225	2,025	319,225	12,825	161,025	25,425
29	1,955	1,077	2,735	123	166	233	15,129	27,556	54,289	20,418	28,659	38,678
30	2,059	1,108	3,029	227	197	527	51,529	38,809	277,729	44,719	119,629	103,819
31	2,059	813	2,531	227	(98)	29	51,529	9,604	841	(22,246)	6,583	(2,842)
32	2,096	1,101	2,765	264	190	263	69,696	36,100	69,169	50,160	69,432	49,970
33	2,201	1,186	3,074	369	275	572	136,161	75,625	327,184	101,475	211,068	157,300
34	2,016	1,092	2,651	184	181	149	33,856	32,761	22,201	33,304	27,416	26,969
35	2,197	915	3,056	365	4	554	133,225	16	306,916	1,460	202,210	2,216
36	2,083	1,062	3,155	251	151	653	63,001	22,801	426,409	37,901	163,903	98,603
	65,952	32,796	90,072	-	-	-	2,120,780	560,470	5,244,538	730,408	2,880,436	1,411,469
Mean	1,832	911	2,502									

Figure 4.2 Gamma Company calculations for regression with two independent variables.

$$b_1 = \frac{(\sum x_1 y)(\sum x_2^2) - (\sum x_2 y)(\sum x_1 x_2)}{(\sum x_1^2)(\sum x_2^2) - (\sum x_1 x_2)^2}$$

$$= \frac{2{,}880{,}436 \times 560{,}470 - 1{,}411{,}469 \times 730{,}408}{2{,}120{,}780 \times 560{,}470 - 730{,}408^2}$$

$$= 0.8906$$

$$b_2 = \frac{(\sum x_2 y)(\sum x_1^2) - (\sum x_1 y)(\sum x_1 x_2)}{(\sum x_1^2)(\sum x_2^2) - (\sum x_1 x_2)^2}$$

$$= \frac{1{,}411{,}469 \times 2{,}120{,}780 - 2{,}880{,}436 \times 730{,}408}{2{,}120{,}780 \times 560{,}470 - 730{,}408^2}$$

$$= 1.3578$$

$$a = \bar{Y} - b_1 \bar{X}_1 - b_2 \bar{X}_2$$

$$= 2502 - 0.8906 \times 1832 - 1.3578 \times 911$$

$$= -366.46$$

Thus, the regression function for Gamma Company is

$$Y_t = -366.46 + 0.8906\, X_{1t} + 1.3578\, X_{2t} + e_t$$

This is the best estimate of the ULR:

$$Y_t = \alpha + \beta_1 X_{1t} + \beta_2 X_{2t} + u_t$$

The formula for a is the same as that in the case of one predicting variable, except for the addition of the term $b_2 \bar{X}_2$. Also the leftmost terms in the numerator and denominator in the formula for b_1 are those used to compute b in the model with one predicting variable, and the additional terms are those needed to compute the effect of X_2. Finally, the numerators in the formulas for b_1 and b_2 are symmetrical, and their denominators are identical.

The regression coefficients can be determined by an alternative procedure that is more intuitively appealing. An explanation of that procedure follows.

In the simple model derived in Chapter 3, in which X_1 is the only predicting variable, the extent to which X_1 has failed to explain the behavior of Y is represented by the residuals from that function. Thus, if X_2 has the potential to improve the estimates of Y, it must contribute information about the previously unexplained behavior of Y. In other words, X_2 must be correlated with the residuals.

The information that can be contributed by X_2 may overlap somewhat with information that has already been contributed by X_1. To determine the *marginal* contribution of X_2, it is first necessary to remove the influence of X_1 from X_2. This is done by regressing X_2 as a test variable against X_1. The residuals from that regression represent the marginal information content of X_2. The ideal situation is to have a very low degree of correlation between X_1 and X_2 because then the overlap will be minimal.

The correlation between the two sets of residuals (from Y vs. X_1 and from X_2 vs. X_1) represents the marginal influence of X_2. In fact, the coefficient b_2 can be calculated by regressing the residuals from Y versus X_1 as the test variable against those from X_2 versus X_1 as the predicting variable.

In the Gamma Company example (explained in Chapter 3), Y is regressed against X_1, and the regression function is

$$\hat{Y}_t = 13.78 + 1.3582\ X_{1t}$$

The residuals from this function are

$$e_t = Y_t - (13.78 + 1.3582\ X_{1t})$$

If X_2 is regressed against X_1, the function is

$$\hat{X}_{2t} = 280.05 + 0.3444\ X_{1t}$$

The residuals from this function (designated by f to distinguish them from those previously designated by e) are

$$f_t = X_{2t} - (280.05 + 0.3444\ X_{1t})$$

Finally, if e is regressed as the test variable against f as the predicting variable, the resulting regression function is

$$\hat{e}_t = 1.3578 f_t$$

The point of interest in the last function is that the coefficient of f is the same as the coefficient of X_2 in the regression function with two predicting variables. (Readers may also note that this coefficient is very close to 1.3582, the coefficient of X_1 in the original regression function with one predicting variable. This closeness is purely coincidental, and readers should not attribute any significance to it.)

There is no regression constant in the function relating e and f. This is because a regression function always passes through the mean of the variables, and because the variables in this case are actually residuals from previous regressions, their means are zero. As a result, the regression line for this regression passes through the point (0,0).

The coefficient of correlation between e and f is 0.65. This is called the *partial correlation coefficient between Y and X_2 after removing the influence of X_1*. It is a measure of the degree to which X_2 explains the variability that remains after the initial regression of Y against X_1.

It has been shown how to calculate the coefficient of X_2 given that X_1 has already been included in the function. If the respective subscripts and narrative references in the previous discussion are reversed, the same procedure can be used to calculate the coefficient of X_1 given that X_2 has been included.

Figure 4.3 shows the summary of the alternative procedure illustrated in this subsection; the illustration is extended to include the reverse calculations.

4.2.2 Other Regression Statistics

The other regression statistics for the model with two predicting variables closely parallel those for the model with one predicting variable. Therefore, the results are presented with minimum comment.

Total variation can be analyzed as follows:

Explained sum of squares	$\sum \hat{y}_t^2$	4,481,633
Residual sum of squares	$\sum e_t^2$	762,905
Total sum of squares	$\sum y_t^2$	5,244,538

The standard error of the regression function is

First Set of Regressions Regression Number	R_1	R_2	R_3	R_4
Variables				
Test	Y	X_2	Y	X_1
Predicting	X_1	X_1	X_2	X_2
Regression Function				
Constant	13.78	280.05	207.77	644.78
Coefficient	1.3582	0.3444	2.5184	1.3032
Correlation	0.86	0.67	0.82	0.67

Second Set of Regressions Regression Number	R_5		R_6
Variables - residuals from the regressions above:			
Test	R_1		R_3
Predicting	R_2		R_4
Regression Function:			
Constant	-		-
Coefficient - Applicable in three-variable model to:			
X_1			0.8906
X_2	1.3578		-
Partial Correlation	0.65		0.74

Figure 4.3   Interaction between the variables in the Gamma Company example.

$$s_u = \sqrt{\frac{\sum e_t^2}{n - k - 1}} = \sqrt{\frac{762,905}{33}} = 152.0418$$

The number of degrees of freedom is 33, which is 1 less than for the function with one predicting variable. The coefficient of determination is

$$R^2 = \frac{\sum \hat{y}_t^2}{\sum y_t^2} = \frac{4,481,633}{5,244,538} = 0.8545$$

The coefficient of correlation is

$$R = \sqrt{R^2} = 0.92$$

4.2.3   Comparison of Examples

Figure 4.4 shows a comparison of the regression statistics for the models with one and two predicting variables, respectively.

	One Variable	Two Variables
Regression constant	13.78	-366.46
Regression coefficients		
X_1	1.3582	0.8906
X_2	-	1.3578
Standard error of regression function	197.9557	152.0418
Coefficient of Correlation	0.86	0.92

Figure 4.4   Gamma Company comparison of regression statistics for one and two predicting variables, respectively.

4.3   MANY PREDICTING VARIABLES

The basic concepts explained for the model with two predicting variables hold also for extensions to three or more predicting variables. However, the complexity of the formulas expands exponentially as more variables are added. For such models, the concise notation of matrix algebra and more efficient computational methods are needed. Presented in Chapter 9, for readers who are interested, are a matrix formulation of regression analysis and a detailed account of the computational procedure that is used in the STAR Program. In this section, an intuitive treatment of the same subject matter is provided.

When a large set of predicting variables is available to the auditor, a decision has to be made about which particular subset results in the "best" regression function. One extreme is to use all the variables; another is to use none or perhaps only one. Between these two extremes, there is a wide range of choices. For example, if 15 predicting variables are available, over 32,000 different regression functions could be developed.

Some method must be used for selection of the "best" regression function from among the many possibilities. On the one hand, there is an inclination to include as many of the predicting variables as possible, because it is desirable that the regression function should explain as much as possible about the behavior of the test variable. On the other hand, there is a cost associated with each additional predicting variable, so the conflicting inclination is to use a smaller set of predicting variables. Clearly, a compromise is needed.

The ideal is a small but powerful set of predicting variables. Variables that are superfluous because they do not contribute much to the explanatory power of the regression function should be left out, but variables that make a significant contribution should be included. The STAR Program incorporates a variable selection procedure that ensures the selection of such a set. The statistical basis for this selection process is discussed in Chapter 8. The audit decisions that should precede and follow the automatic selection process are discussed in Chapter 6.

There are various statistical procedures for selecting the best regression function. One rather cumbersome approach is to have the computer generate all possible regressions and then to select the "best" one judgmentally. Another approach is to compute the regression function that includes all the predicting variables and then use a *backward elimination* procedure to eliminate, one by one, the variables that make the least significant contribution. After each elimination, the regression function is recomputed. The procedure ends when the least significant variable in the regression function nevertheless still makes a statistically significant contribution.

Yet another approach is to start with no variables in the regression and use a *forward selection* procedure to enter, one by one, the variables that make the most significant contribution to the regression. After each admission of a variable, the regression function is recomputed. The procedure ends when the most significant remaining variable would make only a statistically insignificant contribution to the regression were it to be included in the function.

The STAR Program uses a procedure that includes a forward selection procedure for admitting new variables one at a time, as well as a backward elimination procedure for removing variables that become redundant as a result of subsequent admissions. Known as *stepwise regression,* this procedure is widely regarded as one of the best procedures currently available. Its goal is to ensure that all the predicting variables that are included in the final regression function contribute significantly to it in a statistical sense.

In Figure 4.5, a STAR Program printout is shown for a Gamma Company model in which TIME AT STANDARD (X_1), EXPENSES (X_2), and COST OF SERVICES (X_3) were specified as the predicting variables. In the stepwise regression procedure, X_3 was the first predicting variable to be admitted to the function, because it is the one that correlates most highly with Y. Thereafter, X_1 and X_2 were admitted, in that order. Finally, in a backward elimination process, X_3 was eliminated from the function, because it had been rendered redundant by the combined effect of X_1 and X_2. The net result is the regression function with two predicting variables that was discussed in Section 4.2. This example will be explained in greater detail in Chapter 9.

```
Variables Specified:
Y    Revenue                                        TEST
X1   Time at Standard                            PREDICTING
X2   Expenses                                     PREDICTING
X3   Cost of Services                             PREDICTING
```

```
========================================================================
Stepwise Multiple Regression Model
                              Input Data              Regression Function
                        ---------------------------  --------------------------

                                       Standard      Constant or   Standard
      Description            Mean        Error        Coefficient    Error
----------------------  -------------  -----------   -----------   -----------
Constant                                               -366.46

Predicting Variables
X1   Time at Standard      1,832.00       246.16        0.8906        0.1406
X2   Expenses                911.00       126.54        1.3578        0.2736

Test Variable
Y    Revenue               2,502.00       387.10
Y'   Expectation                                      2,502.00      152.0418

Coefficient of Correlation (100% = Perfect)              92%
```

```
Expectation [Y'(t)] for observation t :
Y'(t) = -366.46 + 0.8906*X1(t) + 1.3578*X2(t)
```

Figure 4.5   Gamma Company. In this application, three predicting variables were specified. In the stepwise multiple regression procedure, X_3, COST OF SERVICES, was the first variable to be admitted to the function because it is the variable that is most highly correlated with Y. In the following steps, X_3 was eliminated because that variable was rendered redundant by the joint effect of X_1 and X_2.

4.4   STATISTICAL ASSUMPTIONS, TESTS, AND TRANSFORMATIONS

The soundness of an inference based on a model is usually affected by the validity of certain assumptions about that model. In regression analysis, certain statistical assumptions are implicit in the use of the model. Although the expectation that these assumptions will be appropriate for most applications is reasonable, the assumptions ordinarily cannot be proven to be true or false for any particular analysis. Nevertheless, statistical tests can be made to determine whether they appear to be reasonable. These tests help to ensure that the auditor is alerted to problems that may affect the usefulness of the application.

In this section, an introduction to the statistical assumptions, tests, and transformations of regression is presented. A more detailed and mathematical treatment is set forth in Chapter 8.

4.4.1   Discontinuity of the Regression Function

One assumption that is implied in the linear model is that of *continuity*, that is, that the same underlying linear relationship applies through the range of the observations. Its opposite, *discontinuity*, can occur within the base period or between the base period and the audit period. The STAR Program applies tests for both types of discontinuity to time-series applications.

The data shown in Figure 4.6 display discontinuity. These data relate to the production of a chemical for 1972, 1973, and 1974. The two variables are PRODUCTION COSTS and QUANTITY PRODUCED. A significant discontinuity occurred after the price of oil began to skyrocket in late 1973. The discontinuity is apparent from Figure 4.7, where it can be seen that the regression function that best represents the first 24 months is very different from the function that represents the last 12 months; and neither coincides with the function that best represents the full 36 months of the base period.

A partial STAR printout for the regression is shown in Figure 4.8. A complete printout is included as Printout B.2 in Appendix B. The discontinuity clearly shows up in the graph of the residuals.

A statistical indication of discontinuity within the base period can sometimes occur in situations in which the practical significance of the discontinuity is negligible. These situations can arise when, in spite of the discontinuity, the regression function still manages to fit the observations for the entire base

	1972			1973			1974	
		Prod			Prod			Prod
	Quant	Costs		Quant	Costs		Quant	Costs
Obs. #	X	Y	Obs. #	X	Y	Obs. #	X	Y
1	388	312	13	739	568	25	581	414
2	392	320	14	604	448	26	614	528
3	422	320	15	787	613	27	1,152	1,010
4	494	363	16	644	452	28	733	699
5	721	512	17	734	540	29	916	831
6	470	334	18	653	531	30	673	638
7	567	390	19	815	621	31	707	675
8	263	185	20	467	363	32	750	710
9	683	528	21	698	515	33	692	711
10	483	395	22	825	605	34	742	723
11	499	380	23	717	546	35	679	660
12	496	375	24	805	629	36	626	633

Figure 4.6   Universal Chemicals data for 1972 to 1974.

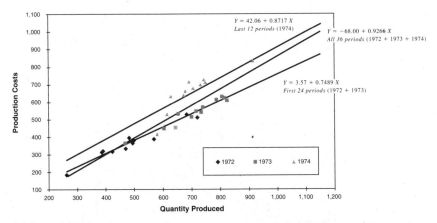

Figure 4.7 Universal Chemicals. The scatter diagram relates PRODUCTION COSTS to QUANTITY PRODUCED. The points on the diagram are represented by the number of the year in which the observation occurred. Three regression functions are shown.

a. $\hat{Y} = 3.7545 + 0.7489X$. This is the line of best fit for the first 24 periods (years 1 and 2).

b. $\hat{Y} = 42.0620 + 0.8717X$. This is the line of best fit for the last 12 periods (year 3).

c. $\hat{Y} = -67.9933 + 0.9266X$. This is the line of best fit for the entire 36 periods (years 1, 2, and 3).

The discontinuity between the data for the first 24 months and the last 12 months is apparent.

period very well. As a result, the STAR Program does not test for discontinuity when the coefficient of correlation is 95% or greater.

Discontinuity is typically caused by changes in conditions. If these are anticipated when the model is first specified, the problem of discontinuity can sometimes be avoided. If discontinuity occurs, the cause can sometimes be found by reviewing the residuals. This review could suggest a new predicting variable, the inclusion of which might eliminate the discontinuity. It might suggest, however, that the discontinuity is best eliminated by discarding the observations for the first year in the base profile. Because the consequences of discontinuity within the base period can be quite significant, the STAR Program does not allow a model that is discontinuous in the base period to be used for audit purposes.

The test for discontinuity between the base period and the audit period is similar in concept to the test for discontinuity within the base period, although the mechanics are somewhat different.

When discontinuity is detected between the base period and the audit period, the STAR Program prints a message to alert the auditor. The presence of such discontinuity should not be interpreted to mean that the regression

Plot of Residuals

Obs No	Recorded Amount	Regression Estimate	Residual (Difference)	Residuals Graphed in Units of One Standard Error
				-4 -3 -2 -1 0 1 2 3 4
				-|--+--+--+-- |--+--+--+-- |-
1	312	297	15	`*`
2	320	301	19	`*`
3	320	329	-9	`*`
4	363	395	-32	`*`
5	512	603	-91	`*`
6	334	373	-39	`*`
7	390	462	-72	`*`
8	185	158	27	`*`
9	528	568	-40	`*`
10	395	385	10	`*`
11	380	399	-19	`*`
12	375	396	-21	`*`
				-|--+--+--+-- |--+--+--+-- |-
13	568	619	-51	`*`
14	448	496	-48	`*`
15	613	663	-50	`*`
16	452	532	-80	`*`
17	540	615	-75	`*`
18	531	540	-9	`*`
19	621	689	-68	`*`
20	363	361	2	`*`
21	515	490	25	`*`
22	605	698	-93	`*`
23	546	599	-53	`*`
24	629	680	-51	`*`
				-|--+--+--+-- |--+--+--+-- |-
25	414	474	-60	`*`
26	528	505	23	`*`
27	1,010	998	12	`*`
28	699	614	85	`*`
29	831	782	49	`*`
30	638	559	79	`*`
31	675	590	85	`*`
32	710	629	81	`*`
33	711	576	135	`*`
34	723	622	101	`*`
35	660	564	96	`*`
36	633	516	117	`*`
				-|--+--+--+-- |--+--+--+--|-

Figure 4.8 Universal Chemicals. This is a plot of the residuals from a regression function that relates PRODUCTION COSTS to QUANTITY PRODUCED. The regression function has been based on the full 36 months. Note the discontinuity that occurs at around period 26. This was due to the increase in the price of oil at about that time.

function is inappropriate for performing analytical review. In many cases the reason for the apparent discontinuity is the very effectiveness of the regression function in identifying that errors or unusual transactions occurred in the audit period. All the facts of the particular circumstance should be considered in deciding whether the application is appropriate for the auditor's analytical review objective.

4.4.2 Autocorrelation

An assumption that is implicit in the ULR is that the disturbances from the ULR are statistically independent of one another over time. In other words, a regression estimate in period t could not be improved by knowledge of what the residual was in period $t - 1$ or any other prior period.

In the business world, events frequently move in a time-related pattern. When those events are the minor factors that underlie the behavior of the residuals, a pattern in the residuals may result. In this case, the assumption of statistical independence is not valid, because regression estimates can be improved by factoring in the pattern in the residuals.

A systematic pattern of interdependence over time is known as *autocorrelation*, or *serial correlation*, of the disturbances. It ordinarily results in a visible pattern in the residuals from the regression function. If significant autocorrelation is ignored and the ordinary regression function is used, two things could happen. First, the regression projections might not be as good as they could be because the pattern would be ignored rather than factored in. Second, the calculations of the standard error might be distorted. It is desirable therefore to test for autocorrelation and, if possible, to circumvent the problem that autocorrelation can cause.

Because significant autocorrelation is a potentially serious problem, the STAR Program automatically tests for it and then, if necessary, adjusts for it by calculating a so-called *generalized regression function.* This test is performed only in time-series applications (not in cross-sectional applications), because autocorrelation relates to patterns over time.

Although it is possible to consider patterns that are highly complex, a satisfactory assumption for most purposes is that autocorrelated disturbances follow a so-called *first-order autoregressive scheme.* This means that the disturbance in period t consists of a part that depends on the residual in period $t - 1$, the previous period, and a part that is random and independent.

Figure 4.9 contains three graphs showing zero autocorrelation and two

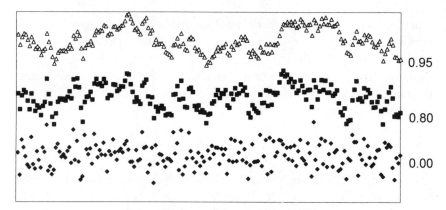

Figure 4.9   Three graphs show residuals generated by different autoregressive schemes. The autoregressive parameters (coefficients of autocorrelation) that have been used are 0.0, 0.6, and 0.9. Note how the pattern in the residuals gets more pronounced as the coefficient of autocorrelation increases.

different degrees of first-order autocorrelation. The coefficients of autocorrelation that are illustrated are positive numbers between 0 and 1. Accordingly, the related patterns are such that runs of positive residuals and runs of negative residuals are observed. A scatter diagram in which the residuals were plotted against themselves lagged by one period would show noticeable positive correlation.

Negative autocorrelation is also possible. In that case, the coefficient of autocorrelation is a negative number between 0 and −1, and successive residuals tend to flip-flop between positive and negative to a greater extent than they would when there is no autocorrelation. A scatter diagram of the residuals plotted against themselves lagged one period would show a negative correlation. Negative autocorrelation is seldom a factor in business data and therefore is not dealt with in the STAR Program or in this book.

To illustrate what STAR does about autocorrelation, the data for a company called Autocorp Inc. are shown in Figure 4.10. Figure 4.11 shows how the STAR Program handled the application, in which WAGES was regressed against HOURS WORKED. The residuals from the generalized function show very little pattern, whereas the residuals from the original function show a strong pattern. A complete STAR Program printout is included as Printout B.3 in Appendix B.

The generalized function for the Autocorp application is shown in Figure 4.11. How it was calculated is explained in detail in Chapter 8. The function

	Obs *	Wages Y	Hours X
Base	1	649	287
	2	660	303
	3	766	355
	4	747	347
	5	804	356
	6	686	299
	7	709	312
	8	745	319
	9	904	370
	10	968	384
	11	824	342
	12	806	328
	13	928	373
	14	884	346
	15	881	362
	16	901	396
	17	986	411
	18	863	346
	19	987	393
	20	989	377
	21	945	389
	22	980	401
	23	885	363
	24	942	390
	25	986	406
	26	887	370
	27	989	401
	28	1,042	425
	29	943	394
	30	905	383
	31	963	382
	32	945	419
	33	820	352
	34	862	378
	35	786	360
Audit	36	805	417
	37	867	442
	38	925	482
	39	1,200	537
		34,364	14,697

Figure 4.10 Autocorp Inc. wages and hours-worked data.

shows that, for periods 2 through 39, regression estimates are made with the formula

$$\hat{Y}_t = 118.85 + 2.0386 \, X_t + 0.6209 \, e_{t-1}$$

where 0.6209 is the coefficient of autocorrelation and

Obs No	Y	Est	e	Plot of Residuals from Ordinary Least Squares Regression Function	Est	e	Plot of Residuals from Generalized Least Squares Regression Function
				-4 -3 -2 -1 0 1 2 3 4			-4 -3 -2 -1 0 1 2 3 4
1	649	665	-16		661	-12	
2	660	706	-46		702	-42	
3	766	839	-73		795	-29	
4	747	819	-72		779	-32	
5	804	842	-38		795	9	
6	686	696	-10		703	-17	
7	709	729	-20		729	-20	
8	745	747	-2		741	4	
9	904	877	27		858	46	
10	968	913	55		921	47	
11	824	806	18		857	-33	
12	806	770	36		792	14	
13	928	885	43		891	37	
14	884	816	68		854	30	
15	881	857	24		894	-13	
16	901	944	-43		941	-40	
17	986	982	4		941	45	
18	863	816	47		842	21	
19	987	936	51		944	43	
20	989	895	94		929	60	
21	945	926	19		975	-30	
22	980	957	23		957	23	
23	885	860	25		886	-1	
24	942	929	13		930	12	
25	986	969	17		964	22	
26	887	877	10		898	-11	
27	989	957	32		945	44	
28	1,042	1,018	24		1,018	24	
29	943	939	4		957	-14	
30	905	911	-6		913	-8	
31	963	908	55		901	62	
32	945	1,003	-58		1,014	-69	
33	820	831	-11		819	1	
34	862	898	-36		879	-17	
35	786	852	-66		836	-50	
36	805	998	-193		928	-123	
37	867	1,061	-194		918	-51	
38	925	1,164	-239		1,007	-82	
39	1,200	1,304	-104		1,104	96	

Figure 4.11   Autocorp Inc. The ordinary least squares regression is

$$\hat{Y} = -68.0822 + 2.5554X$$

The generalized regression function (after the second iteration) is

$$\hat{Y}_1 = 118.85 + 2.0386 \, X_1 + \sqrt{1 - 0.6209^2} \, e_1$$

$$\hat{Y}_1 = 118.85 + 2.0386 \, X_1 + 0.6209 \, e_{t-1}, \text{ for } t > 1$$

where $e_t = Y_t - (118.85 + 2.0386 \, X_t)$

Note how the pattern that is apparent in the left-hand plot has been eliminated in the right-hand plot.

$$e_t = Y_t - (118.85 + 2.0386\ X_t)$$

The generalized function works rather like an ordinary regression function except that it includes a term that factors in the previous residual. For example, to calculate the regression estimate for period 38, it is necessary first to calculate e_{37}.

$$e_{37} = 867 - (118.85 + 2.0386 \times 442) = -153$$

Then the generalized regression estimate is

$$\hat{Y}_{38} = 118.85 + 2.0386 \times 482 + 0.6209 \times (-153) = 1107$$

In period 1, because the previous residual is not known, the regression estimate is made with a different formula ($Y_1 = 649$ and $X_1 = 287$):

$$e_1 = 649 - (118.85 + 2.0386 \times 287) = -55$$
$$\hat{Y}_1 = 118.85 + 2.0386 \times 287 + \sqrt{1 - 0.6209^2} \times (-55) = 661$$

If the adjustment works, the generalized function will not be autocorrelated. If, however, the generalized regression function is autocorrelated, the function is treated only as a first approximation and the procedure is repeated, and this time the generalized function is treated as if it were the original ordinary function. The result is a new generalized regression function. The STAR Program goes through three iterations like this. If the function is still autocorrelated after the third iteration, the application is treated as fatally flawed. In the Autocorp application, the program took two iterations to develop an approximation to the coefficient of autocorrelation that was sufficiently good to eliminate the autocorrelation. These iterations will be explained in Chapter 8.

Autocorrelation can often be attributed to a major cause. In such cases, it is ordinarily better to include in the regression function a variable that accounts for the cause of the autocorrelation than to use the generalized function.

4.4.3   Heteroscedasticity

Another assumption made in ordinary regression analysis is that the standard error is constant from point to point along the ULR. This condition is called *homoscedasticity*. To illustrate this condition, assume that it is possible to select any X value along the ULR and, while holding it constant, observe a large number of Y values corresponding to that X. The standard error of the disturbances could be calculated at that point. Homoscedasticity means that standard errors calculated in this way would be the same at all points of the ULR.

In practice, disturbances are not always homoscedastic. For example, in a cross-sectional analysis of sales across the branches of a retail company, the sales of large stores might fluctuate more from the ULR (the disturbances will have a greater standard error) in terms of absolute dollars than the sales of small stores. Disturbances from the ULR that do not have a constant standard error are said to be *heteroscedastic*. Heteroscedasticity can also be observed in a time-series analysis in which the size of the variables increases over time because of either growth or inflation. Disturbances are heteroscedastic if their standard error varies in absolute dollar terms, even though it may not vary in relative terms.

The scatter diagrams in Figure 4.12 illustrate the difference between well-behaved homoscedastic disturbances and heteroscedastic disturbances. When the disturbances are homoscedastic, the standard error of the regression function can be used as an estimate of the standard error of the disturbances from the ULR. When they are heteroscedastic, the standard error of the regression function cannot be used without modification. In the example of heteroscedastic residuals shown in Figure 4.12, the standard error of the regression function will tend to overestimate the standard error of the smaller disturbances and to underestimate that of the larger disturbances.

Heteroscedasticity can take many different forms. For audit applications of regression analysis, however, it is ordinarily reasonable to assume that, where heteroscedasticity exists, the size of the disturbances will vary in proportion to one of the independent variables. This is the assumption made in the STAR Program, and it provides the basis on which the Program tests for and compensates for heteroscedasticity. Where there is significant heteroscedasticity, STAR performs *weighted regression*, in which the observations are weighted to compensate for the effect of the independent variable on the standard error.

An example of heteroscedasticity is provided by the Heteroco application in which RENT COST and FLOOR AREA are regressed against SALES in a cross-sectional application. A printout of the data for this application is shown in Figure 4.13. In this example, the OLS function computed from the original variables is

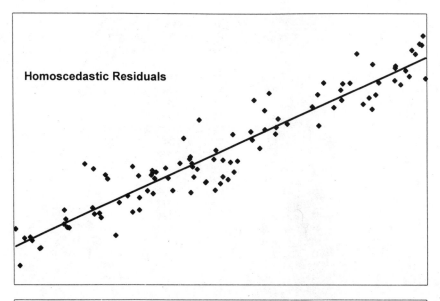

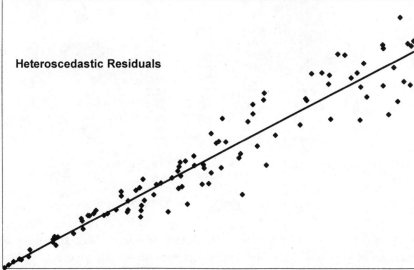

Figure 4.12 These two scatter diagrams contrast homoscedasticity (*top*) and heteroscedasticity (*bottom*). Homoscedastic residuals show approximately the same standard error from observation to observation. Heteroscedastic residuals typically show a standard error that increases as the independent variable increases.

Obs. #	Sales Y	Rent Cost X_1	Floor Area X_2	Absolute Residuals $|e|$
1	2,787	347	2,050	15
2	3,095	437	2,052	56
3	3,184	517	1,944	0
4	2,084	139	1,978	15
5	2,287	189	2,022	4
6	3,228	551	1,901	20
7	4,842	1,076	2,058	84
8	2,210	194	1,912	4
9	2,565	276	2,081	24
10	2,494	297	1,912	15
11	2,422	241	2,030	21
12	3,090	444	2,077	10
13	2,287	229	1,899	11
14	2,669	297	2,151	41
15	3,204	467	2,123	17
16	2,105	171	1,886	11
17	2,440	229	2,096	23
18	3,126	479	1,970	32
19	4,776	1,002	1,951	158
20	2,030	100	2,035	2
21	2,070	138	1,963	14
22	4,949	1,144	1,945	82
23	2,862	371	2,087	12
24	2,347	185	2,082	25
25	2,912	388	2,030	36
26	2,259	234	1,875	33
27	2,730	393	1,822	14
28	2,106	153	1,944	6
29	2,274	200	1,967	4
30	2,444	212	2,087	38
31	2,200	300	2,000	392

Figure 4.13 Heteroco Inc. cross-sectional data across operating units.

$$Y_t = 29.72 + 2.9450X_{1t} + 0.8393X_{2t} + e_t$$

A strong correlation between the absolute residuals and X_1 in the Heteroco example is apparent from the scatter diagram shown in Figure 4.14. The weighted regression function is

$$Y_t = -97.52 + 2.9701 X_{1t} + 0.8987 X_{2t} + e_t$$

Its standard error is $0.0860 X_{1t}$ for observation t. The inclusion of X_{1t} ensures that the standard error will vary from observation to observation. A complete

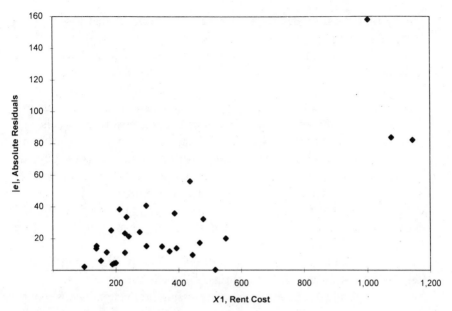

Figure 4.14   Heteroco Inc. Scatter diagram of ABSOLUTE RESIDUALS against RENT COST. There is a strong positive correlation between them, indicating heteroscedasticity.

STAR Program printout for this application is included as Printout B.4 in Appendix B.

4.4.4   Abnormality

In Section 3.6 strong theoretical grounds were presented for believing that disturbances from the ULR will tend to be normally distributed. There is no real way to confirm that a particular disturbance is normally distributed because, ordinarily, only one residual is observed for that period. If it were possible to hold a value of the predicting variable constant for period t and observe repeated values of the residual, a frequency distribution of the residual could be prepared and tested against the normal distribution. Because this cannot be done, the only practical way to test for normality is to test the distribution of the collective residuals with the understanding that each residual should actually relate to a separate distribution. The STAR Program performs such a test and alerts the auditor to the presence of apparent *abnormality* (also known in statistical literature as *nonnormality*) in the base-period residuals.

The STAR Program describes the type of abnormality that has been encountered as *left skewness, right skewness,* or *kurtosis. Skewness* means that the distribution of the residuals is asymmetrical rather than symmetrical like the normal bell-shaped curve. In left skewness, the mean occurs to the left of the mode, or distribution peak. It is ordinarily caused by one or more extreme negative residuals. In right skewness, the mean occurs to the right of the mode, ordinarily because of one or more extreme positive residuals.

Kurtosis means that the distribution is either unusually peaked or unusually flat (the latter case is rare). A peaked distribution may be caused by one or more larger residuals on one side or on each side of the mean. These large residuals tend to inflate the standard error of the regression estimate to the extent that the other residuals appear unusually small in relative terms and appear to cluster tightly around the regression line, creating the appearance of a peaked distribution.

Figure 4.15 contains cross-sectional PRODUCTION QUANTITIES and HOURS WORKED data for Paranormal Production Inc. Figure 4.16 shows a plot of the residuals that result from regressing production against hours.

Obs. #	Production Y	Hours X	Obs. #	Production Y	Hours X
1	31	39	21	52	70
2	32	39	22	51	83
3	32	42	23	55	72
4	36	49	24	62	81
5	41	72	25	41	58
6	33	47	26	53	61
7	39	57	27	100	134
8	19	26	28	70	85
9	53	68	29	82	106
10	40	48	30	65	79
11	38	50	31	67	86
12	38	50	32	61	92
13	56	74	33	71	84
14	45	60	34	72	91
15	62	79	35	66	83
16	45	64	36	62	76
17	55	73	37	82	97
18	53	65	38	60	72
19	61	82	39	60	73
20	37	47	40	37	47

Figure 4.15 Paranormal Production Inc. cross-sectional production quantities and hours-worked data.

Plot of Residuals

Obs No	Recorded Amount	Regression Estimate	Residual (Difference)	Residuals Graphed in Units of One Standard Error
				-4 -3 -2 -1 0 1 2 3 4
				- |--+--+--+--|--+--+--+--| -
1	31	30	1	- * -
2	32	30	2	- * -
3	32	32	0	- * -
4	36	38	-2	- * -
5	41	55	-14	- * -
6	33	36	-3	- * -
7	39	44	-5	- * -
8	19	20	-1	- * -
9	53	52	1	- * -
10	40	37	3	- * -
11	38	38	0	- * -
12	38	38	0	- * -
13	56	57	-1	- * -
14	45	46	-1	- * -
15	62	61	1	- * -
16	45	49	-4	- * -
17	55	56	-1	- * -
18	53	50	3	- * -
19	61	63	-2	- * -
20	37	36	1	- * -
21	52	54	-2	- * -
22	51	64	-13	- * -
23	55	55	0	- * -
24	62	62	0	- * -
25	41	44	-3	- * -
26	53	47	6	- * -
27	100	103	-3	- * -
28	70	65	5	- * -
29	82	81	1	- * -
30	65	61	4	- * -
31	67	66	1	- * -
32	61	70	-9	- * -
33	71	64	7	- * -
34	72	70	2	- * -
35	66	64	2	- * -
36	62	58	4	- * -
37	82	74	8	- * -
38	60	55	5	- * -
39	60	56	4	- * -
40	37	36	1	- * -
				- |--+--+--+--|--+--+--+--| -

```
                          -4 -3 -2 -1  0  1  2  3  4
                     Frequency of Residuals
                     0011010023669442100000 0

                9-              *
                8-              *
                7-              *
                6-            ***
                5-            ***
                4-           *****
                3-          ******
                2-         ********
                1-  *  *  * *********
                0-|--+--+--+--|--+--+--+--|-
                  -4 -3 -2 -1  0  1  2  3  4
                     Approximately
                     Normal Distribution
                     of 40 Residuals
                             *
                            ***
                         *******
                         *******
                        *********
                      *************
                 -|--+--+--+--|--+--+--+--|-
```

Figure 4.16 Paranormal Production Inc. Plot of residuals from the regression function $\hat{Y}_t = -0.0131 + 0.7662X_t$. The large negative residuals in periods 5, 22, and 32 have caused the apparent left skewness and kurtosis in the residuals.

The figure also shows a frequency distribution of the residuals and, for comparative purposes, an approximately normal distribution. A complete STAR Program printout for this application is included as Printout B.5 in Appendix B.

Abnormality generally results from the presence of outliers in the residuals. Sometimes, however, the underlying distribution of the disturbance terms may be genuinely nonnormal. In such cases, it may be difficult, if not impossible, to modify the model to deal with the abnormality. A more fruitful approach may be to abandon the assumption that the disturbances are basically normal in favor of an alternative method that requires no assumption about their distribution. Such an approach changes the mathematics of the audit interface, including the calculation of excesses to be investigated (dealt with in Chapter 5). Methods for dealing with an underlying nonnormal distribution are discussed in Section 8.6 and a numerical example that uses the data in Figure 4.15 is given for one of the methods.

4.4.5   Multicollinearity

Multicollinearity, a high correlation between two or more predicting variables, is a condition that is significant in many applications of regression analysis. The principal effect of multicollinearity is to increase the standard error of the regression coefficients of those variables that are highly correlated. In practical terms, multicollinearity makes it difficult to disentangle the effects of those variables to arrive at reliable separate estimates of their coefficients.

In auditing applications of regression analysis, regression estimates of the test variable usually are more important than estimates of the coefficients of the predicting variables. In such applications, therefore, multicollinearity is seldom a problem even when it occurs. In addition, where a set of predicting variables is multicollinear, the stepwise selection procedure used by the STAR Program (see Section 4.3) will usually ensure that significant multicollinearity is not present within the set of selected variables. For these reasons, no specific test for multicollinearity has been included in the STAR Program.

GENERAL REFERENCES

S. Chatterjee, *Regression Analysis by Example,* 2nd ed. New York: Wiley, 1991.

N. R. Draper and H. Smith, *Applied Regression Analysis,* 2nd ed. New York: Wiley, 1981.

M. Ezekiel and K. A. Fox, *Methods of Correlation and Regression Analysis,* 3rd ed. New York: Wiley, 1959.

A. Koutsoyiannis, *Theory of Econometrics,* 2nd ed. London: Macmillan, 1977.

M. S. Lewis-Beck, *Applied Regression: An Introduction.* Beverly Hills, CA: Sage Publications, 1980.

J. Neper, *Applied Linear Regression Models.* Homewood, IL: R. D. Irwin, 1983.

K. W. Smillie, *An Introduction to Regression and Correlation.* New York: Academic Press, 1966.

5

THE AUDIT INTERFACE

5.1 INTRODUCTION

The technique the STAR Program uses to detect significant fluctuations from the ULR by the test variable is explained in this chapter. This technique, which blends statistics and quantified audit judgments, represents the *audit interface*. The three audit parameters that the auditor must provide in the audit interface are the monetary precision (MP), the reliability factor (R), and the direction of test (i.e., overstatement or understatement). These parameters are discussed in Chapters 1 and 6.

5.2 BASIC CONCEPTS

The primary purpose of the audit interface is to achieve a specified level of reliability that one or more observations containing errors will be identified for investigation if the amount of accounting errors affecting the recorded total of the test variable in a specified direction is at least as much as the monetary precision. As used here and later in this book, *errors* includes both intentional irregularities and unintentional mistakes in the amounts or in the application of accounting principles.

The basic concept underlying the audit interface is that the recorded amounts of the test variable in the projection period may have been materially affected by accounting errors, whereas the estimates projected from the regression model should not be so affected (because the model is based on observations that have been audited or obtained from sources considered reliable). Residuals in the audit period therefore are expected to have been caused by:

- The random variation that is inherent in business operations and in estimates made by using a regression model

- Errors or unusual events that affect the recorded amount of the test variable in the projection period

STAR sets a *threshold* for each residual in the projection period. If the residual exceeds the threshold, the excess is treated as an excess to be investigated. This is illustrated in Figure 5.1. The computation of the threshold involves the quantified audit parameters and certain statistics, in particular the standard error of the residual (see Section 3.5).

The computation of the threshold is complicated by the fact that the way in which material error might be spread among the values of the test variable is unknown. For example, it could all be bunched in 1 month or it could be spread throughout 12 months. Fortunately, there is always a certain spread of error that is *most adverse* in the sense that it is the most difficult to detect. STAR computes this most adverse spread of error and uses it in the calculation of the threshold. This results in thresholds that are conservative if the error is not spread in the most adverse way.

If STAR identifies an excess to be investigated, then, until further audit work is performed, the auditor's level of reliability will be less than required. If a satisfactory explanation of the excess cannot be obtained, the auditor would ordinarily need to increase the extent of the tests of details of the affected observation. The STAR Program calculates how many extra items should be sampled to bring the auditor's reliability back to the required level. How this sample size is calculated is explained in the next section.

In Chapter 3, the concept of the standard error of the residual, the standardized residual (the residual divided by its standard error), and the t distribution were introduced. The standard error of the residual for period 48 for the Gamma Company application was calculated. It is 214.4938, and the standardized residual is

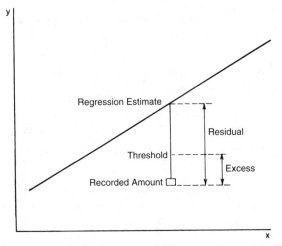

Figure 5.1   Excess to be investigated. This diagram shows that the excess to be investigated is the difference between the recorded amount and the threshold point.

$$\frac{e_{48}}{s(e_{48})} = \frac{-266}{214.4938} = -1.24$$

This statistic is distributed as t with 34 degrees of freedom. These concepts and statistics will be used in this chapter as will the fact that the monetary precision, MP, has been set at \$600,000 (shown as \$600 on the STAR printout in Figure 2.3, because the dependent variable is in thousands of dollars), the reliability factor, R, has been set at 3.0, and the direction of test is *understatement*.

5.3   IDENTIFYING EXCESSES TO BE INVESTIGATED

In this section, it is explained how thresholds and excesses to be investigated are calculated. Also illustrated are the principles involved, using as an example the period-48 data for the Gamma Company, as this example was used in previous sections and many of the factors have already been calculated.

An important factor in the calculation of a threshold is the most adverse spread of error between individual observations. That such a thing as the most adverse spread of error should exist may not be immediately obvious.

The key to understanding why it does exist is to recognize that there are two opposing factors that determine the probability of detecting error.

- The size of the individual error taintings. The smaller the error tainting of a particular observation, the less probable it is that the observation will be identified.

- The number of error-tainted observations. The more error-tainted observations there are, the more likely it is that at least one will be identified.

It can be shown that the interaction of these two opposing factors ensures that a certain spread of error will result in the most conservative threshold. This spread is the most adverse spread of error because any other will allow a threshold that is less stringent.

The most adverse spread of error is dependent on two main factors: the size of the MP relative to the standard error of the residual and the required reliability level. The greater the relative MP, and the lower the required reliability level, the greater the most adverse spread of error.

In the analysis that follows, all of the calculations will be expressed in terms of "standardized" dollars. That is, dollar amounts will be divided by the standard error of the residual for period 48. This will make it unnecessary to flip back and forth between standardized dollars (which are needed for t distribution calculations) and real dollars. At any point, standardized dollars can be translated back into real dollars by multiplying by the standard error. The symbol "s$" will be used to denote standardized dollar amounts. The standardized residual is $-s\$1.24$, as shown in the Section 5.2. The standardized MP is $\$600/214.4938 = s\$2.80$.

The following subsections will show how thresholds could be set for successively thinner spreads of error if those spreads were known. The important thing is that the thresholds will get closer to the regression line for a few iterations and then begin to move further away. The most conservative threshold, the one closest to the regression line in this example, will be the one used by the STAR Program. (The final section in this chapter contains a discussion of a relatively unusual condition where the threshold may not be the one closest to the regression line.)

In the following analysis, it will be assumed that such error as exists will be spread equally throughout those observations that contain errors. Although there is no basis for this assumption, it can be shown that it results in the most conservative threshold for the given number of error-tainted observations.

Because the reliability factor set for the exercise is $R = 3.0$, the reliability level required is 95% (see Figure A.1 in Appendix A). In other words, 5% is the maximum risk that the auditor is prepared to accept that no error-tainted observations will be identified if the total understatement is s$2.80 or more.

5.3.1 Spread of One

If it is assumed that the total error of s$2.80 (if it exists) will taint only one observation, then the threshold must be set such that there is only a 5% risk that the error-tainted observation will not be identified.

The first step is to establish a *risk point* such that 95% of all *correct Y* values (standardized) will fall below it (i.e., 95% of the residuals will fall below it on the hypothesis that there is no error in the data). Then the threshold is simply set at a distance of s$2.80 below the risk point. If 95% of all *correct Y* values fall below the risk point, then 95% of all *recorded* values that understate the correct Y value by s$2.80 or more must fall below the threshold. Thus, any observation with an understatement of s$2.80 or more will be identified with 95% reliability.

Determining the risk point is equivalent to determining that point on the t distribution (the one with 34 degrees of freedom) such that 95% of all t values fall below it. The STAR Program uses a formula to calculate t values. Some of these are shown in Figure A.2 for illustrative purposes. The t value is 1.69. The threshold is therefore

$$s\$1.69 - s\$2.80 = -s\$1.11$$

The complete process is illustrated in Figure 5.2. Thus, residuals that are larger than $-s\$1.11$ in the negative direction (i.e., $-s\$1.11 \times 214.4938 = -\$238$ or larger, in real dollars) will be treated as excessive.

5.3.2 Spread of Two

If it is assumed that the total understatement of s$2.80 (if it exists) will affect two separate observations by s$1.40 each, then the threshold must be set so that at least one of those observations will be identified with 95% reliability. Put differently, the auditor can accept a maximum 5% risk that both error-

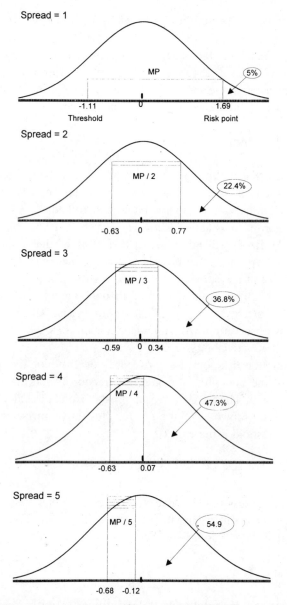

Figure 5.2 Finding the most adverse spread of error. Thresholds for successively thinner spreads of error get closer to the regression line to start with and then get further away. This example shows how the calculations are made for period 48 of the Gamma Company data. In this case, the most adverse spread of error is 3, as that spread results in the most conservative threshold, that is, −0.59 in standardized dollars.

tainted observations will escape identification. The risk that both such observations may escape identification is the product of the risks that each escapes. Because 22.4% × 22.4% = 5%, 22.4% is the acceptable risk that a particular error-tainted observation is not identified.

The risk point must be set such that 77.6% (100% − 22.4%) of all correct standardized *Y* values will fall below it, and the threshold must be set at a distance of s$1.40 (one-half standardized *MP*) below it. If 77.6% of all *correct Y* values fall below the risk point, then 77.6% of all *recorded* values that understate the correct *Y* value by s$1.40 or more will fall below the threshold. Thus, given any error of understatement of s$1.40 or more, the risk is not more than 22.4% that the error-tainted observation will not be detected.

The *t* value that corresponds to a risk of 22.4% is 0.77. The threshold is therefore

$$\text{s\$0.77} - \text{s\$1.40} = -\text{s\$0.63}$$

This is illustrated in Figure 5.2.

5.3.3   Spread of Three

If it is assumed that the total understatement of s$2.80 (if it exists) will affect three separate observations by s$0.93 each, then, because 36.8% × 36.8% × 36.8% = 5%, 36.8% is the acceptable risk that a particular error-tainted observation will not be identified.

The *t* value that corresponds to a risk of 36.8% is 0.34. The threshold is therefore

$$\text{s\$0.34} - \text{s\$0.93} = -\text{s\$0.59}$$

This is illustrated in Figure 5.2.

5.3.4   Spreads of Four, Five, and More

If the error is assumed to affect four observations equally by one-fourth of *MP* (i.e., s$0.70), the acceptable risk of not identifying a particular error-tainted observation is 47.3% (47.3% × 47.3% × 47.3% × 47.3% = 5%).

The *t* value that corresponds to a risk of 47.3% is 0.07. The threshold is therefore

$$s\$0.07 - s\$0.70 = -s\$0.63$$

For a spread of five, the individual risk is 54.9%, the t value is $-s\$0.12$, and the threshold is

$$-s\$0.12 - s\$0.56 = -s\$0.68$$

These are illustrated in Figure 5.2.

5.3.5   Most Adverse Spread of Error

Figure 5.3 shows a summary of the thresholds that would be required for various known spreads of error. It is clear from this summary that the most conservative threshold is $-s\$0.59$, the one that corresponds to three error-tainted observations. The thresholds that correspond to one or two, or to four or five, such observations are all further away. If this exercise were to be continued for even more thinly spread error, the trend would continue. Accordingly, three is the most adverse spread of error, and $-s\$0.59$ is the most conservative threshold.

Initially, it might seem that the maximum number of observations over which a material error might be spread should be limited by the number of observations in the projection period. For example, if the application uses monthly data, the need to consider the risk of spreading a material error over more than 12 observations in the projection period might appear doubtful. The STAR Program, nevertheless, does not place any upper limit on the most adverse spread of error, and the calculation is performed separately for each observation. Spreads ranging into the thousands are possible.

Spread	Risk	Risk Point (t)	Error Tainting	Threshold
1	5.0%	1.69	2.80	(1.11)
2	22.4%	0.77	1.40	(0.63)
3	*36.8%*	*0.34*	*0.93*	*(0.59)*
4	47.3%	0.07	0.70	(0.63)
5	54.9%	(0.12)	0.56	(0.68)

Most Adverse Spread of Error

Figure 5.3   Gamma Company setting the threshold for observation 48.

This approach to calculating the most adverse distribution helps to ensure that the statistical assurance provided by STAR is not diluted over multiple STAR applications. For example, if the calculation did not consider the possibility that a material error could be spread over 60 observations, the risk that material error could be spread over five different STAR applications that use monthly data might be higher than the nominal level. Another consequence of the way in which the most adverse spread of error is calculated is that the monetary precisions specified for designing multiple STAR applications may be considered noncumulative with respect to the combined applications.

Figure 5.3 shows how the threshold gets closer to the regression line as the error affects more observations. However, if it affects more than three observations, the threshold can be relaxed. An error exactly equal to *MP* is most adversely spread when it affects three observations equally. The error, the risk points, and the thresholds are expressed in standardized dollars. Standardized dollars can be translated into normal dollars by multiplying by the standard error, which is 214.4938 in this case.

5.3.6   Excess to Be Investigated

As explained previously, the threshold that will be most conservative for the period-48 residual for Gamma Company is −s$0.59. This translates to

$$-s\$0.59 \times 214.4938 = -\$127$$

in real dollars (expressed in thousands). Accordingly, the residual of −$266 is excessive by $139. The STAR printout in Figure 2.3 shows $138, the difference being due to rounding.

5.4   OPTIONAL SAMPLE DATA

Besides identifying thresholds and excesses to be investigated, the audit interface module of the STAR Program also designs supplementary statistical samples that may be used to test details of those recorded amounts of the test variable that have been determined to contain excesses. Such samples are appropriate when no adequate explanation of an "excess to be investigated" can be obtained. Their purpose is to "close the gap" between the specified reliability level and the achieved reliability level.

The remainder of this section is a demonstration of how the STAR Program calculates the optional sample data for the excess to be investigated, which was discussed in the previous section. The observed residual in that case was −s$1.24. The auditor's concern is that the true residual (i.e., the residual excluding any error component) might be understated by s$0.93 or more. Put another way, the auditor is concerned that the true residual might fall above −s$0.31. Thus, −s$0.31 is called the *effective risk point.* The risk that the true residual is above −s$0.31 (the *effective risk*) can be calculated from the *t* distribution. It is 61.9%, as illustrated in Figure 5.4. It exceeds the *target risk* level for the observation, which is 36.8% (see Section 5.3.3).

The optional sample must be designed so as to reduce the effective risk to the target risk for the observation. Thus, the appropriate risk level for the optional sample is 36.8%/61.9% = 59.5%. Put another way, the product of the effective risk and the optional sample risk must equal the target risk.

A reliability factor of *R* = 0.52 (see Figure A.1) is equivalent to a reliability level of 40.5% (the complement of the optional sample risk, 59.5%). Based on the implied precision limit and reliability factor, the STAR Program determines a maximum sample size and a selection interval to test the recorded amount for that observation. The sampling approach contemplated by the STAR Program in designing this sample is a probability-proportional-to-size technique, which is embodied in an audit sampling plan widely used in D&T as a companion technique to the STAR Program (see Section 7.3.2.)

In terms of this sampling plan, an appropriate monetary sampling interval

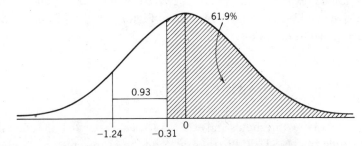

Figure 5.4 Calculating effective risk. The residual period 48 in the Gamma Company example is −s$1.24. There is a 61.9% probability that the true residual for this observation will be more than one-third of *MP* (s$0.93) above this amount. Because the threshold point has been set to detect errors of one-third *MP,* 61.9% is the effective risk associated with the result.

for the tests of details can be calculated by dividing the reliability factor into the required precision. The precision limit is $200 ($MP$ divided by 3, the most adverse spread of error). Hence, sample size will be based on a selection interval of $200/0.52 = $384 (rounded down for conservatism).

As will be discussed further in Chapter 7, the population to be sampled depends on the direction of the test. The recorded value of the test variable itself may be sampled if the audit objective relates to overstatement errors. If that were the case, the maximum sample size would be the recorded value of the test variable divided by the selection interval. As it is, because the audit objective relates to understatement errors, the sample should be taken from a population that could reveal understatements or omissions in the recorded amounts of the test variable. Because the best estimate of the test variable for period 48 is $3,259 (Figure 2.3), the regression estimate, the best estimate of the maximum extra sample required, is $3,259/$384 = 8.49 items. STAR rounds this to 8 items and recalculates the actual selection interval to be used as $3,259/8 = $407.

5.5   EXCESSES GREATER THAN RESIDUALS

Under some circumstances, the STAR Program will indicate an excess to be investigated that is larger than the residual. At first this might seem contrary to common sense—after all, the residual is the difference between the recorded value and the best estimate of the test variable. Clearly, such an excess is unlikely to be identified in a conventional analytical review. Such excesses are referred to as *paradoxical excesses.*

To understand how paradoxical excesses arise, it is necessary to remember that the STAR Program sets thresholds on the basis of the monetary precision, the reliability level, the direction of test, and the statistical characteristics of the regression function (the standard error of the residual, in particular). In general, the more stringent the audit requirements, the tighter the thresholds and the greater the excesses to be investigated. At a certain point, the auditor's requirements may become so demanding relative to the statistical characteristics of the regression function that thresholds cross to the opposite side of the regression estimates and paradoxical excesses might be identified.

For example, if a regression model with a standard error of $1,000 were to be used to obtain 95% assurance that sales are not understated by more than $100, then, because the audit objectives are so demanding in relation to the predictive ability of the regression model, it is likely that paradoxical excesses would be identified.

Paradoxical excesses occur infrequently, and their presence suggests that the precision and reliability that have been specified are relatively difficult to achieve through analytical review. The related regression model should be assessed to determine whether or not it is the best model practicable under the circumstances. As statistical objectives become more demanding, the auditor should be prepared to invest more effort in developing a model of sufficient quality to achieve those objectives efficiently. In a figurative sense, paradoxical excesses indicate that the auditor may be trying to "squeeze blood from a turnip."

The audit response to paradoxical excesses is, in theory, no different from that for other excesses to be investigated. However, because an analytical explanation is ordinarily not feasible for the entire excess, the usual response should be to increase the tests of details by the size of the optional sample designed by the STAR Program. If part of the excess can be explained analytically, the Program should be rerun with the explained part removed from the recorded amount. The revised optional sample would then be the appropriate one to use.

PART THREE

AUDITING APPLICATIONS OF REGRESSION ANALYSIS

6

DESIGNING AUDIT MODELS

6.1 INTRODUCTION

An auditor can use STAR in planning an audit and for performing substantive procedures. During the planning phase, STAR can be run by using interim financial information to identify account balances with large or unusual fluctuations. Because these fluctuations may indicate a possible error, it is important to identify them at the planning stage so that the auditor can evaluate the potential audit risk and decide on an appropriate method of testing the balance.

For clients whose accounting records are decentralized and when it is not practical to visit all locations, STAR can help the auditor decide which locations (subsidiaries, plants, etc.) should be selected for examination. On many engagements, locations are selected by rotation or by size. Although these selection methods are logical, they are usually not as effective as a selection made by using STAR. STAR can be used to identify locations whose accounts deviate from the expectation, and the selection will thus be based on risk.

In addition to the planning of audits and substantive analytical review procedures, STAR can be used for applications that are not related to auditing. The regression analysis performed by STAR can be used to prepare forecasts of future financial information.

STAR will develop a model, similar to audit applications, based on the predicting and test variables specified. (Test variables are, of course, amounts the user wants to forecast.) Prior period data alone can be used to forecast future information, or the model can be used to perform what-if analysis. What-if analysis can be performed by changing the amounts associated with one or more of the predicting variables and re-running the program.

In performing substantive audit procedures through analytical review, the auditor compares the recorded amounts with an expectation that has been developed using relevant and reliable financial or nonfinancial data. Regardless of the method used to develop the expectation, the substantive analytical review process consists of the following steps.

1.   Develop an expectation of the amount to be tested at an appropriate level of disaggregation (e.g., general ledger account level, by location, by month, etc.) based on relevant financial or nonfinancial data (base data). These data should be reliable (either already tested or obtained from an independent source) and related to the balance to be tested so that they can be reasonably used to develop an expectation.

2.   Determine a threshold amount, which is the maximum error the auditor can tolerate in the recorded amount and conclude that the balance is not materially misstated. The threshold is the maximum difference between the expectation of the amount to be tested and its recorded balance that is acceptable without further investigation. It should be sufficiently small to detect misstatements that could be material, either individually, in aggregate with misstatements in other disaggregated portions of the account tested, or with other components of the financial statements.

3.   Compare the expectation to the recorded amount and identify differences requiring further investigation. Differences that exceed the threshold amount or appear unusual based on the auditor's judgment should be examined.

4.   Obtain explanations for the differences from the client or by performing additional audit work to test the account. It is often unnecessary to investigate the entire difference between the expectation and the recorded balance as long as the unexplained amount is clearly less than the threshold. Verbal explanations obtained from the client must be corroborated by examining supporting documentation or through discussions with individuals considered independent.

5. Evaluate the results of the procedures and determine the reasonableness of the amount tested.

STAR is very helpful to the auditor during the first three steps of the substantive analytical review process.

1. STAR will analyze relationships between the predicting data and amounts to be tested and will develop a model that can be used to calculate an expectation of the recorded amount. This is done through regression analysis.

2. The software will automatically perform mathematical tests to assess the plausibility and predictability of the relationship between predicting data and amounts to be tested.

3. STAR will compute a threshold based on the materiality and level of assurance specified by the auditor and on the precision inherent in the particular regression model.

4. STAR will identify differences between the expectations and the recorded amounts exceeding the threshold.

It should be stressed that STAR does not replace professional judgment. It focuses attention on areas where further analysis is needed and should not be used as an automated answer. The auditor must use common sense and knowledge of the client's business to evaluate critically the reliability of predicting data and the relevance and plausibility of the relationship between the predicting data, the amount to be tested, and the model developed by STAR.

Use of the STAR Program for an audit application consists of the following steps:

- Designing the audit model
- Running the STAR Program
- Reviewing the audit model
- Investigating unusual fluctuations
- Evaluating the audit results

The auditing decisions to be made in designing an audit model are discussed in this chapter, and the remaining steps will be discussed in Chapter 7. A diagram of these decisions is shown in Figure 6.1.

The decisions involved in designing effective and efficient audit models require a blend of audit judgment and statistical techniques. Such decisions should be based on the general and specific audit objectives in the circumstances, the related statistical considerations, and the data available for use as variables. In the next section, the audit and statistical objectives that apply to all audit applications are discussed. In the remainder of the chapter, the specific objectives and other elements of audit models for individual applications are discussed.

6.2   GENERAL AUDIT AND
STATISTICAL OBJECTIVES

The auditing objective of analytical procedures will be accomplished most effectively by a model that provides the best fit that is practicable in the circumstances. Achievement of this objective requires a clear understanding of the factors affecting the company's operations and the underlying data relationships that exist in the company's business. Experimentation in specifying the variables and the data profile to develop a model that best achieves the audit purpose of an application is appropriate and should be encouraged, both in the initial design of the model and, as discussed in Chapter 7, after its review.

6.2.1   Statistical Best Fit

In analytical procedures, the auditor's purpose ordinarily will be to develop a model that will provide the best estimates of the test variable. As explained in Section 3.4.2, "best" is measured by the standard error of the regression function.

Although it is not possible to provide specific guidelines for an acceptable coefficient, the more precise the auditor expects the relationship to be, the closer the coefficient should be to 100%. The auditor should track the coefficient from year to year; if a significant decrease is noted, the auditor should examine the validity of the model. A significant decrease may indicate the presence of a new business factor that is not reflected in the model.

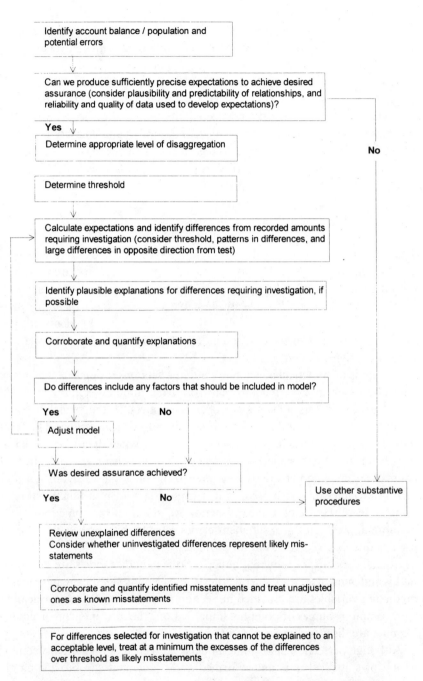

Figure 6.1 Process of designing and performing substantive analytical procedures.

The authors do not recommend any minimum value for the coefficient of correlation as a requirement for use of an audit model in an analytical review application for two reasons. The first is that this statistic is recognized through the standard error, which is used to compute the threshold for excesses to be investigated, as explained in Chapter 5; the compensatory effect of lower correlation is that it tends to require more audit investigation.

The second reason is that the statistical discipline and measurements obtained through regression analysis, regardless of the correlation, will ordinarily result in a better analytical review than nonstatistical techniques applied to the same data.

6.2.2   Practical Constraints

There are two practical constraints on the statistical degree of fit that can be obtained in an audit model for any particular application. First are the inherent characteristics of the operations of the business or organization being audited. Some operations are relatively stable, whereas others are highly volatile in relation to any set of variables that can reasonably be identified. Refinements in the model will not, and indeed should not, obscure real volatility in the underlying operations.

Second is the practical inevitability of imperfections to some degree in any audit model. Such imperfections may arise from limitations in the auditor's knowledge of factors affecting the client's business, in the availability and reliability of predicting data, or from cost-benefit considerations. The term *imperfections* is used here to mean matters that frequently are described in regression literature as *specification errors* and *measurement errors*. In that context, specification errors usually refer to the omission of significant predicting variables or to the use of a less appropriate form of functional relationship (e.g., the use of a linear function when a nonlinear function would be more appropriate); measurement errors refer to inaccuracies in the data used as the observed values of the variables.

Practical means for reducing imperfections in audit models are discussed in this and later chapters. General criteria for selecting significant and reliable predicting variables are provided in Section 6.5, and suggestions for dealing with common sources of potential imperfections that are unique to accounting data are discussed in Section 6.6.

Although perfection in an audit model is unlikely to be achieved, a combination of statistical tests and informed audit judgment can provide ample precaution against the risk of significant imperfections. As a practical matter, the quality of an audit model must be judged against the quality of the available alternatives rather than against some imaginary perfection. Under this criterion, it seems evident that the imperfections remaining in audit models generated by the STAR Program should not be greater, and probably are much less, than those that are present (even if not recognized) in the implicit models used in nonstatistical analytical procedures. Some auditors, who have been content for years to use nonstatistical techniques with no apparent concern for the imperfections inherent in them, tend to become hypersensitive about imperfections in regression models. It is hoped this book will place such concerns in perspective.

6.2.3   Correlation and Causation

The distinction between correlation and causation needs to be understood. Statistical correlation may, but does not necessarily, imply a cause-and-effect relationship between variables. For example, a high correlation might be shown between rainfall and floods. Such correlation would provide a reasonable basis for inferring that rainfall causes floods, but not that floods cause rainfall. As another example, a high correlation has been found between teachers' salaries and sales of alcoholic beverages. In this case, it seems clear that there is no cause-and-effect relationship but that both of the variables are influenced similarly by other socioeconomic variables.

In many cases, the distinction between correlation and causation may be more complex and less apparent, and possibly less relevant for the purpose of the application, than the simple but extreme examples just given. For instance, increases in the physical volume of sales alone would increase total sales and cost of sales, whereas increases in unit costs might decrease the physical volume of sales but increase the unit sales prices and either increase or decrease total sales and cost of sales. The ramifications of cost-price-volume relationships may be a fertile field for regression analysis for management and other economic purposes. It may suffice for the auditor's analytical review purposes, however, to establish that management has been able to maintain a relatively stable relationship between certain variables (e.g., sales and costs) throughout relevant periods, without detailed analysis of the causes of changes in each of the variables unless such analysis is necessary to explain unusual fluctuations.

6.3   SPECIFIC OBJECTIVES OF
AN AUDIT APPLICATION

The auditor defines the specific objectives of an application by making decisions about the following matters and by entering these decisions in the form of specifications for the STAR Program:

- The test variable
- The type and number of observations in the data profile
- The direction of the audit test
- The statistical reliability and precision desired

6.3.1   Test Variable

The specific account, class of transactions, or financial statement component to be tested and the audit purpose of the application determine the test variable to be specified. The audit purpose of an application may be to review fluctuations in income-statement accounts or to review the reasonableness of balances in balance-sheet accounts. In either case, the purpose may relate to accounts at one operating location or at multiple locations.

If the audit purpose is to review fluctuations in accounts at a single location, the test variable might be the monthly amounts of sales, the cost of sales, or the major classifications of operating expenses.

Audit tests of balance-sheet accounts at a single location often include tests of details at some interim date, supplemented by tests or a review of transactions for the intervening period from that date to the end of the year being audited. In such situations, the audit purpose of an application might be to review certain components of the transactions during the intervening period, and the test variable might be the monthly amounts of transactions (e.g., collections on receivables or credits to inventory accounts for cost of sales). The purpose of such review would be to consider the cumulative effect of any unusual fluctuations in such transactions on the ending balance of the related account. The STAR Program achieves this purpose by using the regression estimates of the test variable during the intervening period to project an ending balance and by comparing the projected balance with the recorded balance to determine any excess to be investigated. This type of application is described as an *ending balance projection*. An example of an ending balance projection is included as Printout B.6 in Appendix B.

In audits of companies that operate in multiple locations, the base profile might consist of certain locations that have been, or will be, audited for the current year by other procedures, and the projection profile might include all other locations. The audit purpose of such an application might be to review fluctuations in the yearly total of income-statement accounts or ending balances in balance-sheet accounts in the projection profile and to identify locations to be visited or otherwise investigated because of unusual fluctuations. In such applications, the yearly total or ending balance of a specific account or component for locations not audited by other means would be the test variable. This type of an application is called *cross sectional;* applications based on historical base data are called *time-series applications*. An example of a cross-sectional application can be found in the printout included as Printout B.4 in Appendix B. The model developed for Heteroco Inc. is based on current year observations of rent and floor space (predicting variables) and on sales (test variable) at a number of retail stores, and it is used to estimate sales of other stores owned by the company.

In specifying the test variable, the auditor must also make decisions about the following matters relating to the audit purpose of the application:

• The accounting unit for which the application is to be made
• The level of detail of the accounts to be used

The accounting unit for a particular application might be the consolidated group, one particular company, an operating division, a branch, or some other subdivision of the entity. The level of detail of the accounts might be, for example, total cost of sales or the separate material, labor, and overhead components. In determining the accounting unit and level of detail to be used, the objective should be to achieve the maximum practicable audit effectiveness and efficiency.

To be effective for audit purposes, the accounting unit used should be no larger than the smallest entity on whose financial statements the auditor is to express an opinion. If, for example, the auditor is to express an opinion on the financial statements of each subsidiary company, the accounting unit could be each such company or some subdivision of it, but should not be the consolidated entity.

A similar limitation need not be applied to the level of general ledger accounts or subaccounts unless the auditor is to issue a special report on a particular account. In the usual situation, the auditor expresses an opinion on financial statements in which amounts are stated in broad financial statement components (e.g., cost of sales, selling expenses, and administrative and general expenses). In such cases, these components or their subdivisions may be used as the test variable in applications to test the respective components. If further details of these components are presented as supplementary information, which the auditor does not consider necessary for fair presentation of the financial statements, such details are comprehended in the standard form of opinion only as they relate to those statements taken as a whole. In such circumstances, the auditor may conclude that it is not necessary to use, as a separate test variable, each level of detail that is presented as supplementary information. If an unqualified opinion is to be expressed in a special report on a particular component of the financial statements, however, that component should be used as the test variable in any application that is to be relied on by the auditor for that purpose.

Subject to the limitations in the preceding two paragraphs, both audit effectiveness and efficiency will be improved by specifying an accounting unit and level of detail of accounts that result in the best statistical fit, as discussed in Section 6.2.

In general, models that project results at the detail level tend to be more accurate than those that use total figures, because disaggregation of data usually reduces the standard error of the regression function and increases the coefficient of correlation. It is ordinarily desirable to exclude from an application any accounting units for which there is a known diversity in operating conditions that would be expected to adversely affect the correlation between the variables to be used. Similarly, the level of detail of variables to be used should exclude accounts that would be expected to adversely affect the correlation. For example, operating locations that have been affected by strikes or other disruptions and accounts that have been affected by a change in accounting principles generally should be excluded. Any units or accounts that are excluded should be covered by other STAR applications or by other auditing procedures. Consequently, excessive refinement in making exclusions to improve the correlation in one or more applications may decrease the overall audit efficiency with little, if any, improvement in effectiveness. Thus, audit judgment and an understanding of the business operations are needed in deciding on the accounting unit and level of detail to be used in specifying the test variable.

6.3.2   Type and Number of Observations in the Data Profile

As discussed in the preceding section, the type of data profile to be specified depends on the audit purpose of the application. The two basic types of data profiles are *time-series* and *cross-sectional* data profiles. These terms were defined in Section 2.5.1. In a cross-sectional profile, the units might be subdivisions (e.g., operating locations) of the company. In some applications, a data profile that includes both time-series and cross-sectional observations may be useful; such a combination may be described as a *cross-time* profile. Such a profile might, for example, include monthly observations from several locations.

As discussed in Section 2.5.1 the data profile consists of two parts: the base profile and the projection profile. The base profile includes the set of observations that is used in computing the regression function and other regression statistics; the projection profile includes the set that is used in computing the regression estimates and excesses to be investigated in the current audit period. For time-series applications, the base profile includes observations from prior periods that are deemed reliable. For cross-sectional applications, the base profile ordinarily should consist of selected units whose current or prior period data have been audited or are otherwise deemed reliable. For audit purposes, data is considered reliable if it has been appropriately audited or has been prepared by a party that is independent of the individuals responsible for accounting and financial reporting. Prior period balances may have been audited through nonstatistical analytical procedures, STAR applications, or detail testing.

The number of observations to be included in the base profile is influenced by two conflicting considerations. The general effect of a larger number of observations is to increase the degrees of freedom and thereby to decrease the standard error of the regression estimates. A contrary effect may result, however, from adding earlier periods in a time-series profile or from adding more units in a cross-sectional profile, either of which may have been affected by different operating conditions than those affecting the other base period data and would thus increase the standard error.

For a time-series profile, it ordinarily is desirable to eliminate the oldest observations if operating conditions have changed in more recent periods, because this will help to reduce the standard error. For a cross-sectional profile, it may be appropriate to subdivide or stratify the units into two or more profiles on the basis of size or some other characteristic that reduces the standard error.

Because of the conflicting considerations and variety of circumstances the auditor is likely to encounter the authors do not suggest specific guidelines for the number of observations to be included in the base profile. However, 36 monthly or 20 quarterly observations usually are reasonable for time-series profiles, and 20 observations usually are reasonable for cross-sectional profiles.

The projection profile for time-series applications generally should include observations for all periods of the year being audited, although it may be desirable to run the STAR Program separately for periods preceding and following an interim examination date. For cross-sectional applications, the projection profile should include all units being audited in the STAR application.

6.3.3 Direction of the Audit Test

The direction of the audit test to be specified is either overstatement or understatement. As explained in Chapter 5, this specification is used in the audit interface computation of the threshold point for determining whether there are excesses to be investigated. If the primary audit purpose of the application is to audit the test variable for possible overstatement, the most relevant residuals usually will be those arising from excesses of the recorded amounts over the related regression estimates. In tests for understatement, the most relevant residuals usually will be those in the opposite direction. Exceptions to this rule arise in some situations (paradoxical excesses), which are explained in Section 5.5. The STAR Program can test in either direction.

In the event that the recorded value of the test variable falls beyond the threshold point in the direction of the test, STAR identifies the difference between the recorded amount and the threshold point as a significant difference to be investigated. (Differences are always shown as positive if the recorded amount exceeds the regression estimate and the negative if the reverse is true, regardless of the direction of the test specified.) If the recorded value of the test variable falls beyond the threshold point in the direction opposite that of the test, STAR also identifies the difference as significant. The auditor should evaluate such differences to determine whether they are unusual or unexpected. The size of the difference should also be considered when determining whether it should be examined further. A difference that is in the direction opposite the test may indicate an error in the test variable itself or problems with the predicting variables in the audit period.

Decisions about the direction of test and the types and combinations of auditing procedures necessary to accomplish reasonable tests of financial statement components in both directions are matters of audit judgment that are not unique to STAR applications; they are matters about which different auditors may have different views. Further discussion of this topic per se is beyond the scope of this book, but some of the examples cited throughout the book are indicative of our general views on appropriate types and combinations of auditing procedures.

6.3.4   Statistical Reliability and Precision

The concepts of statistical reliability and precision and their role in auditing were introduced in Chapter 1, and their application to the audit interface was explained in Chapter 5. As indicated earlier, the reliability level (a probability percentage) desired for an application of the STAR Program is specified through a reliability factor. The relationship between reliability levels and reliability factors is shown in Figure A.1 in Appendix A. The monetary precision limit is specified directly as a monetary amount in the same units as the test variable.

These parameters are the connecting link between statistical techniques and audit judgment. The culmination of an auditor's judgment about the ultimate objectives of auditing procedures can be expressed by specifying these parameters for use in designing either an audit model for analytical review or a statistical sample for an audit test of details. For either of these purposes, reliability should be related to the auditor's judgment about audit risks, and monetary precision should be related to his or her judgment about materiality. Monetary precision represents the maximum potential error amount affecting the account that the auditor can tolerate and issue an unqualified opinion.

The matters to be considered in making these judgments are discussed in SAS 39 [1] and SAS 47 [2]. The appendix to SAS 39 discusses and illustrates the combination of risks relating to internal accounting control, analytical review, and tests of details. The material in this appendix is as relevant to analytical review applications as it is to audit sampling applications. The following features of Table 2 in the appendix to SAS 39 relate to the discussion in this book.

- The percentages shown in the table are in terms of "risk," which is the complement of "reliability" as used in this book.
- The column headings in the table show the assumed risk assigned to analytical review (AR); the percentages in the body of the table are the computed risks for tests of details (TD) for the respective assumed levels of internal accounting control risk (IC). For the purposes of this book, the positions of AR and TD in the table could be reversed so that the percentages in the body of the table would become the risks for analytical review applications.

6.4   CLASSIFICATION AND SOURCE OF PREDICTING VARIABLES

Predicting variables can be classified as either *real* or *dummy* variables.

6.4.1   Real Variables

Real variables consist of monetary or other quantitative measures of size, and they can be classified by source as either *internal* or *external* variables.

Internal variables.   These variables consist of values that originate within the organization being audited. They include accounting and operating data expressed in monetary terms or in other quantitative units (e.g., the number of hours worked, the quantity of products shipped, or the number of employees). Accounting and operating reports are the primary source of internal variables.

External variables.   These consist of values that originate outside the company being audited. Examples of external variables include gross national product, price indices, employment statistics, prime interest rates, population data, and specific industry statistics. Government agencies, industry associations, and private research organizations are the primary sources for external variables.

6.4.2   Dummy Variables

Dummy variables are those that are used to differentiate between the absence or the presence of some condition or event that cannot be otherwise quantified as a real variable. They may be used, for example, to differentiate between observations affected or not affected by unusual events (e.g., acquisitions, disposals, fires, and strikes) or by holidays, which are reasonably expected to have an effect on the test variable. Although a real variable is preferable to a dummy variable, including a dummy variable is likely to generate a significantly better model than if the event is simply ignored. For example, suppose one wishes to predict cost of sales based on sales. An initial regression yields the model

$$\text{cost of sales} = 0.9 \text{ sales}$$

This model generates significant differences to be investigated, particularly during the 4 months in the base period when there was a strike.

If a dummy variable is introduced as an additional predicting variable X_2, and a "1" is entered for each month that there was a strike and a "0" is entered for the other months, the regression equation can be improved. STAR will bring the strike month observations into line with the other observations by allocating a coefficient to X_2.

STAR uses stepwise multiple regression. It first accepts SALES (being the strongest predicting variable) into the regression equation, then accepts the additional DUMMY predicting variable, because it has a significant effect on reducing the unexplained variation in cost of sales in the strike months.

The equation becomes

$$\text{cost of sales} = 0.8 \text{ sales} + 52 \, X_2$$

X_2 is the dummy variable, which has a value of 0 in the nonstrike months and 1 in the strike months. Therefore, in a nonstrike month when sales are 100, cost of sales is 80. In a strike month when sales are 10, cost of sales is 60. One has, therefore, successfully modeled the relationship. Dummy variables typically are expressed in terms of the binary numbers 0 and 1, but they may be in terms of any other set of numbers that serve to distinguish one observation from another, based on some characteristic that may be significant in a particular application.

6.4.3   Seasonality

If the relationship among the variables in the model is expected to be affected by seasonal factors, the STAR Program includes options to generate seasonal variables automatically, which are a type of a dummy variable. If these options are specified, the program will test to determine whether there is a significant seasonal pattern in the test variable.

In a monthly model, for example, STAR will generate one predicting variable for each month of the year, S_1 through S_{12}, each of which adjusts for seasonal effects in the month it represents. These variables have the value 1 in the months they represent and 0 for all other months. S_{12}, for example, has the value 1 in months 12, 24, 36, etc., and the value 0 elsewhere. Thus, only the months affected by seasonality will have the effect incorporated into the calculated expectation of the test variable.

Seasonality should be used with caution. If, based on knowledge of the client's business, the user is not aware of seasonal fluctuations, seasonality should not be specified for the model. In addition, when seasonality has been specified, the auditor should review for which months STAR generated the predicting seasonal variables to ascertain that the model corresponds with the user's understanding of the business.

Instead of using seasonal adjustment, it is ordinarily preferable to indicate the months during which a seasonal fluctuation is expected by including a specific real or dummy variable in the model for such months. Examples of months that might be seasonally adjusted are:

- December, for a business in the retail industry, when sales volumes are significantly higher and the relationship to cost of sales is likely to differ from other months of the year
- January, for a business that usually sells its products at a discount during that month and hence has lower profit margins than at other times of the year
- August, if the business shuts down production (for vacation or model changeover), thereby affecting the relationship between the variables in the model.

For seasonality to be specified (instead of specifically using a dummy variable), there needs to be a base period with at least three sets of observations for a seasonal pattern to be identified. In a monthly model, the base must consists of 36 periods, even though STAR normally requires only 20 observations.

To continue the sales–cost of sales example, suppose that the client has a sale every May but has no other seasonal influences. Sales in May are 200 and cost of sales is 170. If seasonal adjustment is requested, STAR will create 12 seasonal variables, S_1 through S_{12}. The variable representing May, S_5, will have values of 1 each May and values of 0 in all other months. (Note that STAR requires at least 3 years of data in the base period if seasonality is used; this example assumes that the base has been increased to 36 months.)

Because STAR uses stepwise multiple regression to ensure that only significant variables are included in the model, it will include only S_5 and exclude the other 11. The regression equation is

$$\text{cost of sales} = 0.8\ \text{sales} + 52X_2 + 10S_5$$

The effects of a dummy variable and seasonality are the same. However, identifying the expected seasonal pattern and developing a model with a dummy variable to incorporate it is usually preferable to specification of seasonality.

6.4.4 Trends

STAR can also generate a trend variable that the program can use to adjust for significant time-related trends. The auditor can specify trend when the relationship between the predicting and test variables is expected to change systematically and in one direction over time. For example, trend can be used in a model to predict cost of sales from sales when costs are increasing but selling price is fixed. Cost of sales is expressed in the model as a fixed percentage of sales plus a markup, which increases each period. The markup is represented by the trend variable and an appropriate coefficient (e.g., cost of sales $= 0.8\ \text{sales} + 0.25X_2$, where X_2 is the trend variable).

The trend variable has the value 1 in the first period of base data, 2 in the second period, and so on. Thus, if there are 36 monthly observations in the base period and 12 in the current period (the period being tested), the last observation in the projection period will have a trend variable value of 48.

6.4.5 Lagged Variables

Lagged variables can be specified to build expected time lags into relationships such as those expected between cash collections and sales or between sales and advertising expenses. For example, if advertising expenses in March were expected to affect June sales, the auditor can specify that advertising expense be lagged by 3 months.

6.5   GENERAL CRITERIA FOR PREDICTING VARIABLES

Once the audit objectives of a STAR application have been defined (as discussed in Section 6.3), the remaining step in designing the audit model is the selection of the predicting variables to be specified. This can be viewed as a three-stage process: (1) the initial selection of the variables, (2) possible refinements of the variables before running the Program, and (3) possible improvements in the audit model after reviewing it and other results shown on the STAR printouts. The first of these stages is discussed in this section, the second is discussed in the next section, and the third is discussed in Chapter 7.

Audit judgment and knowledge of the business being audited are particularly important in specifying the appropriate predicting variables. As explained in Chapter 4, the STAR Program will eliminate any specified variables that are not statistically significant. However, it obviously cannot include significant variables unless they have been specified by the auditor. Entering variables without regard to whether they are predictive of the amount being tested, even though they are likely to be discarded by STAR, is not recommended. The auditor should only enter data expected to have a relationship with the test variable, which should meet the criteria of being plausible, relevant, and independent. However, if predicting variables expected to be related to the test variable are rejected by STAR, the auditor should investigate why the relationship is not acceptable to STAR.

Although it is possible to use up to 24 predicting variables in a STAR model, the auditor should refrain from using more than two or three to prevent the model from becoming too complex to be comprehensible.

6.5.1   Plausibility and Relevance

A relationship between a predicting variable and the test variable should be both plausible and relevant for the audit purpose of an application. These two criteria are discussed together for convenience in dealing with their similarities and differences. A *plausible* relationship is one that may reasonably be expected to exist based on the auditor's understanding of the business and its accounting procedures. The relationship should be plausible with regard to the base profile and to the projection profile.

A relationship that is logically very tenuous or remote would not be plausible, even though the correlation might be high, because the auditor would be unable to explain it on the basis of knowledge of the business. This kind of correlation is known as *spurious correlation.* A corollary effect of spurious correlation is that the auditor would not have a reasonable basis for expecting the relationship to continue to apply to the projection profile of audit interest. A *relevant* relationship is one that affords evidence that is meaningful for the purpose of the application and that, therefore, can be expected to provide projections that will be useful in identifying observations containing errors or irregularities.

Plausibility and relevance are not quite the same thing, although they have similarities. For example, a relationship between gross profit as a test variable and sales and cost of sales as predicting variables obviously is plausible, because gross profit is determined by deducting cost from sales. It is equally obvious, however, that a regression function derived from these variables would not be relevant for audit purposes, because it would only provide evidence of arithmetic accuracy.

Similarly, a relationship between sales and cost of sales is inherently plausible but would not be relevant for audit purposes if (1) there is only one product and it has a known constant cost and selling price or (2) there are several products but periodic cost of sales is determined as a constant estimated percentage of sales. However, the relationship would be relevant if known or estimated costs vary among products.

A relationship between sales and cost of sales is plausible, whether these variables are expressed as gross or net amounts. Some deductions in determining net amounts may, however, affect these variables differently. For example, sales allowances or customer deductions may not involve returned goods that are deducted from cost of sales. Similarly, cash discounts or retroactive quantity discounts may be recorded during accounting periods later than those in which the gross sales and corresponding costs were recorded. If such deductions and the relevant time lag are material, the gross amounts may be more relevant for use as variables. In this case, the deductions should be tested separately by analytical review or otherwise.

If cost of sales is determined at standard costs and variances from actual cost are recorded when purchases and production occur rather than when sales occur, the relationship of sales to standard costs may be more relevant than the relationship to actual costs because of the timing difference in recognizing the variances. The relationship of sales to standard costs may also be more relevant when separate tests of the cost variances are feasible. In such applications, basic raw material prices or indexes, labor rates, and production or sales volume would be plausible and relevant variables.

A relationship between sales and inventory purchases or production is also plausible and may be relevant for some audit purposes. Such a relationship, however, ordinarily would require use of observations of purchases or production of earlier periods to reflect the usual inventory turnover experience. Variations from the latter, resulting from strikes or other interruptions in the operations of the client, may be useful as real or dummy variables.

A relationship between sales and selling expenses is also plausible and relevant, even though the expenses may include relatively fixed components that do not vary significantly with sales. Such components will be comprehended in the constant in the regression function when selling expenses are the test variable. The preceding comments concerning selling expenses apply also to administrative and general expenses, although the latter may include a larger proportion of relatively fixed expenses.

In considering the plausibility of relationships between variables, the possibility of time lags in such relationships should be recognized. For example, a time lag may be expected between sales and collections on receivables, depending on the credit terms of the sales. If monthly collections are the test variable, sales for the current and one or more preceding months may be more plausible as the predicting variables than sales for the current month alone.

The plausibility of dummy variables for trend and seasonality depends on whether the auditor thinks such variables may identify changes that might occur in the test variable, either gradually over time (trend) or systematically within each year (seasonality), which are not reflected in any other predicting variable. For example, the relationship between sales and cost of sales may change gradually because of competitive pressures or periodically in a pattern that corresponds with the seasons of the year. However, the relationship may remain relatively stable, although both variables are increasing because of inflation or expanding physical volume or because of a seasonal pattern that affects both somewhat equally.

The effects of trend or seasonality should ordinarily be specified if the auditor has any reason to believe that they may be significant and no real variables are available that might provide a better measure of the effects of these factors. If the dummy variables are not significant, they will simply be excluded from the audit model by the automatic tests performed by the Program. Examples of real variables that might provide better measures include an index of specific prices or of general inflation (if increases in unit prices are changing the relationship between physical volume and total sales) or statistics relating to weather conditions (if such conditions are likely to affect the relationship between sales and costs).

The discussion in this section is merely illustrative of the kinds of factors to be considered in applying the general criteria of plausibility and relevance and does not purport to be exhaustive or definitive. In specifying the predicting variables, there is no substitute for a clear understanding of the business operations and the audit purpose of the application. Appendix C provides examples of relationships between test and predicting variables.

6.5.2   Audit Independence

The audit independence criterion requires that variables specified as predicting variables for statistical purposes should be either (1) obtained from independent sources or (2) tested through other auditing procedures. This criterion encompasses the dual objectives of assuring reasonable accuracy in the data used as observations and avoiding circularity in the logic of applications. It applies to observations in both the base profile and the projection profile.

External variables, by definition, originate from sources outside the company being audited and ordinarily would satisfy the audit independence criterion. Tables of statistics published by government agencies or industry associations should not, however, be used uncritically. The auditor should read any explanations that accompany such a table to understand what it purports to show and to decide whether it is relevant for the intended application. If the company being audited has a dominant effect in the compilation of industry statistics, the auditor should recognize this in considering the relevance of such statistics to the application.

Dummy variables should be based on conditions known to the auditor and thus ordinarily would satisfy the audit independence criterion.

Internal variables that may be treated as being from independent sources are those derived from records that are maintained by persons who are not in a position to manipulate, directly or indirectly, the records of the test variable. Usually, any data obtained from accounting or finance departments are not considered independent or reliable unless the data have been tested by the auditors. Further discussion of this subject, however, is beyond the scope of this book. In addition to the basic accounting records and periodic financial statements, other possible internal sources of independent variables include auxiliary records of production, shipments, number of employees, and other quantitative operating data.

Tests to establish the independence of internal variables through other auditing procedures ordinarily should be for misstatement in the direction that is properly related to the direction of test specified for the test variable. If, for example, machinery and equipment is the predicting variable and depreciation expense is the test variable in an application to test depreciation expense for overstatement, the test to establish the independence of machinery and equipment should also be for overstatement. In this situation, any errors of overstatement in machinery and equipment would have the effect of increasing the regression estimates of depreciation expense. This would tend to obscure errors of overstatement in the depreciation expense by reducing the probability of identifying excesses to be investigated or by reducing the amount of the excesses that are identified.

Tests to establish the independence of internal variables need not be performed separately but can be accomplished through appropriate application and coordination of other auditing procedures. In performing these tests, the auditor must be careful to avoid the problem of circularity. An example of circularity in this context would be the use of salaries and wages as the predicting variable in an application to test payroll tax expense for overstatement and the use of payroll tax expense as the predicting variable in another application to test salaries and wages for overstatement, without any other tests for overstatement of either variable. The following paragraphs provide several examples that show how circularity can be avoided by practical combinations of typical auditing procedures.

Confirmation of accounts receivable from customers, combined with tests for overstatement of credits to such receivables from cash-receipts records and other sources, such as sales returns and allowances records, constitute corollary tests for overstatement of sales. Consequently, sales through the confirmation date could appropriately be used as a predicting variable in applications to test for overstatement of such test variables as cost of sales, selling expenses, and administrative and general expenses.

Tests for overstatement of inventories, through observation and tests of the compilation of physical inventories combined with tests of cutoffs and of transactions charged to inventory accounts, constitute corollary tests for understatement of cost of sales. Consequently, cost of sales through the physical inventory date could appropriately be used as a predicting variable in applications to test for understatement of sales.

If sales for the current year are tested for understatement without cost of sales being used as a predicting variable, sales may be used as a predicting variable in applications to test for understatement of cost of sales. Such applications, following tests of a physical inventory at an interim date, combined with tests for overstatement of charges to inventory during the intervening period, would provide a corollary test for overstatement of inventory at the balance-sheet date. If cost of sales for the current year is tested for overstatement without sales being used as a predicting variable, cost of sales may be used as a predicting variable in applications to test for overstatement of sales. Such applications, following confirmation of accounts receivable at an interim date, combined with the use of sales as a predicting variable to test for understatement of collections and other credits to receivables during the intervening period would provide a corollary test for overstatement of receivables at the balance-sheet date.

6.6   POSSIBLE IMPROVEMENTS IN AUDIT MODELS

The variables selected initially should be considered further to decide whether refinements of them might improve the audit model. Certain factors that sometimes are present in accounting records may provide an opportunity for such refinements. These factors can be classified generally as (1) errors in variables, (2) unusual transactions or events, and (3) changes in conditions. Before discussing these factors further, the general forms of possible refinements and their statistical effect on audit models are considered.

6.6.1   General Forms and Effects of Refinements of Variables

Possible refinements of the initial variables may take the form of (1) adjustment of the observations to eliminate the actual or estimated effects of a factor that has been identified, (2) use of such effects as a separate variable, or (3) use of a dummy variable as a surrogate for the unknown effects.

The general order of preference among these forms of refinement is that actual amounts are preferable to estimates, and adjustment of the observations to eliminate the actual effects is preferable to use of such effects as a separate variable. The choice between estimates and dummy variables, however, generally depends on the availability and expected reliability of the estimates.

The preferability of actual amounts over estimates is obvious. The preferability of adjustment of the observations affected over use of the actual amounts as a separate variable arises from the statistical effects of the latter option. Because of the likelihood of some degree of partial correlation between the new variable and other variables and the loss of 1 degree of freedom in the computations, the results of using a separate variable are likely to approximate reasonably well, but not be equal to, the actual effects of the factor identified.

To compare the use of estimated and dummy variables, consider the latter option first. If an identified factor affects only one observation of the variable involved, using a dummy value of 1 for the observation affected is equivalent to using an estimate of any amount (with zeros being used for the other observations in either case). Although the values of the variables and their coefficients obviously will differ in the two cases, their products will be equal, and therefore the other relevant regression results will be identical.

If more than one observation is affected, the regression results will be the same, whether a dummy value of 1 or some other uniform estimate is used for each affected observation. Nonuniform estimates will either improve or impair the model, depending on how well they approximate the actual factors. In choosing between the use of estimated or dummy variables, the auditor should consider other conditions that affect the application, particularly the availability or difficulty of obtaining estimates. A dummy variable may be as effective as, and easier to obtain than, more completely quantified estimates.

6.6.2 Errors in Variables

Although the objective of analytical procedures is to detect errors in the projection profile that would materially affect the financial statements, possible errors in the base profile used to develop the audit model should be considered. As the data in the base profile ordinarily will have been audited (previously in time-series applications or currently by other means in cross-sectional applications), any errors that would materially affect the financial statements presumably would have been identified and corrected by adjustments. In that event, the adjustments should also be recognized in the data used in the base profile. If previously identified errors were not adjusted because their effects were not considered material to the financial statements, it nevertheless will ordinarily be worthwhile to adjust the data in the base profile to correct such errors unless their effect is negligible.

In addition to the possible errors already discussed, there may be errors in the recording or allocation of amounts between months or quarters that do not affect the aggregate amounts included in the annual financial statements. These may be regarded as *intraperiod timing errors,* in contrast to *interperiod timing differences* (as that term is used in accounting with reference to income tax allocations and certain other matters). For brevity in the remainder of this chapter, such errors are referred to simply as *timing errors.* These errors ordinarily would be systematic, in the sense that they arise from the system or process for recording transactions and periodic allocations. Typical examples include the system or process used for establishing cutoffs for monthly sales and purchase transactions, for recording cost of sales, and for periodic accruals and amortization.

At one extreme, systems may be found in which periodic recording is quite accurate, with only minor (if any) adjustments being required at the end of the year. At the other extreme, systems may be found—especially in smaller businesses—in which little if any effort is made to achieve proper periodic recording, with the result that substantial adjustments are required to prepare financial statements at the end of the year. Between these extremes are intermediate variations in degree, including systems that are designed to provide proper periodic recordings by quarters but not by months. The auditor's general knowledge of the client's systems should be adequate for the purpose of deciding whether refinements of variables are needed because of systematic timing errors.

Probably the most common situations requiring consideration in this respect are the systems for making cutoffs in the recording of accounts payable and purchases and for recording inventories and cost of sales.

Accounts payable and purchases.   In some systems, purchases may be recorded through a voucher system or similar record that provides a continuous balance of accounts payable. In other systems, the primary recording of purchases may be through the cash disbursements records, with accounts payable being recorded only from lists of unpaid invoices at the end of a month, quarter, or year.

If the listing of unpaid invoices is recorded monthly, there would be no systematic differences between the continuous and periodic systems. The results under both systems, however, depend on the accuracy of the monthly cutoffs, and this accuracy may vary if more careful attention is given to cutoffs for the last month in each quarter or year. The effect of more careful attention at such dates ordinarily would be difficult to quantify, but the use of a dummy variable to reflect that effect may improve the model.

If accounts payable are recorded only from quarterly or annual listings of unpaid invoices, the model is likely to be improved by eliminating, from the observations involved, the net effect of recording the current balance and reversing the preceding balance.

Inventories and cost of sales.   Systems for recording inventories and cost of sales can be classified broadly as perpetual inventory systems and periodic inventory systems. For simplicity in this section, the flow of inventory from raw materials through work in process to finished goods or to other accounts is ignored, and comments will be confined to purchases and cost of sales.

In a perpetual system, as its name implies, inventory accounts are continuously debited for the cost of inventory acquired and credited for the cost of sales or other dispositions. These accounts show perpetual balances that purport to represent inventory on hand. Perpetual inventory records ordinarily show the transactions and balances in detail, by reference to descriptions, part numbers, or other identification of inventory items, and the perpetual balances ordinarily are adjusted at least annually to agree with actual balances based on physical inventories.

If the amount of an inventory adjustment is significant, the audit model can be improved by eliminating the effect of that adjustment. Ordinarily, this adjustment will be made in the period in which it is recorded. If the periods to which the adjustment applies are known, however, it is better to adjust those periods.

In a periodic inventory system, the inventory balances are determined solely by periodic physical inventories, and cost of sales is determined from purchases and the changes in the physical inventories. If physical inventories are taken at the end of each month or other period to be used as an observation in a data profile, the results for such periods should be the same as they would be under a perpetual inventory system. In a periodic inventory system, if physical inventories are not taken at the ends of such periods, systematic timing errors are almost certain to exist. The effect of such errors is that recorded cost of sales is the same as purchases for all periods except the one in which an inventory adjustment is recorded, and the recorded costs for that period include both current purchases and the change in inventory that occurred during all periods since the preceding physical inventory.

If the amount of a periodic inventory adjustment is not significant in relation to the aggregate cost of sales for the periods since the last similar adjustment and if there is no reason to believe that the actual (but unknown) inventories have fluctuated significantly within the intervening periods, the audit model can be improved by eliminating the effect of the inventory adjustment, as explained previously.

The conditions described in the preceding paragraph imply that purchases can reasonably be used as a surrogate for cost of sales in the audit model. These conditions are present in many cases. Whether they are present in a particular case depends largely on the client's operating policies and practices with respect to matters such as the lead time for purchases, the basis used for determining purchasing requirements, the policy concerning production for inventory versus specific orders, the typical inventory levels and turnover rates, and seasonal factors affecting production and sales.

If the factors just mentioned or any other factors cause the auditor to expect significant fluctuations in the actual (but unknown) inventories at the end of any of the periods between the physical inventory dates or if the recorded inventory adjustment is significant in relation to the aggregate cost of sales in the intervening period, the auditor should consider additional possibilities for improving the model. In addition to any other improvements that might be suggested by the circumstances in a particular case, these possibilities include the use of seasonal variables, sales backlogs, sales forecasts, or lagged actual sales as variables.

If sales backlogs or forecasts are to be used, the lead time required for purchasing and production should be recognized in order to achieve an appropriate matching of these variables with purchases by periods. If neither of those variables are available, actual sales lagged by the lead time can be used as a variable on the premise that this is a surrogate for management's expectations that generated the inventory purchases.

6.6.3 Unusual Transactions or Events

Unusual transactions or events are those that differ in some significant way from the client's recurring business operations. When unusual transactions are identified and their amounts are known, such amounts should be eliminated from the observations in which they are included. The amounts that are eliminated should be audited as appropriate by other procedures, because they would be effectively excluded from investigation as a part of the analytical review procedures.

For the purpose of this discussion, unusual events are distinguished from unusual transactions because their effects ordinarily are not readily determinable. Typical examples of unusual events include disruptions of operations resulting from causes such as strikes, equipment failures, severe weather conditions, and fires or other physical disasters. If an unusual event affects more than one period and reasonable estimates of its effects can be made, the estimates should be eliminated from the observations affected. Otherwise, the event should be treated as a dummy variable.

If the unusual event affected only one observation, the dummy variable should be 1 for that observation and 0 for the others. If the unusual event affected more than one observation, the dummy variable could also be 1 for each observation affected, which would imply that the event affected each observation approximately equally. If there is some basis for assuming that the relative effects on the observations were different, some reasonable surrogate for the relative effects should be used instead of a constant 1. For example, the number of days a plant was closed during each period because of a strike might be a reasonable surrogate for the relative effects of such an event.

6.6.4   Changes in Conditions

This section is concerned with changes in conditions that have a continuing effect on the business operations or the accounting records after the date of the change. Examples of changes that affect operations include the acquisition or disposal of subsidiaries; the introduction or discontinuance of product lines or major products; the enactment of laws or regulations affecting matters such as sales prices, product quality, production methods, or marketing arrangements; and major changes in competitive conditions. Examples of changes that affect accounting records include those relating to methods of accounting for matters such as inventory, depreciation, pensions and fringe benefits, leasing transactions, and capitalization of interest.

For the purpose of specifying an audit model, the treatment of changes in conditions should generally be similar to that of unusual transactions or

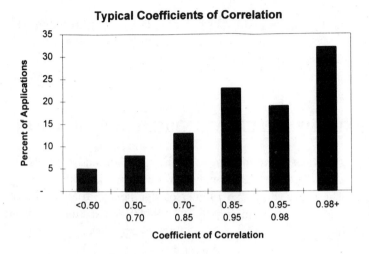

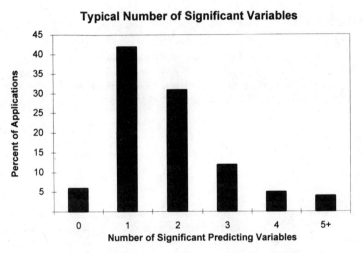

Figure 6.2   Statistical results from typical applications.

events, as discussed previously. If new subsidiaries, operating locations, or products involve operations under significantly different conditions, the results of such operations should be segregated, if feasible, and audited through separate applications of the STAR Program or by other procedures. Changes in volume alone need not be treated as changes in conditions unless the operating relationships being considered are particularly sensitive to volume. If it is not appropriate or feasible to segregate the effects of changes in conditions so that they can be audited by other applications or procedures, the use of reasonable estimates as a separate quantitative variable or of a dummy variable to reflect the effect of such changes ordinarily will improve the audit model.

6.7   EXPERIENCE FROM TYPICAL APPLICATIONS

Figure 6.2 provides some indication of the range of statistical results that reasonably may be expected from typical audit applications of the STAR Program. The figure shows the number of significant variables and the co-efficient of correlation from slightly over 9,000 actual audit applications. These results are a good cross section of actual experience.

REFERENCES

1. American Institute of Certified Public Accounts, "Audit Sampling." *Statement on Auditing Standards* 39, 1981.
2. American Institute of Certified Public Accountants, "Audit Risk and Materiality in Conducting an Audit." *Statement on Auditing Standards* 47, 1983.

7

COMPLETING AUDIT APPLICATIONS

7.1 INTRODUCTION

After the audit model has been designed and the observations to be used in the data profile have been obtained, the auditor's next steps are to (1) run the STAR Program, (2) review the resulting report (and possibly revise the model), (3) investigate any unusual fluctuations identified by the program, and (4) evaluate any errors discovered through such investigation. How to run the STAR Program is discussed in the STAR Program user documentation. Steps 2, 3, and 4 are the subject of this chapter.

7.2 REVIEWING THE PROGRAM REPORT

The auditor should review the STAR Program report before proceeding with the investigation of any excesses identified for that purpose. As will be explained, however, some of the information shown in the report may not require any further action by the auditor.

7.2.1 Specifications and Observations

The specifications should be reviewed to determine that they were entered as intended. The auditor should obtain totals for the observation data prior to entering it into the program and then compare the totals to the totals calculated by STAR.

7.2.2   Regression Function and Other Regression Statistics

The section of the report that displays the results of the regression analysis of the variables in the base profile shows the regression function and other regression statistics. Some of the statistics that are shown, and others that are not, are used in the audit interface segment of the Program to accomplish its purposes. They are included on the report primarily for audit documentation, for use in possible applications of the Program for nonauditing purposes, and because it is customary statistical practice to do so. From an audit point of view, it is not essential that they be evaluated, although a review of them may suggest possible improvements in the model that could lead to greater audit efficiency. The meaning and computation of these results was explained in Chapter 3.

Ideally, all possibilities for improvement in the audit model should have been exhausted when the model was specified originally. Realistically, however, a review of the regression results may suggest possible improvements that were not apparent originally. The development of an audit model, therefore, can be regarded as an iterative process in which the auditor specifies an audit model, runs the Program, reviews the regression results for possible improvements in the model, and, if necessary, makes those improvements and reruns the Program. At a certain point, preferably early in the process, the model is deemed to be good enough for its intended purpose. For typical audit applications, the review for possible improvements should focus on the coefficient of correlation and on the pattern of the residuals. It is also important for the auditor to review the regression function developed by STAR to determine that it indeed reflects the intended relationships between the predicting variables, the test variable, and any dummy variables. The model should represent logical business relationships. One variable's impact on a relationship should not be duplicated by another variable. For example, units shipped and cost of sales should ordinarily not be used as two predicting variables in the same application.

7.2.3   Coefficient of Correlation

Although the statistical validity of the regression results does not depend on the magnitude of the coefficient of correlation, smaller coefficients are likely to be accompanied by more and greater excesses to be investigated, which will reduce audit efficiency. Possible improvements in the audit model should therefore be considered if the coefficient of correlation is smaller than expected from experience with similar applications (e.g., applications in prior years or on other audit engagements). If the auditor anticipates a very precise model, a coefficient as high as 90% may not be acceptable. If, however, the auditor knows that the model is as precise as practical and that the relationship between the variables is valid, a lower coefficient may be acceptable. If a coefficient is too small to allow any reliance, STAR will not use the model and will report that it has found no predicting variables.

Review of the coefficient of correlation, the residuals, and any error or warning messages on the STAR printouts may indicate possible refinements that should or could be made to the STAR model. The auditor should give these refinements serious consideration, because very often a good model becomes unusable in subsequent periods because model refinements were not made in prior years. In addition, a low coefficient of correlation may suggest that a significant variable is missing from the model; or if the user examines the graph of the residuals and finds a large positive residual followed by a negative residual of similar size, this may indicate a cutoff error. Possibilities for improving the model were discussed in Chapter 6.

7.2.4   Residuals

One of the most useful printouts that the STAR Program produces is a plot of the residuals. In a time-series application, it shows how the residuals behave over time. In a cross-sectional application, it shows how the residuals relate to operating units. A review of this graph can sometimes give the auditor insights into the nature of the data and ideas for improving the model that are not otherwise easily obtained. The pattern may suggest a trend or seasonal factor, an omitted variable, an unusual transaction or event, or a change in conditions.

A pattern in which a sequence of predominately positive (or negative) residuals for earlier observations is followed by a sequence of residuals predominately of the opposite sign could indicate a trend that could be represented by a real or dummy variable. A pattern that recurs with some regularity might indicate seasonality. An unusually large individual residual could suggest an unusual transaction or event. A sequence of somewhat random positive and negative residuals, followed by a sequence with predominately one sign, might indicate a change in conditions. Other possibilities may be suggested by the pattern of residuals in a particular application.

An example of a pattern caused by changes in conditions occurred in an application that related sales in a hotel restaurant to cost of sales during a period of high inflation. In this case, the residual plot displayed a jagged pattern in the residuals. Further investigation revealed that the pattern resulted from the fact that menu prices were increased only every few months, whereas costs kept rising steadily. The gradual decline in the gross profit ratio would be halted abruptly when the menu prices were increased and then start declining again. As a result of the review of residuals, the model was improved by use of an index of menu prices as an additional variable.

7.2.5   Warning Messages

Explanations of the warning messages produced by the STAR Program are contained in Appendix D.

7.3   INVESTIGATING SIGNIFICANT DIFFERENCES

Significant differences identified by the STAR Program are designated on the printout as *excesses to be investigated*. How they are calculated by the STAR Program was explained in Chapter 5. In determining whether any of the differences are significant, STAR considered (1) materiality; (2) the required assurance that, if a material misstatement exists in total, the analytical procedure will detect the misstatement; (3) the amount of difference that it would be reasonable to expect due to the inherent imprecision of the model; and (4) the direction of test. Where the Program has identified an excess to be investigated, the recorded amount of the test variable should be tested for possible misstatement in that direction. An excess to be investigated may be caused by:

- An error in the recorded amount of the test variable
- An unusual transaction or event, or a change in conditions
- An error in a predicting variable, some imperfection in the audit model, or an extreme random fluctuation

A particular excess may be investigated by obtaining a satisfactory analytical explanation for the excess and corroborating the explanation by examining some independent evidence. If the auditor cannot obtain and corroborate explanations for significant differences, he should evaluate whether the data used to develop the expectations was reliable and plausible. If not, he should consider whether the application as a whole has any credibility. If it is not efficient to improve the expectations by considering additional predicting variables, he may need to perform tests of details to obtain substantive assurance, either for the entire balance or, if the application appears generally reliable, for those portions of the balance containing unexplained differences.

The fact that STAR identifies a significant difference to be investigated does not necessarily mean that something is wrong. Rather, it indicates that the auditor does not have the desired assurance that something is *not* wrong. The difference could be caused by an unusual transaction or event or by a number of ordinary occurrences that just happen to combine to cause a significant difference. Until the reason for the difference has been determined, corroborated, and quantified, however, the desired level of assurance from the analytical procedure has not been achieved.

In addition, the auditor should check whether differences between expectations and recorded amounts, even if not individually significant, follow any pattern that might indicate potential material misstatement in the aggregate. For example, the auditor should be concerned if most differences were in one direction and if many were close to the threshold.

When an investigation of differences identifies a potential correction to the base data used in the model, the STAR application should be refined, even though the explanation may be sufficient for the current-year audit purposes. In subsequent years, the model is likely to be less precise and, therefore, may identify more and larger excesses if it is not updated for discovered discrepancies.

7.3.1   Analytical Explanation

When an analytical explanation for an excess is used, the excess should be satisfactorily explained as being attributable to some specific cause and the impact of the cause on the recorded amount should be quantified. Reasonable approximations of amounts attributable to such causes are satisfactory, but unquantified vague explanations are not.

The auditor should maintain a healthy degree of skepticism in accepting explanations of excesses. Before accepting an explanation, the auditor should be satisfied that (1) it is reasonable and could account for at least the amount of the excess and (2) it is not based on some factor that has already been reflected in the model. To illustrate the latter, a change in sales volume ordinarily would not be a valid explanation for an excess if sales or cost of sales was used in the model as a predicting variable.

Inevitably, there is a large element of judgment in a decision to accept an explanation of an excess and an associated risk that the judgment may be incorrect. However, this is no different from the risk inherent in the use of nonstatistical techniques for analytical review or in the evaluation of evidence obtained by other auditing procedures.

The working papers documenting the investigation of excesses should indicate the evidential matter examined and the computations made to corroborate representations by management or any other explanations obtained.

7.3.2   Tests of Details

Although it is preferable to obtain a satisfactory analytical explanation of an excess to be investigated, often it is not possible to do so, particularly if the excess is small in relation to the recorded amount of the test variable. The fact that no error was found does not mean that none exists; conversely, the failure to find the cause of an excess does not mean that the cause is an error. In these circumstances, the auditor has not obtained sufficient evidence from analytical procedures to support a conclusion at the reliability level specified for the application. Therefore, additional tests of details are needed as an alternative. If the excess is relatively small, the auditor may decide initially that an analytical explanation is unlikely and elect to perform additional tests of details as the first alternative.

When additional tests of details are to be performed, the tests should be made from records that are pertinent to the recorded amounts of the test variable and appropriate for the direction of test. Because an excess may have been caused by errors at any stage, from initial recording through final summarization in the general ledger, the tests of details should encompass all of those functions.

The STAR Program designs a statistical sample that could be used to perform the additional tests of details. As explained in Chapter 5, the sample design is integrated with the results of the STAR Program to preserve the level of assurance that was specified for the application. The sample should be selected through the sampling technique known variously as *cumulative monetary amounts* (CMA) sampling, *dollar unit sampling* (DUS), *monetary attribute sampling* (MAS), and sampling with *probability proportional to size* (PPS).

The records to be treated as the population for the additional tests of details depend on the direction of test specified for the STAR application. If the test is for overstatement, the population consists of the records that support the observations of the test variable. Selections are made from accounting records and are tested by agreeing to independent source information. These records are referred to as the *primary population*. Any errors of overstatement obviously will be included in this population.

Because errors of understatement can arise from the omission of transactions that should have been recorded (and from errors in recorded transactions), the auditor should make selections from some source of information that can reasonably be expected to indicate transactions that should have been recorded. Such a source of information is referred to as a *reciprocal population*. The use of reciprocal populations for tests of details is common in auditing, although the descriptive term may not be. Typical examples include the use of disbursement checks and vendors' invoices recorded after the end of the year in tests for unrecorded costs, expenses, and payables at the balance-sheet date and the use of sales orders or shipping documents in tests for unrecorded sales and receivables. In this last example, and in some other reciprocal populations, the records may not show monetary amounts. In such cases, the test of details necessarily must be made from a numerical sample rather than from a monetary sample.

To facilitate the selection of sample items, the STAR Program reports the selection interval and the sample size for each observation that includes an excess to be investigated. The selection interval is expressed in monetary amounts in the same units as the test variable (e.g., $1,000s). This information can be used to select a monetary sample from either a primary or a reciprocal population. The simplest procedure for this purpose, which results in *systematic* selection with a random start, is outlined in four steps.

1. Enter a random starting number (which must be no greater than the selection interval) as a negative amount in an adding machine, calculator, or computer.

2. Enter the population items as positive amounts until the cumulative amount equals or exceeds zero. Select the last item entered as a sample item.

3. Enter the selection interval as a negative amount. If the cumulative amount is not negative, repeat this step until it is negative.

4. Repeat the process described in steps 2 and 3 until all population items have been entered.

7.4 EVALUATING AUDIT RESULTS

The final step in a STAR application is the evaluation of the audit results. If the STAR Program does not identify any excesses to be investigated, the objective of the application will have been achieved, and therefore no further evaluation is necessary. If excesses are identified, the need for further evaluation depends on whether any errors are found through the audit investigation, and this may depend on the auditor's definition of "error." If errors are found, the nature, cause, and effect of the errors should be considered in evaluating their qualitative and quantitative implications.

7.4.1 Definition of Errors

The definition of errors to be used depends on the auditor's objective for the particular application, which is indicated by the decisions made in specifying the audit model. As discussed in Chapter 6, the auditor's objective is related to the level of detail of accounts or accounting units to be presented in the financial statements or other information being audited. Therefore, any condition that causes the amount of an item presented in such information to be incorrect should be regarded as an error to be evaluated.

This definition excludes misclassifications of entries within groups of accounts that are combined into the same financial statement line. Such misclassifications are excluded because they would not affect the auditor's opinion on the basic financial information presented, although they might be the subject of comments or suggestions to management. The size of errors is not an element in their definition but should be considered in their evaluation, as discussed later.

Other matters to be considered in applying this definition include the distinction between errors, changes in accounting estimates, differences in judgment, and unauthorized transactions. The considerations concerning these matters in STAR applications are the same as those in applying any other auditing procedures and, therefore, are not dealt with here.

7.4.2   Evaluation of Errors

The nature, cause, and effect of errors may affect either their qualitative or quantitative implications. Errors may arise, for example, because accounting principles or policies are incorrectly applied or because the incorrect principles or policies were adopted in the first place. Errors may be intentional or unintentional. They may result from weaknesses in the design of the system of internal accounting control, from the limitations that are inherent in such systems, or from lack of compliance with the system.

The qualitative characteristics of errors may influence the auditor's judgment about their materiality, the need for their disclosure in the financial statements, or about comments or suggestions to be made to management. These considerations, however, are the same whether errors are detected in STAR applications or by other auditing procedures and, therefore, are not discussed further in this book.

In determining the quantitative implications of errors, the auditor should consider the nature and cause of the errors that have been detected. Depending on these characteristics, the auditor may conclude that such implications (1) are restricted to the isolated transactions or events that gave rise to the errors or to an identifiable category of similar transactions or events or (2) extend to the entire set of observations used in the application. The auditor should exercise careful professional judgment and healthy skepticism in deciding whether the quantitative implications of errors detected can reasonably be regarded as isolated.

The statistical evaluation of a STAR application for analytical review is analogous to that of a statistical sample for a test of details. For both types of auditing procedures, the evaluation should be based on the sample items or the regression observations in which the errors were detected, and it should include an estimate and an upper precision limit with respect to the total errors in the population or projection profile being audited.

The audit decisions made in designing the sample or regression model determine the probability of selection desired for both procedures, but the means by which those decisions are implemented are different. For an audit sample, the probability desired is achieved by computing the required sample size or selection interval, and this computation is based on the variability in the results that could be obtained from all possible samples of a given size. For a STAR application, the probability desired is achieved by computing the required threshold for identifying excesses to be investigated (as explained in Chapter 5), and this computation is based on the variability in the underlying process that generates the observations of the test variable. Therefore, it is evident that the threshold computations can also be used to determine the probabilities needed for a statistical evaluation of the audit results of a STAR application.

The following equation represents a simple method that may be conservative but ordinarily satisfactory for computing the estimate of the total error in the projection profile.* The basic formula for this purpose is

$$E = \sum_{t=1}^{n'} E_t m_t$$

where E = estimated total errors in the projection profile;

n' = number of observations in which errors were detected;

*To the best of the authors' knowledge, the first public presentation of this method of estimation was made at a conference at the University of North Carolina in May 1982. The method was described by Gary Holstrum (a partner in the authors' firm at that time) in his comments as a discussant on a paper by W. R. Kinney Jr. and G. L. Salamon, "Regression Analysis in Auditing: A Comparison of Alternative Investigation Rules." During the evening preceding the conference, Gary Holstrum and Kenneth W. Stringer learned from Stephen J. Aldersley that he had independently developed a similar method. That method, together with a refinement of it, was described in a draft of a paper that he furnished to Holstrum and Stringer at that time and revised in June 1982. The refinement of that method was described briefly in a paper by S. J. Aldersley and D. A. Leslie on "Models for Multilocation Audits," which was presented at a symposium at the University of Illinois on November 9–10, 1984. The authors of this book have benefited from discussions with those individuals about their observations in the course of the study and their use of the STAR Program.

E_t = amount of errors detected analytically in an observation t or estimated from an optional sample by use of the next formula; and

m_t = error estimation multiplier for the applicable observation t,
which is $1/(1 - \text{most adverse risk for the observation})$.

The most adverse risk is the risk associated with the "risk point" (as illustrated in Chapter 5). It can be found for a particular application by obtaining
a report in the form illustrated in Printout B.7 in Appendix B. The complement of the most adverse risk is the probability of selection (identification of
an excess to be investigated) of the applicable observation. The reciprocal of
this probability is the multiplier m_t to be used in extrapolating errors detected.

If errors are detected in an observation through use of an optional sample
of details as indicated on the STAR report rather than through an analytical
investigation, an estimate of the total errors in the observation should be
made from the sample and used as indicated in the preceding formula. The
formula for this estimate is

$$E_t = \sum_{i=1}^{j} E_{ti} \left(\frac{I_t}{A_{ti}} \right)$$

where E_t = estimated total errors in the observation t;

j = number of sample items in which errors were detected;

E_{ti} = amount of error detected in a sample item i from observation t;

I_t = selection interval for the optional sample from observation t
(shown on the STAR report); and

A_{ti} = recorded amount of the sample item in which the error was detected.

To maintain the reliability level specified for a STAR application, the upper precision limit specified initially must be adjusted to include both the
estimated total errors and their incremental effect on the precision limit. A
simple and conservative method that is ordinarily satisfactory for this purpose is given in the following formulas:

$$MP' = MP + E'$$

$$E' = \sum_{t=1}^{n'} E_t m_t P_t$$

where MP' = adjusted upper monetary precision limit;
    MP = specified upper precision limit;
    E' = precision-adjusted estimate of errors;
    P_t = precision adjustment factor for the applicable observation (as shown in Figure A.7);

and other notations are as shown previously.

The relationship between the initial precision limit specified, the effects of errors detected, and the final evaluation of the results of an application can be summarized as follows:

	Precision limit specified	Effects of errors detected	Final evaluation of results
Estimated errors	None	E	E
Precision limit	MP	$(E' - E)$	$MP + (E' - E)$
Total	MP	E'	MP'

There is an important distinction between the two components of the adjusted precision limit. The estimate of the errors is a statistical measure of the condition of the records comprising the projection profile, and this estimate is not affected by the reliability level specified for the application. In contrast, the precision limit is not related to the condition of the records but is a measure of the statistical assurance that can be attributed to the results of the application, and this is affected directly by the reliability level specified. Thus, the estimate of errors relates to the financial statements being audited, whereas the reliability and precision relate to the basis for the auditor's opinion on those statements. For further discussion of the consideration to be given by an auditor to the estimate of total errors and the risk that actual errors may exceed that estimate, readers are referred to SAS 39 and 47.

The methods presented earlier are simply a regression analogue of monetary sample evaluation methods. Certain refinements or variations are possible in applying the basic concept underlying these methods. One possible refinement is to revise all of the audit interface computations to give effect to the errors detected. The net effect of this revision would be revised values for the error estimation multipliers m_t, and these could then be used as indicated in the formulas given previously. Another possible refinement would be to use binomial probabilities for computing the precision adjustment factors P_t instead of the Poisson probabilities used for computing those shown in Figure A.7. A third variation would be to use the method known as DUS cell evaluation [1]. Further discussion of these alternatives is not included because they involve significant complications or other considerations and are unlikely to alter the audit decisions that would be made on the basis of the simpler methods presented here.

The method developed for computing monetary precision limits has been the subject of extensive research by academicians and practitioners. The upper limit computed by this method is often referred to in that context as the *Stringer bound* or *limit*. Most of this research has dealt with the known conservatism of the method under some conditions and with possibilities for reducing such conservatism without sacrificing the mathematical rigor that the method was designed to achieve. A review of this research literature or further exposition of the underlying method is beyond the scope of this book, but references to selected portions of this literature are included [2].

REFERENCES

1. D. A. Leslie, A. D. Teitlebaum, and R. J. Anderson, *Dollar-Unit Sampling: A Practical Guide for Auditors,* Toronto: Copp Clark Pitman, 1979.
2. (a) R. J. Anderson and A. D. Teitlebaum, "Dollar-Unit Sampling: A Solution to the Audit Sampling Dilemma," *CA Magazine,* April 1973.
   (b) S. E. Fienberg, J. Neter, and R. A. Leitch, "Estimating the Total Overstatement Error in Accounting Populations," *Journal of the American Statistical Association,* June 1977.
   (c) W. R. Kinney Jr. "Integrating Audit Tests: Regression Analysis and Partitioned Dollar-Unit Sampling," CICA Auditing Research Symposium, 1977.
   (d) J. H. McCray, "Evaluating Dollar Unit Sampling Upper Bounds," unpublished manuscript, 1981.
   (e) G. R. Meikle, "Example of a Sampling Plan," *Statistical Sampling in an Audit Context, an Audit Technique Study.* Toronto: Canadian Institute of Chartered Accountants, 1972.
   (f) J. Neter and J. K. Loebbecke, *Behavior of Major Statistical Estimators in Sampling Populations—An Empirical Study.* American Institute of Certified Public Accountants, 1975.
   (g) J. Neter, R. A. Leitch, and S. E. Fienberg, "Dollar Unit Sampling: Multinomial Bounds for Total Overstatement and Understatement Errors," *The Accounting Review,* January 1978.
   (h) J. Neter, H. S. Kim, and L. E. Graham, "On Combining Stringer Bounds for Indepen-

dent Monetary Unit Samples from Several Populations," *Auditing: A Journal of Practice and Theory,* Fall 1984.

(i) F. F. Stephan, "Some Statistical Problems Involved in Auditing and Inspection," *Proceedings of the American Statistical Association,* 1963.

(j) K. W. Stringer, "Practical Aspects of Statistical Sampling in Auditing," *Proceedings of the American Statistical Association,* 1963.

PART FOUR

MORE ADVANCED STATISTICAL CONCEPTS AND TECHNIQUES

8

STATISTICAL TESTS AND TRANSFORMATIONS

8.1 INTRODUCTION

This chapter utilizes some of the mathematical and computational aspects of the material that was covered in Chapter 4. First, the concepts of statistical inference and statistical significance are discussed. Second, how to apply tests of significance of independent variables in the stepwise regression algorithm used in the STAR Program is shown. Third, the statistical tests for discontinuity, autocorrelation, heteroscedasticity, and abnormality are explained and illustrated.

These tests all follow a common pattern. First, a *test statistic* is computed that measures the condition being tested (e.g., the degree of autocorrelation). The formula for the test statistic is designed in such a way that it is possible to determine what range of values is plausible for the statistic, under the hypothesis that the condition is *not* present. (The hypothesis that the condition is not present is often called the *null hypothesis*.) The endpoints of the range of plausible values are called *critical values*. If the value of the test statistic falls outside the range of plausible values, the implication is that the null hypothesis is incorrect. In other words, there is prima facie evidence that the condition being tested for is present.

The critical values for a test statistic are determined from the probability distribution of the statistic (this distribution is known from statistical theory) and the tester's decision about what constitutes a *significant* level of improbability. In statistical work, 5% and 1% are two often-used *significance levels.* To say that "the test statistic is significant at the 5% level" means that the probability is 5% or less that the value that has been calculated for the test statistic could occur if the null hypothesis were correct.

A number of different probability distributions are used to describe the behavior of test statistics. The test statistics that are of principal interest in this chapter are so-called *F statistics* that follow the *F distribution* (both named after Sir Ronald Fisher, a great British statistician). *F* statistics are ordinarily expressed as a ratio of two other statistics (and for that reason are sometimes also called *F ratios*). Both the numerator and the denominator of the ratio have degrees of freedom associated with them, and those two parameters determine the shape of the particular *F* distribution that applies. An example of the *F* distribution with a typical critical value is shown in Figure 8.1. Tables, such as those shown as Figures A.3 and A.4, are available to determine the critical value for *F*, given its two parameters and the required significance level.

8.2 SIGNIFICANCE OF INDEPENDENT VARIABLES

The statistic that is used to test for the statistical significance of an independent variable is based on the ratio of the sum of squares explained by the new variable to the residual (unexplained) sum of squares.

$$F = \frac{\text{sum of squares explained by new variable}/1}{\text{residual sum of squares}/(n - k - 1)}$$

The greater this *F* ratio, the more significant the variable being tested. It can be shown that *F* behaves according to the *F* distribution. Thus, the variable is judged to be significant when the *F* ratio exceeds a critical value determined by the *F* distribution and the level of significance at which the test is conducted. The numerator of this statistic has 1 degree of freedom, and the denominator has $n - k - 1$ degrees of freedom. Therefore, the statistic has an *F* distribution with 1 and $n - k - 1$ degrees of freedom. To illustrate the significance test, assume a 5% significance level because that is the level that the STAR Program uses.

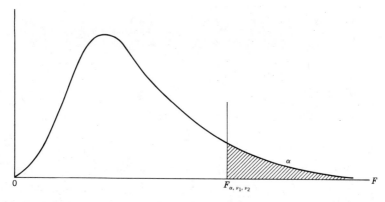

Figure 8.1 F distribution with v_1 and v_2 degrees of freedom. A critical value corresponding to a significance level of α is also shown.

The F ratio depends on two things:

1. The ratio of the variation explained by the new variable to the residual variation. The greater this ratio, the greater the F ratio.
2. The degrees of freedom associated with the residual variation ($n - k - 1$). The greater the degrees of freedom, the greater the F ratio.

The calculations for testing TIME AT STANDARD for significance in the Gamma Company application are shown in Figure 8.2. This is an example of an *analysis-of-variance* table. The statistics in the table come from Section 3.4.1.

The test statistic for the admission of X_1 is

$$F = \frac{3,912,198/1}{1,332,340/(36 - 1 - 1)} = 99.84$$

The critical value for a ratio with 1 degree of freedom for the numerator and 34 for the denominator is 4.13 at the 5% significance level (this can be interpolated from Figure A.4). Because the computed ratio of 99.84 exceeds this critical value, the independent variable is significant at the 5% level. This means that the risk that the variable is not really significant, but through a random occurrence appears to be so, is 5% or less (much less than 5% in this case, because the ratio is very high).

The F test can easily be extended to test the significance of the marginal

Type of Variation	Sum of Squares	Degrees of Freedom	Mean Square	F Ratio
Explained	3,912,198	1	3,912,198	99.84
Unexplained	1,332,340	34	39,186	
Total	5,244,538	35		

Figure 8.2   Gamma Company analysis of variance—one independent variable.

effect of using one or more additional independent variables. When used for this purpose, the test is applied progressively to each new variable being considered for admission to the regression function. This is illustrated in Figure 8.3, which is based on the Gamma Company statistics that were developed in Section 4.2.2. In that section, the residual sum of squares after the admission of X_2 was shown to be 762,905, and the explained sum of squares was shown to be 4,481,633. Because the explained sum of squares after the admission of X_1 was 3,912,198 (see Figure 8.2), the marginal improvement brought about by the admission of X_2 is 4,481,633 − 3,912,198 = 569,435. The test statistic is therefore

$$F = \frac{569,435/1}{762,905/(36 - 2 - 1)} = 24.63$$

The critical F value at the 5% level for a ratio with 1 and 33 degrees of freedom is 4.14. Because the computed ratio of 24.63 exceeds the critical value, the marginal effect of X_2 may be accepted as significant at the 5% level.

Just as the F test can be used to test whether a variable should be admitted to the regression function, it can also be used to test the significance of a

Type of Variation	Sum of Squares	Degrees of Freedom	Mean Square	F Ratio
Explained				
Effect of X_1	3,912,198	1	3,912,198	99.84
Marginal Effect of X_2	569,435	1	569,435	24.63
Joint Effect	4,481,633	2	2,240,817	
Unexplained	762,905	33	23,118	
Total	5,244,538	35		

Figure 8.3   Gamma Company analysis of variance—two independent variables.

variable that is already in the regression function. Thus, it can be used to test whether a variable that is in should remain in or be eliminated.

The F ratio can also be expressed in terms of partial correlation coefficients (see Section 4.2.1, where the concept was introduced). The partial correlation coefficient between a dependent variable Y and an independent variable X represents the marginal contribution of X to explaining Y. To calculate this coefficient, it is necessary to exclude the combined effect of all the other variables from both X and Y. This is done by separately regressing both X and Y against all of the other independent variables and taking the residuals. The partial correlation coefficient between X and Y is obtained by correlating the two sets of residuals.

If the residuals that result from regressing Y against $X_2, X_3, \ldots, X_k$ are denoted by e_t and the residuals that result from regressing X_1 against X_2, $X_3, \ldots, X_k$ are denoted by f_t, then the partial correlation coefficient between Y and X_1 after removing the influence of $X_2, X_3, \ldots, X_k$ is denoted by

$$R_{Y1 \cdot 23 \ldots k} = \frac{\sum e_t f_t}{\sqrt{\sum e_t^2} \sqrt{\sum f_t^2}}$$

where, in $R_{Y1 \cdot 23 \ldots k}$, $Y1$ indicates that the correlation is between Y and X_1 and $23 \ldots k$ indicates that the influence of the variables $X_2, X_3, \ldots, X_k$ has been removed. In general, the partial correlation between Y and X_i, after both have been adjusted for the other variables, is

$$R_{Yi \cdot 12 \ldots (i-1)(i+1) \ldots k}$$

The F ratio for testing the significance of X_1 given that $X_2 \ldots X_k$ are in the regression function can be expressed in terms of the partial correlation coefficient as

$$F = \frac{R_{Y1 \cdot 23 \ldots k}^2 / 1}{(1 - R_{Y1 \cdot 23 \ldots k}^2)/(n - k - 1)}$$

where $n - k - 1$ is the number of degrees of freedom that the regression function will have if the new variable is admitted. This formula is equivalent to the original one previously introduced, and therefore F has an F distribution with 1 and $n - k - 1$ degrees of freedom.

8.2.1   Stepwise Regression

As explained in Chapter 4, the STAR Program uses a stepwise regression algorithm that employs a forward selection procedure coupled to a backward elimination procedure. The following steps are used.

1. Calculate the coefficient of correlation between Y and each of the specified X variables. Find the X variable with the highest coefficient. This is the first candidate for admission.

2. Calculate an F ratio and see if it is significant. If it is, admit the candidate variable to the function. If it is not, stop the procedure and proceed on the basis that there are no significant variables. Go to step 7.

3. If all of the specified variables are in the regression, stop the procedure and go to step 7. Otherwise, calculate the partial correlation coefficient between Y and each of the remaining X variables after removing the influence of the admitted variables. Find the X variable with the highest coefficient. This is the next candidate for admission.

4. Calculate an F ratio and see if it is significant. If it is, admit the candidate variable to the function. If it is not, stop the procedure and go to step 7.

5. If more than two independent variables are in the regression, the backward elimination procedure comes into play. Otherwise, the program continues with the forward selection procedure in step 3.

6. Backward elimination procedure: Calculate the partial coefficient of correlation between Y and each X variable in the regression after removing the influence of the other X variables in the regression. Find the X variable with the lowest coefficient. Form an F ratio and test it for significance. If it is significant, go to step 3 and flip back into the forward selection mode. If it is not, the variable has evidently been made redundant by the admission of the other variables. Eliminate it. Go to step 5 to see if any other variables need to be eliminated at this point.

7. The stepwise procedure ends when all redundant variables have been eliminated from the function and any variables that have not been admitted are insignificant.

A detailed account of the computations that are necessary to implement the stepwise regression algorithm is given in Chapter 9.

8.3   DISCONTINUITY OF THE REGRESSION FUNCTION

In Chapter 4, the concepts of discontinuity in the base period and discontinuity between the base and audit periods were introduced. In this section, the Universal Chemicals example is used to show how the calculations are made to test for discontinuity in the base. The calculations for discontinuity between the base and audit periods are fairly similar, and a specific example of the calculations is not included.

8.3.1   Discontinuity within the Base Period

The following calculations are used to test for discontinuity within the base period.

1. Divide the observations for the base period into two subperiods—the last year and all preceding years.
2. Use the stepwise regression procedure to generate an overall regression function from the entire base.
3. Compute separate regression functions for each of the two subperiods using the independent variables used in step 2.
4. Calculate the residual sum of squares for the overall regression and for both of the separate regressions.

If there is no discontinuity in the data, all three regression functions will more or less coincide. In that case, the combined residual sum of squares for the two separate regressions will about equal the residual sum of squares for the overall regression. Conversely, if the data are discontinuous, the regression functions will not all coincide, and the combined separate functions will provide a tighter fit than the overall function. The combined residual sum of squares for the separate regressions will be significantly less than the residual sum of squares for the overall function.

The statistic that is used to test for discontinuity is

$$F = \frac{[\text{SUMOVERALL} - (\text{SUM}_1 + \text{SUM}_2)]/(k + 1)}{(\text{SUM}_1 + \text{SUM}_2)/(n + n_2 - 2k - 2)}$$

where SUMOVERALL is the residual sum of squares for the overall function, SUM_1 and SUM_2 are the residual sums of squares for the two separate regressions, n_1 and n_2 are the number of base observations in each of the separate subsets, and k is the number of independent variables.

Because the regression functions that are fitted separately to the two sub-parts of the base must always fit at least as well as the overall function, F can never be negative. In the ideal situation, the three functions will be identical, SUMOVERALL will equal $SUM_1 + SUM_2$, and, consequently, F will be zero. When the data are discontinuous, the two separately fitted regression functions will fit better than the overall function; SUMOVERALL will be larger than $SUM_1 + SUM_2$ and therefore F will be positive. F therefore is a measure of the discontinuity of the data.

It can be shown that F has an F distribution with $(k + 1)$ and $(n_1 + n_2 - 2k - 2)$ degrees of freedom. This means that discontinuity can be tested by comparing F with a percentage point of the appropriate F distribution. The STAR Program tests for discontinuity at the 1% level. This means that, if there is no discontinuity in the base, the probability is only 1% that the actual observations and resulting F statistic will lead to a conclusion that the data are discontinuous. The test for discontinuity was developed and published by Chow [1] (see also Fisher [2]).

For the data shown in Figure 4.6, the overall function, based on 36 observations, is

$$Y_t = -68.00 + 0.9266X_t + e_t$$

and the sum of the squared residuals is

$$\text{SUMOVERALL} = 146{,}576$$

The function for the first 24 base observations is

$$Y_t = 3.57 + 0.7489X_t + e_t$$

and the sum of the squared residuals is

$$\text{SUM}_1 = 9{,}631$$

The function for the last 12 base observations is

$$Y_t = 42.06 + 0.8717X_t + e_t$$

and the sum of the squared residuals is

$$SUM_2 = 31{,}029$$

The three regression lines that correspond to these three functions are shown in Figure 4.7. The F ratio is

$$F = \frac{[146{,}576 - (9{,}631 + 31{,}029)]/(1 + 1)}{(9{,}631 + 31{,}029)/(24 + 12 - 2 - 2)}$$

$$= 41.68$$

The 1% significance point for a variable having an F distribution with 2 and 32 degrees of freedom is 5.35 (Figure A.3). Because F is greater than this, the data are judged to be significantly discontinuous.

8.3.2   Discontinuity between Base and Audit Periods

The following steps are used to test for discontinuity between the base period and the audit period.

1.   Compute the regression function from the base data.
2.   Use the same independent variables as in step 1 to compute a regression function based on an *augmented* set of data consisting of the base data plus the audit period data.
3.   Compare the sum of the squared residuals from the regression functions computed in steps 1 and 2. If they are significantly different, this suggests that there has been a shift away from the original function during the audit period.

The F ratio used for this test is

$$F = \frac{(SUM_A - SUMOVERALL)/(n_A - n)}{SUMOVERALL/(n - k - 1)}$$

where SUM_A and n_A are the sum of the squared residuals and the number of observations, respectively, in the augmented set, and the other statistics are as defined in the previous subsection. This statistic has an F distribution with $n_A - n$ and $n - k - 1$ degrees of freedom.

8.4   AUTOCORRELATION

As explained in Section 4.4, a first-order autoregressive scheme is one in which the disturbance in period t consists of a part that depends on the disturbance in period $t - 1$ and a part that is random and independent. This can be expressed in terms of the disturbances from the ULR as

$$u_t = \rho u_{t-1} + v_t$$

where ρ (rho) is the *coefficient of autocorrelation,* or the *autoregressive parameter;* u_t is $Y_t - (\alpha + \beta X_t)$; and v_t is the random independent disturbance.

In practice, an estimate r of ρ is calculated from the residuals from the regression function. Thus,

$$e_t = r e_{t-1} + f_t$$

expresses the autoregressive scheme in terms of the observable residuals. The coefficient r measures the extent to which residuals depend on their previous value and is an estimate of ρ. If r is close to 0, there is little autocorrelation and no pattern will be noticeable. If r is close to 1 (say 0.9), the autocorrelation will be high and a time graph of the residuals will reveal a marked pattern. This is apparent from the graphs in Figure 4.9.

When significant first-order autocorrelation is present, the correct underlying model (assuming just one independent variable) is

$$Y_t = \alpha + \beta X_t + \rho u_{t-1} + v_t$$

This is called a *generalized linear model,* in contrast with an ordinary linear model, because it incorporates a more general assumption about the behavior of the residuals. In fact, the ordinary linear model is just a special case of the generalized model in which $\rho = 0$.

8.4.1   Estimating the Coefficient of Autocorrelation

The estimated coefficient of autocorrelation, r, is the coefficient that relates e_t to e_{t-1} in the equation

$$e_t = re_{t-1} + f_t$$

In this equation, r plays the same role the coefficient b plays in the regression function $Y_t = a + bX_t + e_t$. Thus, the formula for calculating r is similar to the least squares formula used for the calculation of b:

$$r = \frac{\sum_{t=2}^{n} e_t e_{t-1}}{\sum_{t=2}^{n} e_t^2}$$

8.4.2   Test for Autocorrelation

The test that the STAR Program applies for autocorrelation is known as the Durbin–Watson test. It is based on the relative size of the sum of the squared differences between successive residuals. When positive autocorrelation is present, the Durbin–Watson statistic is small, indicating that successive residuals tend to be significantly closer together than they would be were they independent. The statistic developed by Durbin and Watson [3] to test for first-order autocorrelation is

$$d = \frac{\sum_{t=2}^{n} (e_t - e_{t-1})^2}{\sum_{t=1}^{n} e_t^2}$$

The value of the d statistic ranges between 0 and 4. Ideally, its value should be 2, which indicates no autocorrelation. The closer it gets to 0, the stronger the positive autocorrelation; the closer it gets to 4, the stronger the negative autocorrelation. This can be demonstrated quite easily for the situation where d is based on a large number of observations, but not so easily for where n is small. The simpler case will be demonstrated.

The numerator in the formula for d can be expanded to give the expression

$$d = \frac{\sum_{t=2}^{n} e_t^2 - 2 \sum_{t=2}^{n} e_t e_{t-1} + \sum_{t=2}^{n} e_{t-1}^2}{\sum_{t=1}^{n} e_t^2}$$

When the number of observations is large, one observation more or less makes very little difference to the sum of the squared residuals. So the three sums of squares that appear in the expression are approximately equal. Therefore,

$$d \simeq \frac{\sum_{t=2}^{n} e_t^2 - 2 \sum_{t=2}^{n} e_t e_{t-1} + \sum_{t=2}^{n} e_t^2}{\sum_{t=2}^{n} e_t^2}$$

$$\simeq \frac{2 \sum_{t=2}^{n} e_t^2}{\sum_{t=2}^{n} e_t^2} - \frac{2 \sum_{t=2}^{n} e_t e_{t-1}}{\sum_{t=2}^{n} e_t^2}$$

Hence,

$$d \simeq 2 \left(1 - \frac{\sum_{t=2}^{n} e_t e_{t-1}}{\sum_{t=2}^{n} e_t^2} \right)$$

So, by definition of r,

$$d \simeq 2(1 - r)$$

Because r varies between -1 and $+1$, d varies between 0 and 4. Furthermore, when

$$r = 1, \quad d = 0$$
$$r = 0, \quad d = 2$$
$$r = -1, \ d = 4$$

Because only positive autocorrelation is likely in accounting data, the range 0 to 2 is important, and the situation in which d lies between 2 and 4 can be ignored. The particular point between 0 and 2 at which the value of d will be judged to indicate serious positive autocorrelation depends on the significance level at which the test is to be conducted and on the degrees of freedom associated with the d statistic. STAR, for example, tests at the 1% level. The d statistic is closely related to the F statistic and, like F, has two parameters. The degrees of freedom for the numerator and the denominator of d are k and n, respectively.

Although the exact distribution of d is not known, Durbin and Watson established that it lies between the known distributions of two other statistics, d_L (lower limit) and d_U (upper limit). They tabulated the values for these two statistics at the 5% and 1% levels of significance for various values of n and k. Positive autocorrelation is clearly significant if d is less than d_L and not significant if d is greater than or equal to d_U. If d falls between d_L and d_U, however, the test is inconclusive. STAR conservatively regards d less than d_U as a significant indication of positive autocorrelation. Figures A.5 and A.6 show critical values of d_U and d_L suitable for performing tests at the 1% and 5% levels of significance, respectively.

8.4.3 Generalized Regression

Just as ordinary regression analysis is used to estimate the parameters of the ordinary linear model, generalized regression analysis is used to estimate the generalized linear model. The generalized regression function (also called a *generalized least squares,* or GLS, function) is

$$Y_t = a + bX_t + re_{t-1} + f_t$$

This is an estimate of the ULR:

$$Y_t = \alpha + \beta X_t + \rho u_{t-1} + v_t$$

Because, by definition,

$$e_{t-1} = Y_{t-1} - (a + bX_{t-1})$$

the GLS function can (after some rearrangement of the terms) be expressed as

$$Y_t - rY_{t-1} = a(1 - r) + b(X_t - rX_{t-1}) + f_t$$

This can be written as

$$Y_t^* = a^* + bX_t^* + f_t$$

where it is understood that

$$Y_t^* = Y_t - rY_{t-1}$$

$$X_t^* = X_t - rX_{t-1}$$

and

$$a^* = a(1 - r)$$

When the function is written in this way, it looks just like an ordinary regression function, except that it involves Y^* and X^* rather than Y and X. In fact, this suggests the method that STAR uses to calculate a generalized regression function.

The first step is to calculate a set of transformed variables:

$$Y_1^* = \sqrt{1 - r^2}\, Y_1 \qquad X_1^* = \sqrt{1 - r^2}\, X_1$$

$$Y_2^* = Y_2 - r\, Y_1 \qquad X_2^* = X_2 - r\, X_1$$

$$Y_3^* = Y_3 - r\, Y_2 \qquad X_3^* = X_3 - r\, X_2$$

$$Y_4^* = Y_4 - r\, Y_3 \qquad X_4^* = X_4 - r\, X_3$$

$$\cdot \qquad\qquad\qquad \cdot$$
$$\cdot \qquad\qquad\qquad \cdot$$
$$\cdot \qquad\qquad\qquad \cdot$$

$$Y_n^* = Y_n - r\, Y_{n-1} \qquad X_n^* = X_n - r\, X_{n-1}$$

The first observation is transformed differently from the rest because there is no preceding observation. An alternative is simply to drop the first observation. That approach, however, would reduce the degrees of freedom by one. It can be shown that the transformation applied by the STAR Program in period 1 maintains the degrees of freedom (see Kadiyala [4]).

The next step is to use ordinary regression analysis to calculate a regression function

$$Y_t^* = a^* + bX_t^* + f_t$$

based on the transformed variables.

Finally, the generalized function is computed. The regression coefficient b is the same as the coefficient of the ordinary function that relates the transformed variables. The constant is calculated from the formula

$$a = \frac{a^*}{1 - r}$$

and a term is added to include the previous residual. The GLS function is therefore

$$\hat{Y}_t = a + bX_t + re_{t-1}$$

in periods $t = 2,3,4, \ldots$, and

$$\hat{Y}_1 = a + bX_1 + \sqrt{1 - r^2}\, e_1$$

in period 1. In all periods ($t = 1,2,3,4, \ldots$), $e_t = Y_t - (a + bX_t)$.

Because the generalized regression function includes a factor to take account of the pattern in the original residuals, the residuals from that generalized function should not show a pattern. That is, they should not be autocorrelated. In practice, however, they may be, either because the form of the autocorrelation has been misspecified (it is more complex than first-order autocorrelation) or because r, the estimated coefficient of autocorrelation, underestimates the true coefficient, ρ. The latter situation is quite common, because r has to be calculated on the basis of the observed residuals rather than on the disturbances from the ULR.

The estimate of the coefficient of autocorrelation can be improved by treating it as a first approximation and repeating the process. More specifically, the STAR Program works as described in the following steps.

1. Calculate r and a generalized regression function

$$Y_t = a + bX_t + re_{t-1} + f_t$$

2. Test the residuals f_t for autocorrelation. If they are not significantly autocorrelated, the function is satisfactory. Stop here.

3. If the residuals are autocorrelated, r is probably not a good estimate.

Treat the generalized function as if it were the original ordinary function (i.e., just use $\hat{Y}_t = a + bX_t$) and return to step 1.

It can be shown that this procedure yields values of r that get successively closer to the value of the true parameter ρ. As a practical matter, the approximations do not get significantly better after the first few iterations. STAR stops the process after three. If after three iterations the residuals are still autocorrelated, the presumption is that the form of the autocorrelation is not first order, as was originally assumed. The STAR Program gives a warning message that the function is not usable for audit purposes.

8.4.4   Illustrative Calculations

The tests and transformations are illustrated using the Autocorp application of Section 4.4. The following factors can be derived from the residuals shown in Figure 4.11. They will be needed in the calculations that follow:

$$\sum_{t=2}^{n} (e_t - e_{t-1})^2 = 63,101$$

$$\sum_{t=1}^{n} e_t^2 \qquad\quad = 95,514$$

$$\sum_{t=2}^{n} e_t e_{t-1} \qquad = 45,300$$

$$\sum_{t=2}^{n} e_t^2 \qquad\quad = 95,248$$

The coefficient of autocorrelation is

$$r = \frac{\displaystyle\sum_{t=2}^{n} e_t e_{t-1}}{\displaystyle\sum_{t=2}^{n} e_t^2} = \frac{45,300}{95,248} = 0.4756$$

Therefore, the estimated autoregressive scheme is

$$e_t = 0.4756 e_{t-1} + f_t$$

The d statistic used to test the significance of the autocorrelation is

$$d = \frac{\sum\limits_{t=2}^{n} (e_t - e_{t-1})^2}{\sum\limits_{t=1}^{n} e_t^2} = \frac{63,101}{95,514} = 0.66$$

The parameters of this d statistic are $k = 1$ and $n = 36$. Figure A.5 shows $d_U = 1.32$. Because $d < d_U$, the conclusion is that the residuals are auto-correlated.

The next step is to transform the variables using the coefficient of autocorrelation ($r = 0.4756$). The Y variable is transformed as

$$Y_1^* = \sqrt{1 - 0.4756^2} \times 649 = 571$$
$$Y_2^* = 660 - 0.4756 \times 649 = 351$$
$$Y_3^* = 766 - 0.4756 \times 660 = 452$$
$$\cdot$$
$$\cdot$$
$$\cdot$$
$$Y_{36}^* = 805 - 0.4756 \times 786 = 431$$

The X variable is similarly transformed:

$$X_1^* = \sqrt{1 - 0.4756^2} \times 287 = 252$$
$$X_2^* = 303 - 0.4756 \times 287 = 167$$
$$X_3^* = 355 - 0.4756 \times 303 = 211$$
$$\cdot$$
$$\cdot$$
$$\cdot$$
$$X_{36}^* = 417 - 0.4756 \times 360 = 246$$

When ordinary least squares regression is applied to the transformed variables, the regression function that results is

$$\hat{Y}_t^* = a^* + bX_t^* = 55.03 + 2.0796X_t^*$$

The standard error of this regression function is

$$s_v^* = 41.8710$$

The constant of the GLS function is

$$a = \frac{55.03}{1 - 0.4756} = 104.93$$

The function is therefore

$$Y_t = 104.93 + 2.0796X_t + 0.4756e_{t-1} + f_t$$

This can be compared with the original ordinary least squares function

$$Y_t = -68.08 + 2.5554X_t + e_t$$

shown in Figure 4.11.

It can be seen from the preceding discussion that the original ordinary least squares function can be regarded as a GLS function in which $\rho = 0$. This original function can be denoted by GLS^0. So far, GLS^0 has been transformed to GLS'. It is now necessary to consider whether GLS' needs to be transformed into GLS'', and GLS'' in turn to GLS'''. As indicated earlier, the STAR Program does not look beyond GLS''' because in practice this is seldom worthwhile.

To test whether GLS' successfully circumvents the problem of autocorrelation, it is necessary to test whether the new residuals f_t are autocorrelated. Once again the Durbin–Watson test is used. The calculations are similar to those that were made in the first iteration. The factors that are required are

$$\sum_{t-2}^{n} (f_t - f_{t-1})^2 = 69,668$$

$$\sum_{t=1}^{n} f_t^2 = 59,564$$

where the residuals are those from GLS'. The Durbin–Watson statistic is therefore

$$d = \frac{\sum\limits_{t=2}^{n} (f_t - f_{t-1})^2}{\sum\limits_{t=1}^{n} f_t^2} = \frac{69,668}{59,564} = 1.17$$

Because the 1% critical value is $d_U = 1.32$, as before, and $d < d_U$, the autocorrelation is significant at the 1% level.

The GLS′ function has evidently not overcome the problem of autocorrelation. However, it can be regarded as a first approximation to GLS″. The next step is refinement of the estimate of the coefficient of autocorrelation. This is done by calculating a new coefficient based on GLS′. The required factors are

$$\sum_{t=2}^{n} e_t e_{t-1} = 63,713$$

$$\sum_{t=2}^{n} e_t^2 = 102,607$$

where the residuals are formed from the GLS′ function by treating it as if it were the OLS function. That is,

$$e_t = Y_t - (104.93 + 2.0796X_t)$$

Therefore the coefficient of autocorrelation is

$$r' = \frac{\sum\limits_{t=2}^{n} e_t e_{t-1}}{\sum\limits_{t=2}^{n} e_t^2} = \frac{63,713}{102,607} = 0.6209$$

This is a better approximation to the true coefficient of autocorrelation than the first approximation. The new coefficient of autocorrelation is now used to transform the original variables in the same way as before. The application of OLS to these new transformed variables gives

$$\hat{Y}_t^* = a^* + bX_t^* = 45.05 + 2.0386X_t^*$$

The standard error of this function is

$$s_v^* = 39.5844$$

The constant for the generalized function is

$$a = \frac{45.05}{1 - 0.6209} = 118.85$$

(The calculation does not work out exactly as shown because the coefficient of autocorrelation shown here has been rounded to four decimal places.) Therefore, the new generalized least squares regression function GLS″ is

$$Y_t = 118.85 + 2.0386X_t + 0.6209e_{t-1} + f_t$$

Once again, autocorrelation is tested for by applying the Durbin–Watson test. The factors are

$$\sum_{t=2}^{n} (f_t - f_{t-1})^2 = 79,350$$

$$\sum_{t=1}^{n} f_t^2 = 53,391$$

Therefore,

$$d = \frac{\sum_{t=2}^{n} (f_t - f_{t-1})^2}{\sum_{t=1}^{n} f_t^2} = \frac{77,350}{53,391} = 1.45$$

Because this exceeds the critical value of 1.32, the conclusion is that the auto-correlation is not significant at the 1% level, that the function GLS″ has successfully circumvented the problem of autocorrelation, and that the final generalized least squares regression function is

$$Y_t = 118.85 + 2.0386X_t + 0.6209e_{t-1} + f_t$$

This is the GLS function shown in Figure 4.11. If GLS″ had not worked, STAR would have gone through one more iteration using GLS″ as an approximation to GLS‴. If GLS‴ had not worked, the Program would have regarded the autocorrelation as fatal for audit purposes.

The standard error of the residual in a projection period is the same as the standard error of the residual from the OLS function that relates the transformed variables. This is the same as the standard error of f_t from the GLS function. Thus,

$$s(f_t) = s_v^* \sqrt{1 + \frac{1}{n} + \frac{(X_t^* - \bar{X}^*)^2}{\sum x_t^{*2}}}$$

For example, in period 39 for the Autocorp example,

$$s(f_{39}) = 39.5844 \sqrt{1 + \frac{1}{36} + 0.2474} = 44.7009$$

The remaining audit interface calculations are the same as for the nonauto-correlated case.

8.5 HETEROSCEDASTICITY

A reasonable assumption for most audit applications of regression analysis (and the one that is built into the STAR Program) is that, where heteroscedasticity exists, the standard error of the disturbances in period t is proportionate to one of the independent variables. That is,

$$\sigma_t = \sigma_u X_t$$

where σ_u is some constant, X is one of the independent variables, and σ_t is the standard error of the disturbance for observation t.

In this situation, large values of X tend to have proportionately larger values of u associated with them than do small values of X. Therefore, a model that is weighted by the reciprocal of X will tend to have disturbances with a constant standard error. For example, if in the ordinary linear model

$$Y_t = \alpha + \beta_1 X_{1t} + \beta_2 X_{2t} + u_t$$

it is reasonable to assume that $\sigma_t = \sigma_u X_{1t}$, and then the model

$$\frac{Y_t}{X_{1t}} = \alpha \left(\frac{1}{X_{1t}}\right) + \beta_1 + \beta_2 \left(\frac{X_{2t}}{X_{1t}}\right) + \frac{u_t}{X_{1t}}$$

will have a constant standard error.

The theory behind the tests for, and treatment of, heteroscedasticity is dealt with by Johnston [7, Chapter 7] and by Koutsoyiannis [6, Chapter 9].

The Heteroco application, which was introduced in Chapter 4, will be used to illustrate the test for heteroscedasticity and the use of weighted least squares regression to overcome the problem. In that application, the ordinary least squares function is

$$\hat{Y}_t = 29.72 + 2.9450X_{1t} + 0.8393X_{2t}$$

8.5.1   Test for Heteroscedasticity

The STAR Program tests for heteroscedasticity by calculating the coefficient of correlation between the size (absolute value) of the residuals and each independent variable and by testing whether the highest of those coefficients is significant. The coefficient of correlation will be insignificant if the residuals are homoscedastic, because their size will then not be related to the independent variable. However, finding a significant coefficient of correlation is prima facie evidence that the disturbances are heteroscedastic.

The absolute residuals are denoted by $|e_t|$. The coefficient of correlation between $|e_t|$ and X is

$$R_{|e|X} = \frac{\sum(X_t - \bar{X})(|e_t| - |\bar{e}|)}{\sqrt{\sum(X_t - \bar{X})^2} \sqrt{\sum(|e_t| - |\bar{e}|)^2}}$$

In this case, X_1 is most highly correlated with a coefficient of correlation of 0.7739.

To test the significance of the correlation coefficient between $|e|$ and X is to test the null hypothesis that $R_{|e|X} = 0$. The F ratio for testing this hypothesis is

$$F = \frac{R_{|e|X}^2}{(1 - R_{|e|X}^2) / (n - 2)}$$

It has an F distribution with 1 and $n - 2$ degrees of freedom.

A strong correlation between the absolute residuals and X_1 in the Heteroco example is apparent from the scatter diagram shown in Figure 4.14. Because $R_{|e|X1} = 0.7739$, the F statistic is

$$F = \frac{0.7739^2}{(1 - 0.7739^2)/(30 - 2)} = 41.82$$

This statistic has an F distribution with 1 and 28 degrees of freedom. Its critical value at the 1% level (the level at which the STAR Program tests) is 7.64. Therefore, the correlation coefficient is significant at the 1% level, and, as a result, the residuals are assumed to be heteroscedastic. Furthermore, the pattern of heteroscedasticity is assumed to be

$$\sigma_t = \sigma_u X_{1t}$$

8.5.2 Weighted Least Squares

The first step in weighted regression for the Heteroco application is to transform the variables by dividing them by X_1. Thus,

$$Y^* = \frac{Y}{X_1}$$

$$X_1^* = \frac{1}{X_1}$$

$$X_2^* = \frac{X_2}{X_1}$$

The next step is to use ordinary regression to fit a regression function to the transformed variables Y^*, X_1^*, and X_2^*. This function is called the *transformed function,* and its standard error is a constant. In the Heteroco application, the function is

$$Y_t^* = 2.9701 - 97.5193X_{1t}^* + 0.8987X_{2t}^* + e_t^*$$

and its standard error is 0.0860.

The final step in weighted least squares is to multiply the transformed function by X_1. This retransforms it into familiar terms and means that the regression estimate for observation t is

$$\hat{Y}_t = Y_t^* X_{1t}$$

The end result is a familiar-looking function

$$Y_t = a + b_1 X_{1t} + b_2 X_{2t} + e_t$$

which is the *weighted least squares* (or WLS) function. For the Heteroco application, it is

$$Y_t = -97.52 + 2.9701 X_{1t} + 0.8987 X_{2t} + e_t$$

The standard error of the WLS function is variable and can be calculated for any observation by multiplying the standard error of the transformed function by the value of X_1. Thus, if s_u^* is the standard error of the transformed function, then $s_t = X_{1t} s_u^*$ is the standard error of the WLS function for observation t.

The standard error of an individual residual from a WLS function is calculated in a similar way. It is

$$s(e_t) = X_{1t} s(e_t^*)$$

where $s(e_t^*)$ is the standard error of an individual residual from the transformed function. For example, in period 31 in the Heteroco application, it can be shown that, by following the formulas of Section 3.5, $s(e_{31}^*) = 0.08754$. Because $X_{1,31} = 300$, the standard error for the weighted residual is

$$s(e_{31}) = 300 \times 0.08755 = 26.2638$$

The remaining audit interface calculations are the same as in the homoscedastic case.

8.6 ABNORMALITY

In this section, the Paranormal Productions Inc. application (introduced in Chapter 4) will be used to illustrate the mathematics of the tests for abnormality that are applied by the STAR Program. In addition, methods of dealing with cases in which the underlying distribution of the disturbances is genuinely nonnormal are discussed.

8.6.1   Sample Moments and Cumulants

The statistics that are used to test for abnormality of the residuals are derived from various sample moments and cumulants. The second, third, and fourth sample moments are

$$m_2 = \frac{\sum e_t^2}{n}$$

$$m_3 = \frac{\sum e_t^3}{n}$$

$$m_4 = \frac{\sum e_t^4}{n}$$

In the example, these work out as

$$m_2 = 20.29$$

$$m_3 = -109.97$$

$$m_4 = 2{,}090.68$$

The sample cumulants, assuming v degrees of freedom, are

$$k_2 = \frac{v}{v-1} m_2$$

$$k_3 = \frac{v^2}{(v-1)(v-2)} m_3$$

$$k_4 = \frac{v^2}{(v-1)(v-2)(v-3)} [(v+1)m_4 - 3(v-1)m_2^2]$$

(For more on sample cumulants, see Kendall and Stuart [5].)

   Notice that, because $v - 3$ is a divisor in the calculation of k_4, at least 4 degrees of freedom are required before k_4 can be calculated and the following tests applied. In the example, there are 38 (40 − 2) degrees of freedom and the sample cumulants are

$$k_2 = \frac{38}{37} \times 20.29 = 20.84$$

$$k_3 = \frac{38^2}{37 \times 36} \times (-109.97) = -119.21$$

$$k_4 = \frac{38^2}{37 \times 36 \times 35} \times (39 \times 2{,}090.68 - 3 \times 37 \times 20.29^2) = 1{,}110.42$$

The calculations of the sample cumulants do not work out exactly as shown, because the sample moments have been rounded.

8.6.2   Test for Skewness

The test for skewness that is applied by the STAR Program (described by Kendall and Stuart [5] on page 297) uses the statistic

$$G = \sqrt{\frac{(v - 1)(v - 2)}{6v}} \times \frac{k_3}{k_2^{3/2}}$$

G has an expected value of zero if the residuals are symmetrically distributed (e.g., if they are normal) and a variance of approximately

$$\text{var}(G) = 1 - \frac{6}{v} + \frac{22}{v^2} - \frac{70}{v^3}$$

The probability distribution of G is not known. When v tends to infinity, however, var(G) tends to 1 and the fourth moment of G tends to 3, which is in conformity with a tendency to normality. But the tendency is by no means very rapid. The test value used by STAR is $2.576 \sqrt{\text{var}(G)}$, which is the value suggested by the normal distribution. The null hypothesis that the e_t are not skew is rejected at the 1% level when

$$|G| > 2.576 \sqrt{\text{var}(G)}$$

in favor of the alternative hypothesis that they are skew. Positive G indicates right skewness, negative G indicates left skewness.

In the example, the test statistic for skewness is

$$G = \sqrt{\frac{37 \times 36}{6 \times 38}} \times \frac{-119.21}{20.84^{3/2}} = -3.0$$

The variance of G is

$$\mathrm{var}(G) = 1 - \frac{6}{38} + \frac{22}{38^2} - \frac{70}{38^3} = 0.8561$$

The critical value for skewness is

$$2.576\sqrt{0.8561} = 2.4$$

Because $|G| = 3.0 > 2.4$ and G is negative, left skewness is indicated at the 1% significance level.

8.6.3 Test for Kurtosis

The test for kurtosis applied by the STAR Program (described by Kendall and Stuart [5] on page 305) uses the statistic

$$H = \sqrt{\frac{(v - 1)(v - 2)(v - 3)}{24v(v + 1)}} \times \frac{k_4}{k_2^2}$$

which has an expected value of zero and a variance of approximately

$$\mathrm{var}(H) = 1 - \frac{12}{v} + \frac{88}{v^2} - \frac{532}{v^3}$$

if the distribution is normal. The null hypothesis that the distribution is not kurtic ($H = 0$) is rejected in favor of the alternative that it is kurtic when

$$H > 2.576 \sqrt{\mathrm{var}(H)}$$

In the example, the test statistic for kurtosis is

$$H = \sqrt{\frac{37 \times 36 \times 35}{24 \times 38 \times 39}} \times \frac{1110.42}{20.84} = 2.9$$

Its variance is

$$\text{var}(H) = 1 - \frac{12}{38} + \frac{88}{38^2} - \frac{532}{38^3} = 0.7355$$

The critical value for kurtosis is

$$2.576\sqrt{0.7355} = 2.2$$

Because $H = 2.9 > 2.2$, the frequency distribution is judged to be significantly kurtic at the 1% level.

8.6.4   Audit Interface Considerations

The audit interface calculations in Chapter 5 are based on the assumption that disturbances from the ULR are normally distributed. If there is an indication that the cause of abnormality in the residuals is not simply the presence of explainable outliers but an underlying nonnormal distribution of the disturbances, then an alternative approach to the audit interface calculations may be appropriate.

One way to deal with residuals that are not normally distributed is to find some other probability distribution that is a better approximation than the normal distribution. The approximating distribution should reflect degrees of skewness and kurtosis that are consistent with those found in the base data. This can be an attractive alternative, although nonnormal distributions are generally more complex and less tractable than the normal distribution. Kendall and Stuart [5] deal with methods for finding such probability distributions in their Chapter 12.

A second approach is to transform the residuals into a variable that is approximately normal. This has the advantage of making it possible to deal with the audit interface in familiar, normal distribution terms. For the transformed residuals to be usable, they must be put through an inverse transformation and expressed in terms of the original data. Both the underlying rationale and the calculations required for these transformations are quite complex. Kendall and Stuart [5] discuss such transformations in their Chapter 6.

A third method for dealing with abnormality is based on well-established results in the field of nonparametric statistics, which is concerned with statistical inferences that do not depend on any assumptions about the mathematical form of the underlying distribution. The distribution of interest for the purpose of this discussion is described generally in nonparametric literature as the *empirical distribution* or sometimes as the *statistical image* of the population [8–10]. In this context, the empirical distribution is the distribution of the residuals in the regression base. It can be shown that the empirical distribution function can be used as an estimate of the probability distribution. The data from the Paranormal Productions example introduced in Chapter 4 is used to illustrate how the empirical distribution function can be used in the audit interface calculations.

The first step for this purpose is to tabulate the cumulative empirical distribution (generally known as the *empirical distribution function*) as shown in Figure 8.4. The residuals are the same as those shown in Figure 4.16, except that they are given to two decimal places here for convenience in the following discussion, and they have been sorted into ascending order, from largest negative to largest positive. The cumulative distribution column shows the proportion of residuals that are less than or equal to the corresponding residual. For example, 75% of the residuals are less than or equal to 2.42. Because there are 40 residuals in the example, the cumulative distribution rises in steps of 1/40 or 2.5%.

A graph of the cumulative empirical distribution is shown in Figure 8.5. The graph is rather uneven because it is based on a limited number of residuals. If thousands of residuals had been observed, the graph would have been much smoother. A cumulative normal distribution for the same range of residuals is also shown in Figure 8.5. A comparison of the two graphs shows clearly the effect of left skewness and kurtosis. The long left-hand tail (skewness) and the steep rise in the cumulative distribution around 0 (kurtosis) are evident.

To illustrate the use of the cumulative distribution in the audit interface calculations, assume that the monetary precision is $25, the desired reliability level is 95%, and the test is for overstatement. Just as in the normal case, thresholds are calculated after taking the most adverse spread of error into account.

The process is similar to that explained in Chapter 5. For example, suppose one wants to determine how to set the threshold on the assumption that

Obs. #	Rank	Residual	Cumulative Distribution	Cumulative Normal
5	1	-14.15	0.025	0.001
22	2	-12.58	0.050	0.003
32	3	-9.48	0.075	0.020
7	4	-4.66	0.100	0.157
16	5	-4.02	0.125	0.192
25	6	-3.43	0.150	0.229
6	7	-3.00	0.175	0.258
27	8	-2.66	0.200	0.282
19	9	-1.82	0.225	0.347
21	10	-1.62	0.250	0.363
4	11	-1.53	0.275	0.370
14	12	-0.96	0.300	0.418
17	13	-0.92	0.325	0.421
8	14	-0.91	0.350	0.422
13	15	-0.69	0.375	0.441
11	16	-0.30	0.400	0.474
12	17	-0.30	0.425	0.474
3	18	-0.17	0.450	0.485
23	19	-0.15	0.475	0.487
24	20	-0.05	0.500	0.496
29	21	0.80	0.525	0.569
9	22	0.91	0.550	0.578
40	23	1.00	0.575	0.586
20	24	1.00	0.600	0.586
31	25	1.12	0.625	0.596
1	26	1.13	0.650	0.597
15	27	1.48	0.675	0.626
2	28	2.13	0.700	0.678
34	29	2.29	0.725	0.690
35	30	2.42	0.750	0.700
18	31	3.21	0.775	0.756
10	32	3.24	0.800	0.758
36	33	3.78	0.825	0.793
39	34	4.08	0.850	0.811
30	35	4.48	0.875	0.834
38	36	4.85	0.900	0.853
28	37	4.89	0.925	0.855
26	38	6.27	0.950	0.913
33	39	6.65	0.975	0.925
37	40	7.69	1.000	0.952

Figure 8.4   Paranormal Production. Cumulative empirical distribution.

the total error (if it equals $25) will affect three observations. First, note that the acceptable risk of not identifying a particular one of the three observations is 36.8% (because 36.8% × 36.8% × 36.8% = 5%). Figure 8.4 is used to determine the point in the cumulative distribution that includes the 36.8% point. It occurs at the 15th ranked residual (observation number 13), at which

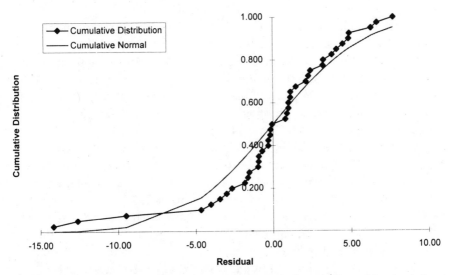

Figure 8.5 Cumulative empirical distribution of the residuals shown in Figure 8.4 and cumulative normal distribution.

Spread	Risk %	Cumulative Distribution	Residual Rank	Risk Point	Threshold
1	5.0	0.050	2	-12.58	12.42
2	22.4	0.225	9	-1.82	10.68
3	36.8	0.375	15	-0.69	7.64
4	47.3	0.475	19	-0.15	6.10
5	54.9	0.550	22	0.91	5.91
6	60.7	0.625	25	1.12	5.29
7	65.2	0.675	27	1.48	5.05
8	68.8	0.705	28	2.13	5.26
9	71.7	0.725	19	2.29	5.07
10	*74.1*	*0.750*	*30*	*2.42*	*4.92*
11	76.2	0.775	31	3.21	5.48
12	77.9	0.800	32	3.24	5.32
13	79.4	0.800	32	3.24	5.16
14	80.7	0.825	33	3.78	5.57
15	81.9	0.825	33	3.78	5.45
16	82.9	0.850	34	4.08	5.64

Most adverse spread of error

Figure 8.6 Computation of the most adverse spread of error based on a cumulative empirical distribution of residuals.

point the cumulative distribution is 37.5%. The risk point is the amount of the residual, that is, -0.69. The threshold is $-0.69 + 25/3 = 7.64$.

The thresholds corresponding to spreads through 16 are shown in Figure 8.6. It can be seen from this figure that the most adverse spread of error is 10, the target risk is 74.1%, and the most conservative threshold is 4.92. If the residual for a projection observation were 7.00, for example, the excess to be investigated would be $7.00 - 4.92 = 2.08$.

Like the calculation of the excess to be investigated, the calculation of the optional sample data parallels the calculations performed in the normal case (see Section 5.4). In the example just given, in which the residual for a projection observation is 7.00, the effective risk point is $7.00 - 25/10 = 4.5$. The effective risk that corresponds to this can be read from Figure 8.4. It is 90%. The target risk is 74.1%, and therefore the appropriate risk level for the optional sample is 74.1%/90% = 82.3%. This translates to a reliability factor of 0.195 and a sampling interval (rounded down) of $(25/10)/0.195 = 12$.

REFERENCES

1. G. C. Chow, "Tests of Equality between Sets of Coefficients in Two Linear Regressions." *Econometrica,* vol. 28, pp. 591–605, 1960.

2. F. M. Fisher, "Tests of Equality between Sets of Coefficients in Two Linear Regressions: An Expository Note." *Econometrica,* vol. 38, pp. 361–366, 1970.

3. J. Durbin and G. S. Watson, "Testing for Serial Correlation in Least-Squares Regression." *Biometrika,* vol. 27, pp. 409–428, 1950, and vol. 38, pp. 157–178, 1951.

4. K. R. Kadiyala, "A Transformation Used to Circumvent the Problem of Autocorrelation." *Econometrica,* vol. 36, pp. 93–96, 1968.

5. Kendall and Stuart, *The Advanced Theory of Statistics.* Vol. 1, 3rd ed. London: Charles Griffin, 1969.

6. A. Koutsoyiannis, *Theory of Econometrics.* London: Macmillan, 1973.

7. J. Johnston, *Econometric Methods,* 2nd ed. New York: McGraw-Hill, 1972.

8. G. E. Noether, *Elements of Nonparametric Statistics.* New York: Wiley, 1969.

9. J. D. Gibbons, *Nonparametric Statistical Inference.* New York: McGraw-Hill, 1971.

10. P. G. Hoel, *Introduction to Mathematical Statistics,* 5th ed. New York: Wiley, 1984.

GENERAL REFERENCES

S. Chatterjee, *Regression Analysis by Example.* New York: Wiley, 1977.

N. R. Draper and H. Smith, *Applied Regression Analysis.* New York: Wiley, 1981.

M. Ezekiel and K. A. Fox, *Methods of Correlation and Regression Analysis,* 3rd ed. New York: Wiley, 1959.

A. Koutsoyiannis, *Theory of Econometrics,* 2nd ed. London: Macmillan, 1977.

M. S. Lewis-Beck, *Applied Regression: An Introduction.* Beverly Hills, CA: Sage Publications, 1980.

J. Neper, *Applied Linear Regression Models.* Homewood, IL: R. D. Irwin, 1983.

K. W. Smillie, *An Introduction to Regression and Correlation.* New York: Academic Press, 1966.

9

MULTIVARIATE REGRESSION
COMPUTATIONS

9.1 INTRODUCTION

In Chapter 4, formulas that deal with two independent variables were introduced. These were quite satisfactory for that purpose, but they only apply to functions with two independent variables. New formulas are needed for the three-variable regression, four-variable regression, and so on. These can all be developed fairly easily, but they are cumbersome and tend to obscure the fact that there really is not much difference in concept between two-variable, three-variable, and k-variable regressions.

Fortunately, *matrix algebra* provides a compact and powerful means of representing and manipulating what are essentially arrays of numbers and symbols. Furthermore, matrix formulas generally do not depend on the number of variables or the number of observations. They apply to one-, two-, three-, or k-variable regressions on n observations.

As an example of how matrix notation can be used to express an idea in regression analysis, consider the two-variable linear model for the Gamma Company that was discussed in Chapter 4. In this example, there are 36 observations on three variables: X_1, X_2, and Y. The regression equation holds that for each observation

$$Y_t = a + b_1 X_{1t} + b_2 X_{2t} + e_t$$

For convenience (because it eliminates the constant term), the equation can be expressed in terms of deviations from the mean. If the 36 equations were written out for each observation, they would look something like

$$y_1 = b_1 x_{11} + b_2 x_{21} + e_1$$
$$y_2 = b_1 x_{12} + b_2 x_{22} + e_2$$

$$\cdot$$
$$\cdot$$
$$\cdot$$

$$y_{36} = b_1 x_{1,36} + b_2 x_{2,36} + e_{36}$$

If the actual observations rather than symbols are used, these equations become

$$-395 = -258b_1 - 109b_2 + e_1$$
$$-587 = -329b_1 - 126b_2 + e_2$$

$$\cdot$$
$$\cdot$$
$$\cdot$$

$$653 = \quad 251b_1 + 151b_2 + e_{36}$$

Without any loss of information, this system of 36 equations can be written as

$$
\begin{bmatrix} -395 \\ -587 \\ \cdot \\ \cdot \\ \cdot \\ 653 \end{bmatrix}
=
\begin{bmatrix} -258b_1 - 109b_2 \\ -329b_1 - 126b_2 \\ \cdot \\ \cdot \\ \cdot \\ 251b_1 + 151b_2 \end{bmatrix}
+
\begin{bmatrix} e_1 \\ e_2 \\ \cdot \\ \cdot \\ \cdot \\ e_{36} \end{bmatrix}
$$

or as

$$
\begin{bmatrix} -395 \\ -587 \\ \cdot \\ \cdot \\ \cdot \\ 653 \end{bmatrix}
=
\begin{bmatrix} -258 & -109 \\ -329 & -126 \\ \cdot & \cdot \\ \cdot & \cdot \\ \cdot & \cdot \\ 251 & 151 \end{bmatrix}
\begin{bmatrix} b_1 \\ b_2 \end{bmatrix}
+
\begin{bmatrix} e_1 \\ e_2 \\ \cdot \\ \cdot \\ \cdot \\ e_{36} \end{bmatrix}
$$

where it is understood that

$$
\begin{bmatrix}
-258 & -109 \\
-329 & -126 \\
\cdot & \cdot \\
\cdot & \cdot \\
\cdot & \cdot \\
251 & 151
\end{bmatrix}
\begin{bmatrix}
b_1 \\
b_2
\end{bmatrix}
=
\begin{bmatrix}
-258b_1 - 109b_2 \\
-329b_1 - 126b_2 \\
\cdot \\
\cdot \\
\cdot \\
251b_1 + 151b_2
\end{bmatrix}
$$

These arrays can be represented by symbols such as

$$\mathbf{Y} = \mathbf{Xb} + \mathbf{e}$$

where the symbols are in bold type to indicate that they refer to arrays of numbers. As long as it is remembered that

$$
\mathbf{Y} =
\begin{bmatrix}
y_1 \\
y_2 \\
\cdot \\
\cdot \\
\cdot \\
y_{36}
\end{bmatrix}
\quad
\mathbf{X} =
\begin{bmatrix}
x_{11} & x_{21} \\
x_{12} & x_{22} \\
\cdot & \cdot \\
\cdot & \cdot \\
\cdot & \cdot \\
x_{1,36} & x_{2,36}
\end{bmatrix}
\quad
\mathbf{b} =
\begin{bmatrix}
b_1 \\
b_2
\end{bmatrix}
\quad
\mathbf{e} =
\begin{bmatrix}
e_1 \\
e_2 \\
\cdot \\
\cdot \\
\cdot \\
e_{36}
\end{bmatrix}
$$

none of the original information has been lost, and the entire system of 36 equations is expressed in a neat, compact notation. The advantage of this notation is that exactly the same symbols can be used, no matter how many variables are included in the model. For example, if there were four independent variables in the model, the system of 36 equations would be

$$
\begin{aligned}
y_1 &= b_1 x_{11} + b_2 x_{21} + b_3 x_{31} + b_4 x_{41} + e_1 \\
y_2 &= b_1 x_{12} + b_2 x_{22} + b_3 x_{32} + b_4 x_{42} + e_2 \\
&\ \cdot \quad\quad \cdot \quad\quad\quad \cdot \\
&\ \cdot \quad\quad \cdot \quad\quad\quad \cdot \\
&\ \cdot \quad\quad \cdot \quad\quad\quad \cdot \\
y_{36} &= b_1 x_{1,36} + b_2 x_{2,36} + b_3 x_{3,36} + b_4 x_{4,36} + e_{36}
\end{aligned}
$$

This system can also be written as

$$\mathbf{Y} = \mathbf{Xb} + \mathbf{e}$$

exactly as before, where

$$
\mathbf{Y} = \begin{bmatrix} y_1 \\ y_2 \\ \cdot \\ \cdot \\ \cdot \\ y_{36} \end{bmatrix}
\qquad
\mathbf{X} = \begin{bmatrix} x_{11} & x_{21} & x_{31} & x_{41} \\ x_{12} & x_{22} & x_{32} & x_{42} \\ \cdot & \cdot & \cdot & \cdot \\ \cdot & \cdot & \cdot & \cdot \\ \cdot & \cdot & \cdot & \cdot \\ x_{1,36} & x_{2,36} & x_{3,36} & x_{4,36} \end{bmatrix}
$$

$$
\mathbf{b} = \begin{bmatrix} b_1 \\ b_2 \\ b_3 \\ b_4 \end{bmatrix}
\qquad
\mathbf{e} = \begin{bmatrix} e_1 \\ e_2 \\ \cdot \\ \cdot \\ \cdot \\ e_{36} \end{bmatrix}
$$

The symbols **Y, X, b,** and **e** each represent an array or *matrix* of numbers (or symbols representing numbers). Matrices can be manipulated in various ways. For example, they can be added together, subtracted from one another, multiplied together, or "inverted." Just as the ordinary rules of algebra determine what can and cannot be done with ordinary numbers, so there are rules of matrix algebra that determine how matrices can be manipulated.

9.2   ELEMENTS OF MATRIX ALGEBRA

A matrix with n rows and k columns such as

$$
\mathbf{A} = \begin{bmatrix} A_{11} & A_{12} & \cdots & A_{1k} \\ A_{21} & A_{22} & \cdots & A_{2k} \\ \cdot & \cdot & & \cdot \\ \cdot & \cdot & & \cdot \\ A_{n1} & A_{n2} & \cdots & A_{nk} \end{bmatrix}
$$

is called a *matrix of order n by k.* It consists of nk elements (numbers or symbols). A matrix may consist of only one row or column, in which case it is sometimes called a *vector.* If, like the vector

$$\mathbf{e} = \begin{bmatrix} e_1 \\ e_1 \\ \cdot \\ \cdot \\ \cdot \\ e_n \end{bmatrix}$$

it consists of only one column of elements, it is called a *column vector.* If, like the vector

$$\mathbf{e} = [e_1 \, e_2 \, \cdots \, e_n]$$

it consists of only one row, it is called a *row vector.*

Two matrices **A** and **B** of order $n \times k$ are said to be *equal* if both contain exactly the same elements in the same positions. Two $n \times k$ matrices can be *added* to produce a third matrix by adding together elements in similar positions. Thus, if

$$\mathbf{A} = \begin{bmatrix} 5 & 0 \\ 7 & -3 \end{bmatrix} \qquad \mathbf{B} = \begin{bmatrix} 2 & -4 \\ -8 & 6 \end{bmatrix}$$

then

$$\mathbf{C} = \mathbf{A} + \mathbf{B} = \begin{bmatrix} 7 & -4 \\ -1 & 3 \end{bmatrix}$$

Similarly, matrices can be *subtracted,* thus

$$\mathbf{C} = \mathbf{A} - \mathbf{B} = \begin{bmatrix} 3 & 4 \\ 15 & -9 \end{bmatrix}$$

A matrix can be *multiplied by a number* (or *scalar,* as such numbers are known in matrix terminology). Thus,

$$2\mathbf{A} = \begin{bmatrix} 10 & 0 \\ 14 & -6 \end{bmatrix}$$

Matrices can be *multiplied* together by following a rather special multiplication rule. Suppose

$$\mathbf{A} = \begin{bmatrix} A_{11} & A_{12} & A_{13} \\ A_{21} & A_{22} & A_{23} \end{bmatrix} \qquad \mathbf{B} = \begin{bmatrix} B_{11} & B_{12} \\ B_{21} & B_{22} \\ B_{31} & B_{32} \end{bmatrix}$$

Then

$$\mathbf{C} = \mathbf{AB} = \begin{bmatrix} C_{11} & C_{12} \\ C_{21} & C_{22} \end{bmatrix}$$

where

$$C_{11} = A_{11}B_{11} + A_{12}B_{21} + A_{13}B_{31}$$
$$C_{12} = A_{11}B_{12} + A_{12}B_{22} + A_{13}B_{32}$$
$$C_{21} = A_{21}B_{11} + A_{22}B_{21} + A_{23}B_{31}$$
$$C_{22} = A_{21}B_{12} + A_{22}B_{22} + A_{23}B_{32}$$

For example, if

$$\mathbf{X} = \begin{bmatrix} 2 & -3 & 0 \\ 1 & 4 & -6 \end{bmatrix} \qquad \mathbf{Y} = \begin{bmatrix} 4 & 1 \\ 2 & 7 \\ 3 & 0 \end{bmatrix}$$

then

$$\mathbf{Z} = \mathbf{XY} = \begin{bmatrix} 8-6+0 & 2-21+0 \\ 4+8-18 & 1+28+0 \end{bmatrix} = \begin{bmatrix} 2 & -19 \\ -6 & 29 \end{bmatrix}$$

Two matrices can be multiplied together only if they are *conformable*. This means that the matrix on the left-hand side of the multiplication must have as many columns as the matrix on the right-hand side has rows. Thus, for example a 2×3 matrix like $\mathbf{X}$ may be multiplied by a 3×2 matrix like $\mathbf{Y}$. The result is a matrix of order 2×2. In general, a matrix of order $n \times k$ may be multiplied by a matrix of order $k \times m$ to give a matrix of order $n \times m$.

In the example, $\mathbf{Y}$ can also be multiplied by $\mathbf{X}$, but the result is not the same as multiplying $\mathbf{X}$ by $\mathbf{Y}$. Thus,

$$\mathbf{YX} = \begin{bmatrix} 8+1 & -12+4 & 0-6 \\ 4+7 & -6+28 & 0-42 \\ 6+0 & -9+0 & 0+0 \end{bmatrix} = \begin{bmatrix} 9 & -8 & -6 \\ 11 & 22 & -42 \\ 6 & -9 & 0 \end{bmatrix}$$

Because **Y** is 3×2 and **X** is 2×3, the resulting 3×3 matrix is **YX,** which is different from the 2×2 matrix **XY.** This *noncommunicative* property of matrix multiplication is one way in which matrix algebra differs from ordinary arithmetic.

Certain types of matrices play an important role in matrix algebra. A *square matrix* is a matrix with as many columns as rows (e.g., a 2×2 matrix). The *unit* or *identity matrix* of order n is the $n \times n$ matrix with 1's in the main diagonal and 0's elsewhere. It is usually written as I_n. For example,

$$
\mathbf{I}_5 = \begin{bmatrix} 1 & 0 & 0 & 0 & 0 \\ 0 & 1 & 0 & 0 & 0 \\ 0 & 0 & 1 & 0 & 0 \\ 0 & 0 & 0 & 1 & 0 \\ 0 & 0 & 0 & 0 & 1 \end{bmatrix}
$$

The identity matrix is important because it plays a role in matrix algebra similar to that played by the number 1 in ordinary arithmetic. If a matrix of suitable order is multiplied by the identity matrix of suitable order, the resulting matrix is the same as the original matrix. For example, if

$$
\mathbf{A} = \begin{bmatrix} 3 & 1 \\ -2 & 5 \\ 1 & 0 \\ 6 & 9 \\ 2 & -3 \end{bmatrix}
$$

then

$$
\mathbf{AI}_2 = \begin{bmatrix} 3 & 1 \\ -2 & 5 \\ 1 & 0 \\ 6 & 9 \\ 2 & -3 \end{bmatrix} \begin{bmatrix} 1 & 0 \\ 0 & 1 \end{bmatrix} = \begin{bmatrix} 3+0 & 0+1 \\ -2+0 & 0+5 \\ 1+0 & 0+0 \\ 6+0 & 0+9 \\ 2+0 & 0-3 \end{bmatrix} = \mathbf{A}
$$

Also

$$
\mathbf{I}_5\mathbf{A} = \begin{bmatrix} 1 & 0 & 0 & 0 & 0 \\ 0 & 1 & 0 & 0 & 0 \\ 0 & 0 & 1 & 0 & 0 \\ 0 & 0 & 0 & 1 & 0 \\ 0 & 0 & 0 & 0 & 1 \end{bmatrix} \begin{bmatrix} 3 & 1 \\ -2 & 5 \\ 1 & 0 \\ 6 & 9 \\ 2 & -3 \end{bmatrix} = \begin{bmatrix} 3 & 1 \\ -2 & 5 \\ 1 & 0 \\ 6 & 9 \\ 2 & -3 \end{bmatrix} = \mathbf{A}
$$

The *transpose* of a matrix **A** is written **A'** and is the matrix that is obtained by interchanging columns and rows. Thus, if

$$\mathbf{A} = \begin{bmatrix} 3 & 1 \\ -2 & 5 \\ 1 & 0 \\ 6 & 9 \\ 2 & -3 \end{bmatrix} \text{ then } \mathbf{A'} = \begin{bmatrix} 3 & -2 & 1 & 6 & 2 \\ 1 & 5 & 0 & 9 & -3 \end{bmatrix}$$

There are some useful rules for dealing with transposed matrices.

- $(\mathbf{A} + \mathbf{B})' = \mathbf{A'} + \mathbf{B'}$. The transpose of the sum of two matrices equals the sum of the transposed matrices.
- $(\mathbf{A} - \mathbf{B})' = \mathbf{A'} - \mathbf{B'}$.
- $(\mathbf{AB})' = \mathbf{B'}\,\mathbf{A'}$. The transpose of the product **AB** equals the transpose of **B** times the transpose of **A**.

A matrix **A** is *symmetric* if its rows and columns are interchangeable, that is, if $\mathbf{A} = \mathbf{A'}$. Clearly, only a square matrix can be symmetric. An example of a symmetric matrix is

$$\mathbf{A} = \begin{bmatrix} 5 & 4 & 7 & 0 \\ 4 & 19 & -2 & 6 \\ 7 & -2 & 3 & 5 \\ 0 & 6 & 5 & -5 \end{bmatrix}$$

In regression analysis, a particular symmetric matrix is especially important. It arises from a matrix of observations on the independent variables, such as the following

$$\mathbf{X} = \begin{bmatrix} x_{11} & x_{21} \\ x_{12} & x_{22} \\ \cdot & \cdot \\ \cdot & \cdot \\ \cdot & \cdot \\ x_{1,36} & x_{2,36} \end{bmatrix}$$

where the x's represent deviations from the means for the two variables X_1 and X_2. The symmetric matrix that arises out of this **X** matrix is **X'X**, that is,

$$\mathbf{X'X} = \begin{bmatrix} \sum x_1^2 & \sum x_1 x_2 \\ \sum x_2 x_1 & \sum x_2^2 \end{bmatrix}$$

$\mathbf{X'X}$ is the matrix equivalent to squaring a number. The importance of this matrix is that it contains all the sums of squares and cross products for the independent variables.

9.2.1   Matrix Inversion

In ordinary arithmetic, the laws of algebra permit one number to be divided by another, provided that the divisor is not equal to 0. Thus, if A, x, and y are ordinary numbers, the equation $Ax = y$ can be solved for x quite simply by dividing both sides of the equation by A (providing that A is not zero). Thus, $x = y/A$ is the solution. Dividing both sides of the equation by A is the same as multiplying both sides by the number A^{-1}. Thus, $A^{-1}Ax = A^{-1}y$ or $1x = A^{-1}y$. For example, if the equation is $3x = 6$, it is solved by multiplying each side by 3^{-1}. Thus, $x = 3^{-1}6 = 2$ is the solution. The number A^{-1} is called the *inverse* of A.

In matrix algebra, the main problem in solving an equation $\mathbf{Ax} = \mathbf{y}$ consists of finding a matrix, called the *inverse* of $\mathbf{A}$ and usually denoted by the symbol $\mathbf{A}^{-1}$, such that $\mathbf{A}^{-1}\mathbf{Ax} = \mathbf{x} = \mathbf{A}^{-1}\mathbf{y}$. Note that $\mathbf{A}^{-1}\mathbf{A} = \mathbf{I}$, the identity matrix, just as in ordinary arithmetic $A^{-1}A = 1$.

As an example of how the inverse of a matrix can be used, consider the problem of solving the simultaneous equations

$$7x_1 + 3x_2 = 36$$
$$6x_1 - x_2 = 13$$

These equations can be written in matrix terms as

$$\begin{bmatrix} 7 & 3 \\ 6 & -1 \end{bmatrix} \begin{bmatrix} x_1 \\ x_2 \end{bmatrix} = \begin{bmatrix} 36 \\ 13 \end{bmatrix}$$

which is a matrix equation of the form $\mathbf{Ax} = \mathbf{y}$. The inverse of $\mathbf{A}$ is

$$\mathbf{A}^{-1} = \begin{bmatrix} 0.04 & 0.12 \\ 0.24 & -0.28 \end{bmatrix}$$

because

$$\mathbf{A}^{-1}\mathbf{A} = \begin{bmatrix} 0.04 & 0.12 \\ 0.24 & -0.28 \end{bmatrix} \begin{bmatrix} 7 & 3 \\ 6 & -1 \end{bmatrix} = \begin{bmatrix} 1 & 0 \\ 0 & 1 \end{bmatrix}$$

Hence, the solution to the equation is

$$\mathbf{x} = \mathbf{A}^{-1}\mathbf{y} = \begin{bmatrix} 0.04 & 0.12 \\ 0.24 & -0.28 \end{bmatrix} \begin{bmatrix} 36 \\ 13 \end{bmatrix} = \begin{bmatrix} 3 \\ 5 \end{bmatrix}$$

The solution $x_1 = 3$, $x_2 = 5$ may be verified by substituting these values into the original equations. The problem of solving the matrix equation $\mathbf{Ax} = \mathbf{y}$ is essentially the problem of inverting $\mathbf{A}$ to get $\mathbf{A}^{-1}$.

Over the years, many ways have been developed to invert matrices. The method to be illustrated is called the Gauss–Jordan method. For the manual inversion of small matrices such as the one just shown, it is not the easiest method to use. It is efficient, however, in computer terms and can be applied to very large matrices. Certain of the precomputer, manual methods, although fine for small matrices, are hopelessly inefficient for large ones. A further advantage of the Gauss–Jordan method is that, when applied to the main inversion problem of multiple regression analysis, it provides some very useful statistics along the way.

As an introduction to the Gauss–Jordan method of matrix inversion, a simple algebraic method will be applied to solve simultaneous equations. The equations are

$$7x_1 + 3x_2 = 36$$

$$6x_1 - 1x_2 = 13$$

In step 1, the first equation is divided by 7. This gives

$$1x_1 + \tfrac{3}{7}x_2 = \tfrac{36}{7}$$

$$6x_1 - 1x_2 = 13$$

Then 6 times the first equation is subtracted from the second equation. This gives

$$1x_1 + \tfrac{3}{7}x_2 = \tfrac{36}{7}$$

$$0x_1 - \tfrac{25}{7}x_2 = -\tfrac{125}{7}$$

In step 2, the second equation is divided by $-\tfrac{25}{7}$

$$1x_1 + \tfrac{3}{7}x_2 = \tfrac{36}{7}$$

$$0 + 1x_2 = 5$$

Then $\tfrac{3}{7}$ times the second equation is subtracted from the first equation. This gives

$$1x_1 + 0 = 3$$

$$0 + 1x_2 = 5$$

The solution, $x_1 = 3$ and $x_2 = 5$, is on the right-hand side of the equations. In matrix terms, the original equation was

$$\begin{bmatrix} 7 & 3 \\ 6 & -1 \end{bmatrix} \begin{bmatrix} x_1 \\ x_2 \end{bmatrix} = \begin{bmatrix} 36 \\ 13 \end{bmatrix}$$

Then in steps 1 and 2, the left-hand side and the right-hand side of the equation were transformed (this is the same as multiplying both sides by some matrix). The ending equation was

$$\begin{bmatrix} 1 & 0 \\ 0 & 1 \end{bmatrix} \begin{bmatrix} x_1 \\ x_2 \end{bmatrix} = \begin{bmatrix} 3 \\ 5 \end{bmatrix}$$

Because the matrix on the left-hand side of the original equation has been transformed into the identity matrix, the transforming matrix must be the inverse of that matrix.

This leads to the Gauss–Jordan method. First, an *augmented* matrix is set up. This is the original **A** matrix, the **Y** matrix, and the identity matrix written side by side. Thus,

$$\left[\begin{array}{cc|c|cc} 7 & 3 & 36 & 1 & 0 \\ 6 & -1 & 13 & 0 & 1 \end{array} \right]$$

The method consists of applying the same transformation to the three components of the augmented matrix so that what started as the **A** component is transformed into the identity matrix, what started as the **Y** component is transformed into the solution vector, and what started as the identity matrix is transformed into $\mathbf{A}^{-1}$, the inverse of **A**.

In step 1, row one is divided by 7 and then 6 times row one is subtracted from row two. This gives

$$\left[\begin{array}{cc|c|cc} 1 & \frac{3}{7} & \frac{36}{7} & \frac{1}{7} & 0 \\ 0 & -\frac{25}{7} & -\frac{125}{7} & -\frac{6}{7} & 1 \end{array}\right]$$

The element used for the transformation (7, in this first step) is called the *pivotal* element. In step 2, row two is divided by $-\frac{25}{7}$, the new pivotal element, and then $\frac{3}{7}$ times row two is subtracted from row one. This gives

$$\left[\begin{array}{cc|c|cc} 1 & 0 & 3 & \frac{1}{25} & \frac{3}{25} \\ 0 & 1 & 5 & \frac{6}{25} & -\frac{7}{25} \end{array}\right]$$

which can also be written as

$$\left[\begin{array}{cc|c|cc} 1 & 0 & 3 & 0.04 & 0.12 \\ 0 & 1 & 5 & 0.24 & -0.28 \end{array}\right]$$

The result of the Gauss–Jordan method is that the left-hand matrix is now the 2×2 identity matrix, the middle two-element vector is the solution vector **x,** and the right-hand matrix is the inverse matrix. The order in which the pivotal elements are chosen makes no difference to the result. The reader might wish to prove this point by reworking the example beginning with -1 as the first pivotal element rather than with the 7.

For a matrix to be inverted, it must be what is called a *nonsingular* matrix. Trying to invert a singular matrix is the matrix equivalent of trying to divide an ordinary number by zero. Singularity is not dealt with further in this text, because the way in which matrices are used for stepwise regression ensures that only nonsingular matrices, or at least only the nonsingular parts of them, are inverted.

The Gauss–Jordan method can be explained in a somewhat more general framework in relation to the problem of solving the 3×3 equation:

$$\begin{bmatrix} A_{11} & A_{12} & A_{13} \\ A_{21} & A_{22} & A_{23} \\ A_{31} & A_{32} & A_{33} \end{bmatrix} \begin{bmatrix} x_1 \\ x_2 \\ x_3 \end{bmatrix} = \begin{bmatrix} y_1 \\ y_2 \\ y_3 \end{bmatrix}$$

The generalization of the method to a $k \times k$ matrix will be obvious. As before, the first step is formation of the augmented matrix.

$$\mathbf{A}_0 = \begin{bmatrix} A_{11} & A_{12} & A_{13} & y_1 & 1 & 0 & 0 \\ A_{21} & A_{22} & A_{23} & y_2 & 0 & 1 & 0 \\ A_{31} & A_{32} & A_{33} & y_3 & 0 & 0 & 1 \end{bmatrix}$$

Three transformations are performed on the augmented matrix to generate a new matrix in which:

- The 3×3 matrix on the left-hand side is $\mathbf{I}_3$, the 3×3 identity matrix
- The 3×1 column vector in the middle is the solution to the original equation
- The 3×3 matrix on the right hand side is $\mathbf{A}^{-1}$, the inverse of $\mathbf{A}$

The pivotal elements can be taken in any order, but for illustrative purposes one can start with A_{11}.

In step 1, row one is transformed by dividing it by the pivotal element A_{11}. Each succeeding row is then transformed by deducting from it the first element in the row times the newly transformed first row. After step 1, therefore, the new augmented matrix is

$$\mathbf{A}_1 = \begin{bmatrix} 1 & B_{12} & B_{13} & v_1 & E_{11} & 0 & 0 \\ 0 & B_{22} & B_{23} & v_2 & E_{21} & 1 & 0 \\ 0 & B_{32} & B_{33} & v_3 & E_{31} & 0 & 1 \end{bmatrix}$$

where

$$B_{12} = \frac{A_{12}}{A_{11}}$$

$$B_{13} = \frac{A_{13}}{A_{11}}$$

$$v_1 = \frac{y_1}{A_{11}}$$

$$E_{11} = \frac{1}{A_{11}}$$

$$B_{22} = A_{22} - \frac{A_{21}A_{12}}{A_{11}}$$

$$B_{23} = A_{23} - \frac{A_{21}A_{13}}{A_{11}}$$

$$v_2 = y_2 - \frac{A_{12}y_1}{A_{11}}$$

$$E_{21} = \frac{-A_{21}}{A_{11}}$$

$$B_{32} = A_{32} - \frac{A_{31}A_{12}}{A_{11}}$$

$$B_{33} = A_{33} - \frac{A_{31}A_{13}}{A_{11}}$$

$$v_3 = y_3 - \frac{A_{31}y_1}{A_{11}}$$

$$E_{31} = \frac{-A_{31}}{A_{11}}$$

In step 2, row two of the new matrix is transformed by dividing it by the pivotal element B_{22}. Then rows one and three are transformed by deducting, from each element, the second element in the row times the newly transformed row two. This gives a new augmented matrix:

$$\mathbf{A}_2 = \begin{bmatrix} 1 & 0 & C_{13} & w_1 & F_{11} & F_{12} & 0 \\ 0 & 1 & C_{23} & w_2 & F_{21} & F_{22} & 0 \\ 0 & 0 & C_{33} & w_3 & F_{31} & F_{32} & 1 \end{bmatrix}$$

In step 3, row three of the new matrix A_2 is transformed by dividing it by the pivotal element C_{33}. Rows one and two are then transformed by deducting, from each element, the third element in the row times the newly transformed row three. This gives a new augmented matrix:

$$A_3 = \begin{bmatrix} 1 & 0 & 0 \\ 0 & 1 & 0 \\ 0 & 0 & 1 \end{bmatrix} \begin{matrix} x_1 \\ x_2 \\ x_3 \end{matrix} \begin{bmatrix} G_{11} & G_{12} & G_{13} \\ G_{21} & G_{22} & G_{23} \\ G_{31} & G_{32} & G_{33} \end{bmatrix}$$

This final matrix contains the complete solution to the problem. The 3×3 matrix on the left-hand side of A_3 is the identity matrix I_3. The column vector x in the middle is the solution vector. The 3×3 matrix G on the right-hand side is the inverse of the original matrix.

9.3   REGRESSION ON TWO INDEPENDENT VARIABLES USING MATRICES

In this section, the material presented in Chapter 4 will be expressed in terms of matrices. This matrix formulation (relating to regression on two independent variables) can be generalized, with almost no change, to a regression on k independent variables.

The underlying linear model can be expressed in matrix terms as

$$Y = X\beta + u$$

Ordinary least squares regression is used to find a vector b that is an estimator of β such that $Y = Xb + e$, and the sum of the squared residuals is a minimum. Now the condition that Σe_i^2 is a minimum can be expressed by saying that $e'e$ must be a minimum. (Note that $e'e$ is a number, not a vector.) Because $e = Y - Xb$, the least squares condition is that

$$e'e = (Y - Xb)'(Y - Xb)$$

must be a minimum. Rearranging the terms using the rules of matrix algebra, including those for transposition, yields

$$e'e = Y'Y - 2b'X'Y + b'(X'X)b$$

Under certain conditions, which are met in this case, rules of differential calculus similar to those applicable to ordinary variables can also be applied to matrices. Thus, to find the vector **b** that minimizes $\mathbf{e'e}$, $\mathbf{e'e}$ is differentiated with respect to **b,** the derivative is set equal to zero, and the resulting equation is solved for **b.** The derivative of $\mathbf{e'e}$ with respect to **b** is

$$\frac{d}{d\mathbf{b}}(\mathbf{e'e}) = -2\mathbf{X'Y} + 2(\mathbf{X'X})\mathbf{b}$$

Setting the right-hand side of this equation to zero gives $\mathbf{X'Xb} = \mathbf{X'Y}$. Because $\mathbf{X'X}$ is a square matrix, it is invertible provided that it is nonsingular. Therefore, the least squares estimator is

$$\mathbf{b} = (\mathbf{X'X})^{-1}\mathbf{X'Y}$$

In the Gamma Company example of Chapter 4,

$$\mathbf{X'X} = \begin{bmatrix} \sum x_1^2 & \sum x_1 x_2 \\ \sum x_2 x_1 & \sum x_2^2 \end{bmatrix} = \begin{bmatrix} 2,120,780 & 730,408 \\ 730,408 & 560,470 \end{bmatrix}$$

Also,

$$\mathbf{X'Y} = \begin{bmatrix} \sum x_1 y \\ \sum x_2 y \end{bmatrix} = \begin{bmatrix} 2,880,436 \\ 1,411,469 \end{bmatrix}$$

Thus, to solve the equation $(\mathbf{X'X})\mathbf{b} = \mathbf{X'Y}$, the following augmented matrix is set up for the Gauss–Jordan transformation:

$$\begin{bmatrix} 2,120,780 & 730,408 & 2,880,436 & 1 & 0 \\ 730,408 & 560,470 & 1,411,469 & 0 & 1 \end{bmatrix}$$

In the first transformation, the first row is divided by the pivotal element 2,120,780. Then the first element (730,408) times the newly transformed first row is deducted from the second row. This gives

$$\begin{bmatrix} 1 & 0.3444054 & 1.358197 & 4.715246E{-07} & 0 \\ 0 & 308913.6 & 419431.5 & -0.3444054 & 1 \end{bmatrix}$$

Scientific notation has been used to represent the number $4.715246E-07$. This is the same as 4.715246×10^{-7} or 0.0000004715246. Scientific notation is often used to represent small numbers such as this.

For the second transformation, the second row is divided by the pivotal element $308{,}913.6$. Then 0.3444054 times the newly transformed second row is deducted from the first row.

$$\begin{bmatrix} 1 & 0 & 0.8905756 & 8.554995E-07 & -1.114892E-06 \\ 0 & 1 & 1.357763 & -1.114892E-06 & 3.237152E-06 \end{bmatrix}$$

The Gauss–Jordan method has produced two matrices of interest. First,

$$\mathbf{b} = \begin{bmatrix} 0.8906 \\ 1.3578 \end{bmatrix}$$

which contains the coefficients of the regression function. These are the same as the coefficients derived in Chapter 4. Second, it has produced the inverse of $\mathbf{X'X}$

$$(\mathbf{X'X})^{-1} = \begin{bmatrix} 8.554995E-07 & -1.114892E-06 \\ -1.114892E-06 & 3.237152E-06 \end{bmatrix}$$

That this matrix is indeed the inverse of $\mathbf{X'X}$ can be verified by multiplying the two together [i.e., $(\mathbf{X'X}) (\mathbf{X'X})^{-1} = \mathbf{I}$].

The regression constant can be calculated from $\bar{Y}$, $\mathbf{b}$, and the vector of means of the independent variables

$$a = \bar{Y} - \mathbf{b}' \bar{\mathbf{X}}$$

$$= 2502 - [0.8906 \ 1.3578] \begin{bmatrix} 1832 \\ 911 \end{bmatrix}$$

$$= -366.4614$$

9.4 MULTIPLE REGRESSION USING THE CORRELATION MATRIX

In the previous section, multiple regression was performed using the matrix of corrected squares and cross products as the starting point. In this section, it will be shown how it can be performed using the matrix of correlation coefficients as the starting point. In the next section, how this approach facilitates the computation will be demonstrated.

The normal equations for a two-independent-variable regression, using corrected data, are

$$b_1 \sum x_1^2 + b_2 \sum x_1 x_2 = \sum x_1 y$$
$$b_1 \sum x_1 x_1 + b_2 \sum x_2^2 = \sum x_2 y$$

These normal equations can be easily changed to equations involving coefficients of correlation instead of corrected squares and cross products. Taking the first equation as an example, the terms on both sides of the equation are first divided by

$$\sqrt{\sum x_1^2} \sqrt{\sum y^2}$$

This gives

$$\frac{b_1 \sum x_1^2}{\sqrt{\sum x_1^2} \sqrt{\sum y^2}} + \frac{b_2 \sum x_1 x_2}{\sqrt{\sum x_1^2} \sqrt{\sum y^2}} = \frac{\sum x_1 y}{\sqrt{\sum x_1^2} \sqrt{\sum y^2}}$$

Next, a "trick" is used in which the second expression on the left-hand side of the equation is multiplied by

$$\frac{\sqrt{\sum x_2^2}}{\sqrt{\sum x_2^2}}$$

After the terms have been rearranged and simplified, the left-hand side of the equation becomes

$$\left(\frac{b_1 \sqrt{\sum x_1^2}}{\sqrt{\sum y^2}} \right) \times 1 + \left(\frac{b_2 \sqrt{\sum x_2^2}}{\sqrt{\sum y^2}} \right) \times \frac{\sum x_1 x_2}{\sqrt{\sum x_1^2} \sqrt{\sum x_2^2}}$$

By definition of the coefficient of correlation, the right-hand side of the equation equals R_{1y} and

$$R_{12} = \frac{\sum x_1 x_2}{\sqrt{\sum x_1^2}\sqrt{\sum x_2^2}}$$

If the expressions in parentheses are denoted by b_1^* and b_2^*, respectively, the first normal equation can be written as

$$b_1^* \cdot 1 + b_2^* R_{12} = R_{1y}$$

where

$$b_1^* = \frac{\sqrt{\sum x_1^2}}{\sqrt{\sum y^2}} b_1$$

and

$$b_2^* = \frac{\sqrt{\sum x_2^2}}{\sqrt{\sum y^2}} b_2$$

Similarly, the second normal equation may be written as

$$b_1^* R_{21} + b_2^* \cdot 1 = R_{2y}$$

Finally, the normal equations may be written in matrix form as

$$\begin{bmatrix} 1 & R_{12} \\ R_{21} & 1 \end{bmatrix} \begin{bmatrix} b_1^* \\ b_2^* \end{bmatrix} = \begin{bmatrix} R_{1y} \\ R_{2y} \end{bmatrix}$$

If these equations are solved for $\mathbf{b}^*$, it is always possible to get back to the original coefficients by decoding them as

$$b_1 = \frac{\sqrt{\sum y^2}}{\sqrt{\sum x_1^2}} b_1^*$$

$$b_2 = \frac{\sqrt{\sum y^2}}{\sqrt{\sum x_2^2}} b_2^*$$

Once b_1 and b_2 have been obtained, the regression constant can be obtained in the usual way as

$$a = \bar{Y} - b_1 \bar{X}_1 - b_2 \bar{X}_2$$

The principal advantage of using the matrix of coefficients of correlation to perform regression analysis is that some useful statistics are generated as part of the stepwise regression procedure. This will become clear in the next section.

In general terms, the normal regression equations can always be written in terms of correlation coefficients and modified regression coefficients:

$$
\begin{aligned}
1b_1^* \quad + R_{12}b_2^* + \cdots + R_{1k}b_k^* &= R_{1y} \\
R_{21}b_1^* + 1b_2^* \quad + \cdots + R_{2k}b_k^* &= R_{2y} \\
&\;\;\vdots \\
R_{k1}b_1^* + R_{k2}b_2^* + \cdots + 1b_k^* &= R_{ky}
\end{aligned}
$$

The coefficient matrix is then not $\mathbf{X'X}$ but

$$
\mathbf{R} =
\begin{bmatrix}
1 & R_{12} & \cdots & R_{1k} \\
R_{21} & 1 & \cdots & R_{2k} \\
\vdots & \vdots & & \vdots \\
R_{k1} & R_{k2} & \cdots & 1
\end{bmatrix}
$$

and the system

$$
\mathbf{Rb^*} =
\begin{bmatrix}
R_{1y} \\
R_{2y} \\
\vdots \\
R_{ky}
\end{bmatrix}
$$

is solved for $\mathbf{b^*}$, that is,

$$b^* = R^{-1} \begin{bmatrix} R_{1y} \\ R_{2y} \\ \cdot \\ \cdot \\ \cdot \\ R_{ky} \end{bmatrix}$$

In solving these new normal equations, the Gauss–Jordan method yields an inverse matrix as a by-product, but this inverse matrix is R^{-1} rather than $(X'X)^{-1}$. Fortunately, to get from R^{-1} to $(X'X)^{-1}$ is not difficult, as will now be demonstrated. First, note that R can be derived from $X'X$: if a matrix M is defined as

$$M = \begin{bmatrix} 1/\sqrt{\sum x_1^2} & 0 & \cdots & 0 \\ 0 & 1/\sqrt{\sum x_2^2} & \cdots & 0 \\ \cdot & \cdot & & \cdot \\ \cdot & \cdot & & \cdot \\ \cdot & \cdot & & \cdot \\ 0 & 0 & \cdots & 1/\sqrt{\sum x_k^2} \end{bmatrix}$$

then $M(X'X)M = R$. Therefore, $X'X = M^{-1}RM^{-1}$. Using the useful property of inverse matrices that $(AB)^{-1} = B^{-1}A^{-1}$ yields

$$(X'X)^{-1} = [(M^{-1}R)M^{-1}]^{-1}$$
$$= (M^{-1})^{-1} (M^{-1}R)^{-1}$$

and therefore

$$(X'X)^{-1} = MR^{-1}M$$

9.5 COMPUTATIONAL PROCEDURE FOR STEPWISE MULTIPLE REGRESSION

Stepwise regression was introduced in Chapter 4 and explained a little more in Chapter 8. In this section, the stepwise regression procedure used in the STAR Program will be described in detail. This procedure was developed by Efroymson [1]. A particularly lucid description of it is also given by Draper and Smith [2]. A STAR Program printout that shows all the mathematical calculations is included as Printout B.7 in Appendix B.

To demonstrate the calculations that are involved, use the Gamma Company variables:

Y REVENUE

X_1 TIME AT STANDARD

X_2 EXPENSES

X_3 COST OF SERVICES

The data are shown in Figure 2.1. The process begins with setting up the augmented matrix of coefficients of correlation. One extra row, however, is added to the matrix, which will prove to be most useful. This row consists of the correlation of Y with itself and the X's plus a sequence of zeros. The matrix is shown as Matrix **A**, below. Notice also that, for convenience, **Y** has been shifted to the leftmost column. The addition of the new row in the augmented matrix will not affect the Gauss–Jordan transformations but will be used to generate factors for calculating partial correlation coefficients and other useful statistics.

Matrix A   Correlation Matrix

	Y	X_1	X_2	X_3	X_1	X_2	X_3
Y	1	0.8636878	0.8232686	0.8693496	0	0	0
X_1	0.8636878	1	0.6699487	0.8617620	1	0	0
X_2	0.8232686	0.6699487	1	0.8480435	0	1	0
X_3	0.8693496	0.8617620	0.8480435	1	0	0	1

For convenience, the successive augmented matrices to be used in the step-wise regression have been labeled **A, B, C, D,** and **E,** where **A** consists of correlation coefficients and **E** is the final matrix. The matrix name plus a subscript will be used to refer to specific elements of the matrix. Thus, for Matrix **A,** the individual elements are referred to as

$$
A = \begin{array}{|c|cccccc|}
\hline
A_{YY} & A_{Y1} & A_{Y2} & A_{Y3} & A_{Y4} & A_{Y5} & A_{Y6} \\
\hline
A_{1Y} & A_{11} & A_{12} & A_{13} & A_{14} & A_{15} & A_{16} \\
A_{2Y} & A_{21} & A_{22} & A_{23} & A_{24} & A_{25} & A_{26} \\
A_{3Y} & A_{31} & A_{32} & A_{33} & A_{34} & A_{35} & A_{36} \\
\hline
\end{array}
$$

For example, $A_{23} = 0.8480435$ is in reality R_{23}, the coefficient of correlation between X_2 and X_3.

9.5.1   Step 1

1. From matrix **A,** calculate a set of so-called V statistics.

$$
\begin{aligned}
V_1 &= A_{Y1}A_{1Y}/A_{11} = 0.745957 \\
V_2 &= A_{Y2}A_{2Y}/A_{22} = 0.677771 \\
V_3 &= A_{Y3}A_{3Y}/A_{33} = 0.755769 \\
V_4 &= A_{Y4}A_{1Y}/A_{14} = 0 \\
V_5 &= A_{Y5}A_{2Y}/A_{25} = 0 \\
V_6 &= A_{Y6}A_{3Y}/A_{36} = 0
\end{aligned}
$$

Note that the statistics V_1 through V_3 are simply the squares of the coefficients of correlation between the dependent variable and the independent variables. The largest V statistic (VMAX) is V_3. Therefore, X_3, the variable that is most highly correlated with Y, is the first variable to be considered for admission. The F ratio used to test the significance of X_3 is

$$
F = \frac{(n - k - 1)\ \text{VMAX}}{A_{YY} - \text{VMAX}}
$$

It can be shown that this statistic has an F distribution with 1 and $n - k - 1$ degrees of freedom. It can also be written as

$$
F = \frac{R^2_{3y}/1}{(1 - R^2_{3y})/(n - k - 1)}
$$

which is the same as the formula presented in Section 8.2. In this case, $n = 36$, and k is the number of variables that will be in the regression if X_3 is admitted. Therefore,

$$F = \frac{34 \times 0.755769}{1 - 0.755769} = 105.21$$

The critical value for an F ratio with 34 degrees of freedom at a 5% level of significance is 4.13 (Figure A.4). Therefore, X_3 is highly significant at the 5% level.

2. Admit X_3 to the regression function. This is done by performing a Gauss-Jordan transformation on Matrix **A** using A_{33} as the pivotal element. The result is Matrix **B**:

Matrix B   Matrix after Transformation Using A_{33} as Pivotal Element

	Y	X_1	X_2	X_3	X_1	X_2	X_3
Y	0.2442313	0.11451540	0.08602229	0	0	0	−0.8693496
X_1	0.11451540	0.25736620	−0.06086306	0	1	0	−0.8617620
X_2	0.08602229	−0.06086306	0.28082220	0	0	1	−0.848035
X_3	0.86934960	0.86176200	0.84804350	1	0	0	1

At this stage, the coefficient of X_3 in the regression function could be found by decoding b_3^*:

$$b_3^* = B_{3Y} = 0.86934960$$

Therefore,

$$b_3 = \frac{\sqrt{\sum y^2}}{\sqrt{\sum x_3^2}} b_3^* = \frac{\sqrt{5{,}244{,}538}}{\sqrt{2{,}141{,}408}} \times 0.86934960 = 1.3605$$

Because $\bar{X}_3 = 1{,}815$ and $\bar{Y} = 2{,}502$, the regression constant at this stage is

$$a = 2{,}502 - 1.3605 \times 1{,}815 = 32.72$$

Therefore, if the regression were to stop at this stage, the regression function would be

$$\hat{Y} = 32.72 + 1.3605X_3$$

Several other statistics of interest may be derived from Matrix **B**. The coefficient of correlation is

$$R = \sqrt{1 - B_{YY}} = \sqrt{1 - 0.2442313} = 0.87$$

which, of course, agrees with the coefficient of correlation between Y and X_3 shown in Matrix **A** (element A_{3Y}). The standard error of the regression function is

$$
\begin{aligned}
S_u &= \sqrt{\frac{B_{YY}\sum y^2}{n - k - 1}} \\
&= \sqrt{0.2442313 \times \frac{5{,}244{,}538}{34}} \\
&= 194.0952
\end{aligned}
$$

The standard error of the regression coefficient b_3 is given by

$$
\begin{aligned}
S_{b3} &= S_u \sqrt{\frac{B_{36}}{\sum x_3^2}} \\
&= 194.0952 \sqrt{\frac{1}{2{,}141{,}408}} \\
&= 0.1326
\end{aligned}
$$

The importance of B_{YY} in these calculations arises from the way in which it was derived. The Gauss–Jordan elimination method ensures that

$$
\begin{aligned}
B_{YY} &= A_{YY} - A_{Y3}\left(\frac{A_{3Y}}{A_{33}}\right) \\
&= R_{YY} - R_{Y3}\left(\frac{R_{3Y}}{R_{33}}\right) \\
&= 1 - R_{Y3}^2
\end{aligned}
$$

Therefore,

$$R_{Y3} = \sqrt{1 - B_{YY}}$$

Also, by definition of the coefficient of correlation,

$$B_{YY} = 1 - R_{Y3}^2$$

$$= 1 - \frac{\sum \hat{y}^2}{\sum y^2}$$

$$= \frac{\sum e^2}{\sum y^2}$$

Therefore,

$$\sum e^2 = B_{YY} \sum y^2$$

Because $s_u = \sqrt{\sum e^2/(n - k - 1)}$, it can be seen that

$$s_u = \sqrt{\frac{B_{YY} \sum y^2}{n - k - 1}}$$

9.5.2   Step 2

1. Using Matrix **B**, calculate the V statistics

$$V_1 = \frac{B_{Y1} B_{1Y}}{B_{11}} = 0.050954$$

$$V_2 = \frac{B_{Y2} B_{2Y}}{B_{22}} = 0.026351$$

$$V_3 = \frac{B_{Y3} B_{3Y}}{B_{33}} = 0$$

$$V_4 = \frac{B_{Y4} B_{1Y}}{B_{14}} = 0$$

$$V_5 = \frac{B_{Y5}B_{2Y}}{B_{25}} = 0$$

$$V_6 = \frac{B_{Y6}B_{3Y}}{B_{36}} = -0.756290$$

Notice that V_6 is negative. The statistics V_4, V_5, and V_6 will be negative when X_1, X_2, and X_3, respectively, are in the regression. This is a consequence of the Gauss–Jordan transformation. (It also provides a convenient way for a computer program to determine whether a particular variable is in the regression at any stage.)

In this case, $VMAX = V_1$. Degrees of freedom, should X_1 be admitted, are $n - k - 1 = 36 - 2 - 1 = 33$.

$$F = \frac{(n - k - 1)VMAX}{B_{YY} - VMAX}$$

$$= \frac{33 \times 0.051524}{0.2442313 - 0.051524}$$

$$= 8.70$$

The critical value for an F ratio with 33 degrees of freedom at a 5% level of significance is 4.14 (Figure A.4). Therefore, X_1 is significant at the 5% level.

An interesting feature of the V statistics is that they are directly proportional to the partial correlation coefficients that are obtained after the influence of the variables in the regression has been removed. In fact, if h_{ij} represents an element in the ith row and the jth column of the matrix, the partial correlation coefficient of X_i and Y after removing the influence of the other variables in the regression is

$$R_{iY\cdot12\ldots(i-1)(i+1)\ldots k} = \sqrt{\frac{h_{iY}^2}{h_{ii}h_{YY}}}$$

From this formula and the formula for V_i (where X_i is not in the regression), it can be seen that

$$V_i = (R_{iY\cdot12\ldots(i-1)(i+1)\ldots k}^2)\, h_{YY}$$

At this stage, for example, where X_3 is the only variable in the regression

$$R_{1Y\cdot3} = \sqrt{\frac{B_{1Y}^2}{B_{11}B_{YY}}}$$

$$= \sqrt{\frac{0.1145154^2}{0.2573662 \times 0.2442313}}$$

$$= 0.46$$

Because the V_i's bear a fixed ratio to the partial correlation coefficients, selecting the variable with the highest partial correlation coefficient is equivalent to selecting the variable with the highest V statistic.

The F statistic, as calculated from the factors generated by the procedure, can easily be shown to be the same as the statistic discussed in Section 8.2. In this latest case,

$$F = \frac{(n - k - 1)V_1}{B_{YY} - V_1}$$

$$= \frac{R_{1Y\cdot3}^2 B_{YY}/1}{(B_{YY} - R_{1Y\cdot3}^2 B_{YY})/(n - k - 1)}$$

$$= \frac{R_{1Y\cdot3}^2/1}{(1 - R_{1Y\cdot3}^2)/(n - k - 1)}$$

2. Because X_1 is to be admitted to the regression, the matrix is now transformed with B_{11} as the pivotal element. This gives Matrix **C**:

Matrix C   Matrix after Transformation Using B_{11} as Pivotal Element

	Y	X_1	X_2	X_3	X_1	X_2	X_3
Y	0.1932776	0	0.1131034	0	−0.4449511	0	−0.4859077
X_1	0.4449511	1	−0.2364843	0	3.8855140	0	−3.3483890
X_2	0.1131034	0	0.2664290	0	0.2364843	1	−1.0518370
X_3	0.4859077	0	1.051837	1	−3.3483890	0	3.8855140

If the regression were terminated at this point, Matrix **C** could be used to provide information about the regression function

$$\hat{Y} = a + b_3 X_3 + b_1 X_1$$

Decoding **b*** gives

$$b_3 = \frac{\sqrt{\Sigma y^2}}{\sqrt{\Sigma x_3^2}} b_3^* = 0.7604$$

$$b_1 = \frac{\sqrt{\Sigma y^2}}{\sqrt{\Sigma x_1^2}} b_1^* = 0.6997$$

$$a = \bar{Y} - b_1 \bar{X}_1 - b_3 \bar{X}_3 = -160.03$$

Therefore, the regression function is

$$\hat{Y} = -160.03 + 0.6997 X_1 + 0.7604 X_3$$

The coefficient of correlation, the standard error of regression, and the other statistics can be calculated in the same way as before.

9.5.3   Step 3

1. From Matrix **C**, calculate the V statistics.

$$V_1 = \frac{C_{Y1} C_{1Y}}{C_{11}} = 0$$

$$V_2 = \frac{C_{Y2} C_{2Y}}{C_{22}} = 0.048014$$

$$V_3 = \frac{C_{Y3} C_{3Y}}{C_{33}} = 0$$

$$V_4 = \frac{C_{Y4} C_{1Y}}{C_{14}} = -0.050954$$

$$V_5 = \frac{C_{Y5} C_{2Y}}{C_{25}} = 0$$

$$V_6 = \frac{C_{Y6}C_{3Y}}{C_{36}} = -0.060765$$

Because X_1 and X_3 are in the regression, V_4 and V_6 are negative. The partial correlation coefficients for the variable not in the regression can be calculated as follows:

$$R_{2Y \cdot 13} = \sqrt{\frac{C_{2Y}^2}{C_{22}C_{YY}}} = 0.50$$

2. Forward selection. This time X_2 is the variable to be considered because it is the variable with the highest V statistic. VMAX $= V_2 = 0.048014$, $n - k - 1 = 36 - 3 - 1 = 32$, and therefore

$$F = \frac{(n - k - 1)\,\text{VMAX}}{C_{YY} - \text{VMAX}} = 10.58$$

The critical value for an F ratio with 32 degrees of freedom at a 5% level of significance is 4.15 (Figure A.4). Therefore, X_2 is significant at the 5% level.

3. Admit X_2 and perform the necessary Gauss–Jordan transformation using C_{33} as the pivotal element. Matrix **D** is

Matrix D   Matrix after Transformation Using C_{22} as Pivotal Element

	Y	X_1	X_2	X_3	X_1	X_2	X_3
Y	0.14526340	0	0	0	-0.5453424	-0.4245159	-0.03938621
X_1	0.54534240	1	0	0	4.0954200	0.8876070	-4.28200700
X_2	0.42451590	0	1	0	0.8876070	3.7533450	-3.94790600
X_3	0.03938621	0	0	1	-4.2820070	-3.9479060	8.03806700

If the regression were to stop at this point, the regression coefficients and constant could be calculated to give the function

$$\hat{Y} = -363.97 + 0.8576X_1 + 1.2986X_2 + 0.0616X_3$$

9.5.4   Step 4

1.   From Matrix **D**, calculate the V statistics.

$$V_1 = \frac{D_{Y1}D_{1Y}}{D_{11}} = 0$$

$$V_2 = \frac{D_{Y2}D_{2Y}}{D_{22}} = 0$$

$$V_3 = \frac{D_{Y3}D_{3Y}}{D_{33}} = 0$$

$$V_4 = \frac{D_{Y4}D_{1Y}}{D_{14}} = -0.072617$$

$$V_5 = \frac{D_{Y5}D_{2Y}}{D_{25}} = -0.048014$$

$$V_6 = \frac{D_{Y6}D_{3Y}}{D_{36}} = -0.000193$$

2.   Backward elimination. VMIN $= V_6 = -0.000193$, and therefore the related F value is

$$F = \frac{(n - k - 1)|\text{VMIN}|}{D_{YY}}$$

$$= \frac{32 \times 0.000193}{0.14526340}$$

$$= 0.04$$

The critical value for an F ratio with 32 degrees of freedom at a 5% level of significance is 4.15 (Figure A.4). Because the calculated F ratio is less than this, X_3 is no longer significant at the 5% level and therefore must be eliminated.

The removal of a variable from the regression function takes exactly the same form as the admission of a variable, except that the pivotal element is taken from the right-hand side of the matrix. In this case, the Gauss–Jordan transformation is applied to **D** using D_{36} as the pivotal element. The result is Matrix **E**.

Matrix E　Matrix after Transformation Using D_{36} as Pivotal Element

	Y	X_1	X_2	X_3	X_1	X_2	X_3
Y	0.145456400	0	0	0.004899960	-0.5663241	-0.4438605	0
X_1	0.566324100	1	0	0.532716000	1.8143260	-1.2155050	0
X_2	0.443860500	0	1	0.491151200	-1.2155050	1.8143260	0
X_3	0.004899960	0	0	0.124408000	-0.5327160	-0.4911512	1

3.　From Matrix **E**, calculate the V statistics.

$$V_1 = \frac{E_{Y1}E_{1Y}}{E_{11}} = 0$$

$$V_2 = \frac{E_{Y2}E_{2Y}}{E_{22}} = 0$$

$$V_3 = \frac{E_{Y3}E_{3Y}}{E_{33}} = 0.000193$$

$$V_4 = \frac{E_{Y4}E_{1Y}}{E_{14}} = -0.176773$$

$$V_5 = \frac{E_{Y5}E_{2Y}}{E_{25}} = -0.108587$$

$$V_6 = \frac{E_{Y6}E_{3Y}}{E_{36}} = 0$$

4.　Backward elimination. VMIN = $V_5 = -0.1085835$, and therefore the related F value is

$$F = \frac{(n - k - 1)\,|\text{VMIN}|}{E_{YY}}$$

$$= \frac{33 \times 0.108587}{0.1454564}$$

$$= 24.63$$

and $n - k - 1 = 33$. The critical value for an F ratio with 33 degrees of freedom at a 5% level of significance is 4.14 (Figure A.4). Because the calculated F ratio exceeds this, X_2 is still significant at the 5% level and therefore must be retained.

    5.   Forward selection. Because there are no further variables to test, the procedure ends at this point with two statistically significant independent variables. The final function is

$$\hat{Y} = a + b_1 X_1 + b_2 X_2$$

As before,

$$b_1 = \frac{\sqrt{\Sigma y^2}}{\sqrt{\Sigma x_1^2}} b_1^*$$

$$= \frac{\sqrt{5,244,538}}{\sqrt{2,120,780}} \times 0.5663241$$

$$= 0.8906$$

$$b_2 = \frac{\sqrt{\Sigma y^2}}{\Sigma x_2^2} b_2^*$$

$$= \frac{\sqrt{5,244,538}}{\sqrt{560,470}} \times 0.4438605$$

$$= 1.3578$$

$$a = \bar{Y} - b_1 \bar{X}_1 - b_2 \bar{X}_2$$

$$= -366.46$$

Therefore,

$$\hat{Y} = -366.46 + 0.8906\, X_1 + 1.3578\, X_2$$

is the final regression function. Furthermore,

$$R = \sqrt{1 - E_{YY}}$$
$$= \sqrt{1 - 0.1454564}$$
$$= 0.92$$

$$S_u = \sqrt{\frac{E_{YY} \sum y^2}{n - k - 1}}$$
$$= \sqrt{\frac{0.1454564 \times 5,244,538}{33}}$$
$$= 152.0418$$

$$S_{b1} = S_u \sqrt{\frac{E_{14}}{\sum x_1^2}}$$
$$= 152.0418 \sqrt{\frac{1.8143260}{2,120,780}}$$
$$= 0.1406$$

$$S_{b2} = S_u \sqrt{\frac{E_{25}}{\sum x_2^2}}$$
$$= 152.0418 \sqrt{\frac{1.8143260}{560,470}}$$
$$= 0.2736$$

9.5.5   A More Efficient Computer Procedure

As the augmented matrix is transformed in each step, some of the columns contain only 0's and 1's, depending on whether a variable is included in or excluded from the regression. In computer terms, the 0's and 1's take up just as much storage as the other numbers. Because the program can determine at any stage whether a particular variable is in or out of the regression by testing the sign of the V statistic, it is really unnecessary to store the trivial 0's and 1's.

The STAR Program, therefore, uses a somewhat more efficient procedure than the one presented. It merges, into one submatrix, the two submatrices that are shown in the example as the middle and the right-hand submatrices. Thus, rather than **E**, the final matrix is

	Y	X_1	X_2	X_3
Y	0.145456400	-0.5663241	-0.4438605	0.004899960
X_1	0.566324100	1.8143260	-1.2155050	0.532716000
X_2	0.443860500	-1.2155050	1.8143260	0.491151200
X_3	0.004899960	-0.5327160	-0.4911512	0.124408000

Whether a variable is in or out of the regression is determined by the sign of the V statistic.

9.5.6   Refinement of the F Test

A refined form of the F test has proved to be quite useful in stepwise regression and is the one actually used by the STAR Program. It results in admission requirements for new independent variables becoming tighter as more variables are admitted. The test is based on *target confidence levels* (probabilities) rather than on critical F values.

Instead of calculating critical F values that correspond to predetermined levels of significance, the STAR Program calculates probabilities that correspond to the calculated F ratios. If there is only one variable to be tested, the F probability that corresponds to the F ratio is computed. If it equals or exceeds 95% the variable is admitted. In the case of only one independent variable, this test is exactly equivalent to the standard F test.

If a second variable is to be tested, however, the target confidence level for its admission is raised from 95% to $T_2 = 95/P_1\%$, where P_1 is the confidence level that corresponds to the F ratio for the admission of the first variable. If the second variable is admitted (at a confidence level of P_2), the target confidence for the third variable is $T_3 = T_2/P_2$. The process continues along these lines. At each step, the target admission requirement for the next variable becomes the previous target divided by the confidence level at which the previous variable was admitted.

The confidence level for eliminating a variable is kept constant at 95% by the STAR Program. If a variable is to be eliminated, the target for the next admission becomes the present target for admission multiplied by the confidence level at which that variable was admitted. This has the effect of reducing the target to what it would have been had the eliminated variable not been admitted in the first place.

9.6   AUDIT INTERFACE CALCULATIONS IN MATRIX TERMS

As regards the audit interface, the only significant difference between regression with one independent variable and multivariable regression is the calculation of the estimated standard error. The number of degrees of freedom will also be less given the same number of observations. Therefore, where the regression function

$$Y_1 = a + b_1 X_{1t} + b_2 X_{2t} + \cdots + b_k X_{kt} + e_t$$

is used to predict a value Y_t, the standardized residual

$$\frac{Y_t - \hat{Y}_t}{s(e_t)}$$

has a t distribution with $n - k - 1$ degrees of freedom (see Chapter 3).
   It can be shown that the standard error of the residual e_t is given by

$$s(e_t) = s_u \sqrt{1 + \frac{1}{n} + \mathbf{c}_t'(\mathbf{X'X})^{-1}\mathbf{c}_t}$$

where $(\mathbf{X'X})^{-1}$ is the inverse of the matrix of corrected squares and cross products, and

$$\mathbf{c}_t = \begin{bmatrix} X_{1t} - \bar{X}_1 \\ X_{2t} - \bar{X}_2 \\ \cdot \\ \cdot \\ \cdot \\ X_{kt} - \bar{X}_k \end{bmatrix}$$

In Chapter 3, the case of one independent variable was discussed. There it was shown that

$$(\mathbf{X'X})^{-1} = \frac{1}{\sum x^2}$$

and

$$\mathbf{c}_t = X_t - \bar{X}$$

The Gauss–Jordan procedure automatically produces the inverse matrix expressed in terms of the coefficients of correlation. In the present example, this is the 2×2 matrix in the middle of $\mathbf{E}$ and corresponds to the variables in the final regression function.

$$\mathbf{R}^{-1} = \begin{bmatrix} 1.814326 & -1.215505 \\ -1.215505 & 1.814326 \end{bmatrix}$$

The Program converts this inverse matrix to one that is expressed in terms of corrected squares and cross products. It uses the relationship $(\mathbf{X'X})^{-1} = \mathbf{MR}^{-1}\mathbf{M}$ derived in Section 9.4. Therefore,

$$(\mathbf{X'X})^{-1} = \begin{bmatrix} \dfrac{1.814326}{2,120,780} & \dfrac{-1.215505}{\sqrt{2,120,780}\,\sqrt{560,470}} \\ \dfrac{-1.215505}{\sqrt{2,120,780}\,\sqrt{560,470}} & \dfrac{1.814326}{560,470} \end{bmatrix}$$

$$= \begin{bmatrix} 0.0000008554995 & -0.0000011148920 \\ -0.0000011148920 & 0.0000032371510 \end{bmatrix}$$

This matrix is used in the calculation of the estimated standard error. For example, in period 48 for Gamma Company,

$$X_{1,48} - \bar{X}_1 = 2,389 - 1,842 = 557$$
$$X_{2,48} - \bar{X}_2 = 1,159 - 911 = 248$$

and therefore

$$\mathbf{c}_t = \begin{bmatrix} 557 \\ 248 \end{bmatrix}$$

The matrix calculation factor $\mathbf{c}_t'(\mathbf{X}'\mathbf{X})^{-1}\mathbf{c}_t$ is

$$[557 \ \ 248] \begin{bmatrix} 0.0000008554995 & -0.0000011148920 \\ -0.0000011148920 & 0.0000032371510 \end{bmatrix} \begin{bmatrix} 557 \\ 248 \end{bmatrix}$$

$$= 0.156502$$

The standard error is therefore

$$s(e_{48}) = 152.0418 \ \sqrt{1 + \frac{1}{36} + 0.156502} = 165.589$$

Hence, $(Y_{48} - \bar{Y}_{48})/165.4589$ has a t distribution with 33 degrees of freedom $(36 - 2 - 1 = 33)$.

All the remaining calculations for identifying excesses and computing optional sample sizes are essentially the same as those set forth in Chapter 5, where they were dealt with in the context of a function with one independent variable.

REFERENCES

1. M. A. Efroymson, *Multiple Regression Analysis.* Article 17 in A. Ralston and H. S. Wilf, Eds., *Mathematical Methods for Digital Computers.* New York: Wiley, 1962.
2. N. R. Draper and H. Smith, *Applied Regression Analysis.* New York, Wiley, 1981.

GENERAL REFERENCES

S. Chatterjee, *Regression Analysis by Example,* 2nd ed. New York: Wiley, 1991.

A. Koutsoyiannis, *Theory of Econometrics,* 2nd ed. London: Macmillan, 1977.

M. S. Lewis-Beck, *Applied Regression: An Introduction.* Beverly Hills, CA: Sage Publications, 1980.

J. Neper, *Applied Linear Regression Models.* Homewood, IL: R. D. Irwin, 1983.

K. W. Smillie, *An Introduction to Regression and Correlation.* New York: Academic Press, 1966.

APPENDIX A

STATISTICAL FIGURES

R	Rel %	R	Rel %	R	Rel %	R	Rel %
0.1	9.5	1.1	66.7	2.1	87.8	3.1	95.5
0.2	18.1	1.2	69.9	2.2	88.9	3.2	95.9
0.3	25.9	1.3	72.7	2.3	90.0	3.3	96.3
0.4	33.0	1.4	75.3	2.4	90.9	3.4	96.7
0.5	39.3	1.5	77.7	2.5	91.8	3.5	97.0
0.6	45.1	1.6	79.8	2.6	92.6	3.6	97.3
0.7	50.3	1.7	81.7	2.7	93.3	3.7	97.5
0.8	55.1	1.8	83.5	2.8	93.9	3.8	97.8
0.9	59.3	1.9	85.0	2.9	94.5	3.9	98.0
1.0	63.2	2.0	86.5	3.0	95.0	4.0	98.2

Reliability factors can be derived from the reliability level percent by the formula $R = -\log(1 - (\text{Rel \%} / 100))$, where log is the natural logarithm

Figure A.1   Reliability factors (R) and related reliability level percentages (Rel %).

Figure A.2 shows the probability that a t-distributed random variable (with degrees of freedom shown in the column heading) will be less than the t value in the leftmost column. For example, the probability that a t variable with 30 degrees of freedom will be less than 0.6 is 72.2%. This represents the area under the curve of the t distribution to the left of 0.6. Because the curve is symmetrical, 72.2% is also the probability that the t variable will be greater than -0.6. The rightmost column represents the cumulative probabilities for the normal distribution because the t distribution is identical to the normal distribution for infinite degrees of freedom.

t	df = 5	df = 10	df = 30	df = 60	df = 120	df = ∞
0.00	50.0	50.0	50.0	50.0	50.0	50.0
0.05	51.9	51.9	52.0	52.0	52.0	52.0
0.10	53.8	53.9	53.9	53.9	54.0	54.0
0.15	55.7	55.8	55.9	55.9	55.9	56.0
0.20	57.5	57.7	57.8	57.9	57.9	57.9
0.25	59.4	59.6	59.7	59.8	59.8	59.9
0.30	61.2	61.5	61.6	61.7	61.8	61.8
0.35	63.0	63.3	63.5	63.6	63.7	63.7
0.40	64.7	65.1	65.3	65.4	65.5	65.5
0.45	66.4	66.9	67.1	67.2	67.3	67.4
0.50	68.1	68.6	68.9	69.0	69.1	69.1
0.55	69.7	70.3	70.6	70.7	70.8	70.9
0.60	71.3	71.9	72.2	72.3	72.5	72.6
0.65	72.8	73.5	73.8	74.0	74.2	74.2
0.70	74.2	75.0	75.4	75.5	75.7	75.8
0.75	75.6	76.5	76.9	77.0	77.3	77.3
0.80	77.0	77.9	78.3	78.5	78.7	78.8
0.85	78.3	79.2	79.7	79.9	80.1	80.2
0.90	79.5	80.5	81.1	81.2	81.5	81.6
0.95	80.7	81.8	82.3	82.5	82.8	82.9
1.00	81.8	83.0	83.5	83.7	84.0	84.1
1.05	82.9	84.1	84.7	84.9	85.2	85.3
1.10	83.9	85.1	85.8	86.0	86.3	86.4
1.15	84.9	86.2	86.8	87.0	87.4	87.5
1.20	85.8	87.1	87.8	88.0	88.4	88.5
1.25	86.7	88.0	88.7	89.0	89.3	89.4
1.30	87.5	88.9	89.6	89.8	90.2	90.3
1.35	88.3	89.7	90.4	90.6	91.0	91.2
1.40	89.0	90.4	91.2	91.4	91.8	91.9
1.45	89.7	91.1	91.9	92.1	92.5	92.6
1.50	90.3	91.8	92.5	92.8	93.2	93.3
1.55	90.9	92.4	93.2	93.4	93.8	93.9
1.60	91.5	93.0	93.7	94.0	94.4	94.5
1.65	92.0	93.5	94.3	94.5	94.9	95.1
1.70	92.5	94.0	94.8	95.0	95.4	95.5
1.75	93.0	94.5	95.2	95.5	95.9	96.0
1.80	93.4	94.9	95.7	95.9	96.3	96.4
1.85	93.8	95.3	96.0	96.3	96.7	96.8
1.90	94.2	95.7	96.4	96.6	97.0	97.1
1.95	94.6	96.0	96.7	97.0	97.3	97.4
2.00	94.9	96.3	97.0	97.3	97.6	97.7

Figure A.2 Cumulative probabilities of the t distribution.

Degrees of freedom for numerator

	1	2	3	4	5	6	7	8	9	10	12	15	20	24	30	40	60	120	∞
1	4,052	5,000	5,403	5,625	5,764	5,859	5,928	5,982	6,023	6,056	6,106	6,157	6,209	6,235	6,261	6,287	6,313	6,339	6,366
2	98.5	99.0	99.2	99.2	99.3	99.3	99.4	99.4	99.4	99.4	99.4	99.4	99.4	99.5	99.5	99.5	99.5	99.5	99.5
3	34.1	30.8	29.5	28.7	28.2	27.9	27.7	27.5	27.3	27.2	27.1	26.9	26.7	26.6	26.5	26.4	26.3	26.2	26.1
4	21.2	18.0	16.7	16.0	15.5	15.2	15.0	14.8	14.7	14.5	14.4	14.2	14.0	13.9	13.8	13.7	13.7	13.6	13.5
5	16.3	13.3	12.1	11.4	11.0	10.7	10.5	10.3	10.2	10.1	9.89	9.72	9.55	9.47	9.38	9.29	9.20	9.11	9.02
6	13.7	10.9	9.78	9.15	8.75	8.47	8.26	8.10	7.98	7.87	7.72	7.56	7.40	7.31	7.23	7.14	7.06	6.97	6.88
7	12.2	9.55	8.45	7.85	7.46	7.19	6.99	6.84	6.72	6.62	6.47	6.31	6.16	6.07	5.99	5.91	5.82	5.74	5.65
8	11.3	8.65	7.59	7.01	6.63	6.37	6.18	6.03	5.91	5.81	5.67	5.52	5.36	5.28	5.20	5.12	5.03	4.95	4.86
9	10.6	8.02	6.99	6.42	6.06	5.80	5.61	5.47	5.35	5.26	5.11	4.96	4.81	4.73	4.65	4.57	4.48	4.40	4.31
10	10.0	7.56	6.55	5.99	5.64	5.39	5.20	5.06	4.94	4.85	4.71	4.56	4.41	4.33	4.25	4.17	4.08	4.00	3.91
11	9.65	7.21	6.22	5.67	5.32	5.07	4.89	4.74	4.63	4.54	4.40	4.25	4.10	4.02	3.94	3.86	3.78	3.69	3.60
12	9.33	6.93	5.95	5.41	5.06	4.82	4.64	4.50	4.39	4.30	4.16	4.01	3.86	3.78	3.70	3.62	3.54	3.45	3.36
13	9.07	6.70	5.74	5.21	4.86	4.62	4.44	4.30	4.19	4.10	3.96	3.82	3.66	3.59	3.51	3.43	3.34	3.25	3.17
14	8.86	6.51	5.56	5.04	4.70	4.46	4.28	4.14	4.03	3.94	3.80	3.66	3.51	3.43	3.35	3.27	3.18	3.09	3.00
15	8.68	6.36	5.42	4.89	4.56	4.32	4.14	4.00	3.89	3.80	3.67	3.52	3.37	3.29	3.21	3.13	3.05	2.96	2.87
16	8.53	6.23	5.29	4.77	4.44	4.20	4.03	3.89	3.78	3.69	3.55	3.41	3.26	3.18	3.10	3.02	2.93	2.84	2.75
17	8.40	6.11	5.19	4.67	4.34	4.10	3.93	3.79	3.68	3.59	3.46	3.31	3.16	3.08	3.00	2.92	2.83	2.75	2.65
18	8.29	6.01	5.09	4.58	4.25	4.01	3.84	3.71	3.60	3.51	3.37	3.23	3.08	3.00	2.92	2.84	2.75	2.66	2.57
19	8.19	5.93	5.01	4.50	4.17	3.94	3.77	3.63	3.52	3.43	3.30	3.15	3.00	2.92	2.84	2.76	2.67	2.58	2.49
20	8.10	5.85	4.94	4.43	4.10	3.87	3.70	3.56	3.46	3.37	3.23	3.09	2.94	2.86	2.78	2.69	2.61	2.52	2.42
21	8.02	5.78	4.87	4.37	4.04	3.81	3.64	3.51	3.40	3.31	3.17	3.03	2.88	2.80	2.72	2.64	2.55	2.46	2.36
22	7.95	5.72	4.82	4.31	3.99	3.76	3.59	3.45	3.35	3.26	3.12	2.98	2.83	2.75	2.67	2.58	2.50	2.40	2.31
23	7.88	5.66	4.76	4.26	3.94	3.71	3.54	3.41	3.30	3.21	3.07	2.93	2.78	2.70	2.62	2.54	2.45	2.35	2.26
24	7.82	5.61	4.72	4.22	3.90	3.67	3.50	3.36	3.26	3.17	3.03	2.89	2.74	2.66	2.58	2.49	2.40	2.31	2.21
25	7.77	5.57	4.68	4.18	3.86	3.63	3.46	3.32	3.22	3.13	2.99	2.85	2.70	2.62	2.53	2.45	2.36	2.27	2.17
30	7.56	5.39	4.51	4.02	3.70	3.47	3.30	3.17	3.07	2.98	2.84	2.70	2.55	2.47	2.39	2.30	2.21	2.11	2.01
40	7.31	5.18	4.31	3.83	3.51	3.29	3.12	2.99	2.89	2.80	2.66	2.52	2.37	2.29	2.20	2.11	2.02	1.92	1.80
60	7.08	4.98	4.13	3.65	3.34	3.12	2.95	2.82	2.72	2.63	2.50	2.35	2.20	2.12	2.03	1.94	1.84	1.73	1.60
120	6.85	4.79	3.95	3.48	3.17	2.96	2.79	2.66	2.56	2.47	2.34	2.19	2.03	1.95	1.86	1.76	1.66	1.53	1.38
∞	6.63	4.61	3.78	3.32	3.02	2.80	2.64	2.51	2.41	2.32	2.18	2.04	1.88	1.79	1.70	1.59	1.47	1.32	1.00

Degrees of freedom for denominator

Interpolation should be performed using reciprocals of the degrees of freedom:

This table is reproduced with the permission of the Biometrika Trustees from M. Merrington, C.M. Thompson, "Tables of percentage points of the inverted beta (F) distribution," *Biometrika*, vol. 33, p. 73, 1943.

Figure A.3 F distribution, upper 1% points.

Degrees of freedom for numerator

denom \ num	1	2	3	4	5	6	7	8	9	10	12	15	20	24	30	40	60	120	∞
1	161	200	216	225	230	234	237	239	241	242	244	246	248	249	250	251	252	253	254
2	18.5	19.0	19.2	19.2	19.3	19.3	19.4	19.4	19.4	19.4	19.4	19.4	19.4	19.5	19.5	19.5	19.5	19.5	19.5
3	10.1	9.55	9.28	9.12	9.01	8.94	8.89	8.85	8.81	8.79	8.74	8.70	8.66	8.64	8.62	8.59	8.57	8.55	8.53
4	7.71	6.94	6.59	6.39	6.26	6.16	6.09	6.04	6.00	5.96	5.91	5.86	5.80	5.77	5.75	5.72	5.69	5.66	5.63
5	6.61	5.79	5.41	5.19	5.05	4.95	4.88	4.82	4.77	4.74	4.68	4.62	4.56	4.53	4.50	4.46	4.43	4.40	4.37
6	5.99	5.14	4.76	4.53	4.39	4.28	4.21	4.15	4.10	4.06	4.00	3.94	3.87	3.84	3.81	3.77	3.74	3.70	3.67
7	5.59	4.74	4.35	4.12	3.97	3.87	3.79	3.73	3.68	3.64	3.57	3.51	3.44	3.41	3.38	3.34	3.30	3.27	3.23
8	5.32	4.46	4.07	3.84	3.69	3.58	3.50	3.44	3.39	3.35	3.28	3.22	3.15	3.12	3.08	3.04	3.01	2.97	2.93
9	5.12	4.26	3.86	3.63	3.48	3.37	3.29	3.23	3.18	3.14	3.07	3.01	2.94	2.90	2.86	2.83	2.79	2.75	2.71
10	4.96	4.10	3.71	3.48	3.33	3.22	3.14	3.07	3.02	2.98	2.91	2.85	2.77	2.74	2.70	2.66	2.62	2.58	2.54
11	4.84	3.98	3.59	3.36	3.20	3.09	3.01	2.95	2.90	2.85	2.79	2.72	2.65	2.61	2.57	2.53	2.49	2.45	2.40
12	4.75	3.89	3.49	3.26	3.11	3.00	2.91	2.85	2.80	2.75	2.69	2.62	2.54	2.51	2.47	2.43	2.38	2.34	2.30
13	4.67	3.81	3.41	3.18	3.03	2.92	2.83	2.77	2.71	2.67	2.60	2.53	2.46	2.42	2.38	2.34	2.30	2.25	2.21
14	4.60	3.74	3.34	3.11	2.96	2.85	2.76	2.70	2.65	2.60	2.53	2.46	2.39	2.35	2.31	2.27	2.22	2.18	2.13
15	4.54	3.68	3.29	3.06	2.90	2.79	2.71	2.64	2.59	2.54	2.48	2.40	2.33	2.29	2.25	2.20	2.16	2.11	2.07
16	4.49	3.63	3.24	3.01	2.85	2.74	2.66	2.59	2.54	2.49	2.42	2.35	2.28	2.24	2.19	2.15	2.11	2.06	2.01
17	4.45	3.59	3.20	2.96	2.81	2.70	2.61	2.55	2.49	2.45	2.38	2.31	2.23	2.19	2.15	2.10	2.06	2.01	1.96
18	4.41	3.55	3.16	2.93	2.77	2.66	2.58	2.51	2.46	2.41	2.34	2.27	2.19	2.15	2.11	2.06	2.02	1.97	1.92
19	4.38	3.52	3.13	2.90	2.74	2.63	2.54	2.48	2.42	2.38	2.31	2.23	2.16	2.11	2.07	2.03	1.98	1.93	1.88
20	4.35	3.49	3.10	2.87	2.71	2.60	2.51	2.45	2.39	2.35	2.28	2.20	2.12	2.08	2.04	1.99	1.95	1.90	1.84
21	4.32	3.47	3.07	2.84	2.68	2.57	2.49	2.42	2.37	2.32	2.25	2.18	2.10	2.05	2.01	1.96	1.92	1.87	1.81
22	4.30	3.44	3.05	2.82	2.66	2.55	2.46	2.40	2.34	2.30	2.23	2.15	2.07	2.03	1.98	1.94	1.89	1.84	1.78
23	4.28	3.42	3.03	2.80	2.64	2.53	2.44	2.37	2.32	2.27	2.20	2.13	2.05	2.01	1.96	1.91	1.86	1.81	1.76
24	4.26	3.40	3.01	2.78	2.62	2.51	2.42	2.36	2.30	2.25	2.18	2.11	2.03	1.98	1.94	1.89	1.84	1.79	1.73
25	4.24	3.39	2.99	2.76	2.60	2.49	2.40	2.34	2.28	2.24	2.16	2.09	2.01	1.96	1.92	1.87	1.82	1.77	1.71
30	4.17	3.32	2.92	2.69	2.53	2.42	2.33	2.27	2.21	2.16	2.09	2.01	1.93	1.89	1.84	1.79	1.74	1.68	1.62
40	4.08	3.23	2.84	2.61	2.45	2.34	2.25	2.18	2.12	2.08	2.00	1.92	1.84	1.79	1.74	1.69	1.64	1.58	1.51
60	4.00	3.15	2.76	2.53	2.37	2.25	2.17	2.10	2.04	1.99	1.92	1.84	1.75	1.70	1.65	1.59	1.53	1.47	1.39
120	3.92	3.07	2.68	2.45	2.29	2.18	2.09	2.02	1.96	1.91	1.83	1.75	1.66	1.61	1.55	1.50	1.43	1.35	1.25
∞	3.84	3.00	2.60	2.37	2.21	2.10	2.01	1.94	1.88	1.83	1.75	1.67	1.57	1.52	1.46	1.39	1.32	1.22	1.00

Degrees of freedom for denominator

Figure A.4 F distribution, upper 5% points.

Interpolation should be performed using reciprocals of the degrees of freedom.

This table is reproduced with the permission of the Biometrika Trustees from M. Merrington, C.M. Thompson, "Tables of percentage points of the inverted beta (F) distribution," *Biometrika*, vol. 33, p. 73, 1943.

	$k' = 1$		$k' = 2$		$k' = 3$		$k' = 4$		$k' = 5$	
n	d_L	d_U	d_L	d_U	d_L	d_U	d_L	d_U	d_L	d_U
15	0.81	1.07	0.70	1.25	0.59	1.46	0.49	1.70	0.39	1.96
16	0.84	1.09	0.74	1.25	0.63	1.44	0.53	1.66	0.44	1.90
17	0.87	1.10	0.77	1.25	0.67	1.43	0.57	1.63	0.48	1.85
18	0.90	1.12	0.80	1.26	0.71	1.42	0.61	1.60	0.52	1.80
19	0.93	1.13	0.83	1.26	0.74	1.41	0.65	1.58	0.56	1.77
20	0.95	1.15	0.86	1.27	0.77	1.41	0.68	1.57	0.60	1.74
21	0.97	1.16	0.89	1.27	0.80	1.41	0.72	1.55	0.63	1.71
22	1.00	1.17	0.91	1.28	0.83	1.40	0.75	1.54	0.66	1.69
23	1.02	1.19	0.94	1.29	0.86	1.40	0.77	1.53	0.70	1.67
24	1.04	1.20	0.96	1.30	0.88	1.41	0.80	1.53	0.72	1.66
25	1.05	1.21	0.98	1.30	0.90	1.41	0.83	1.52	0.75	1.65
26	1.07	1.22	1.00	1.31	0.93	1.41	0.85	1.52	0.78	1.64
27	1.09	1.23	1.02	1.32	0.95	1.41	0.88	1.51	0.81	1.63
28	1.10	1.24	1.04	1.32	0.97	1.41	0.90	1.51	0.83	1.62
29	1.12	1.25	1.05	1.33	0.99	1.42	0.92	1.51	0.85	1.61
30	1.13	1.26	1.07	1.34	1.01	1.42	0.94	1.51	0.88	1.61
31	1.15	1.27	1.08	1.34	1.02	1.42	0.96	1.51	0.90	1.60
32	1.16	1.28	1.10	1.35	1.04	1.43	0.98	1.51	0.92	1.60
33	1.17	1.29	1.11	1.36	1.05	1.43	1.00	1.51	0.94	1.59
34	1.18	1.30	1.13	1.36	1.07	1.43	1.01	1.51	0.95	1.59
35	1.19	1.31	1.14	1.37	1.08	1.44	1.03	1.51	0.97	1.59
36	1.21	1.32	1.15	1.38	1.10	1.44	1.04	1.51	0.99	1.59
37	1.22	1.32	1.16	1.38	1.11	1.45	1.06	1.51	1.00	1.59
38	1.23	1.33	1.18	1.39	1.12	1.45	1.07	1.52	1.02	1.58
39	1.24	1.34	1.19	1.39	1.14	1.45	1.09	1.52	1.03	1.58
40	1.25	1.34	1.20	1.40	1.15	1.46	1.10	1.52	1.05	1.58
45	1.29	1.38	1.24	1.42	1.20	1.48	1.16	1.53	1.11	1.58
50	1.32	1.40	1.28	1.45	1.24	1.49	1.20	1.54	1.16	1.59
55	1.36	1.43	1.32	1.47	1.28	1.51	1.25	1.55	1.21	1.59
60	1.38	1.45	1.35	1.48	1.32	1.52	1.28	1.56	1.25	1.60
65	1.41	1.47	1.38	1.50	1.35	1.53	1.31	1.57	1.28	1.61
70	1.43	1.49	1.40	1.52	1.37	1.55	1.34	1.58	1.31	1.61
75	1.45	1.50	1.42	1.53	1.39	1.56	1.37	1.59	1.34	1.62
80	1.47	1.52	1.44	1.54	1.42	1.57	1.39	1.60	1.36	1.62
85	1.48	1.53	1.46	1.55	1.43	1.58	1.41	1.60	1.39	1.63
90	1.50	1.54	1.47	1.56	1.45	1.59	1.43	1.61	1.41	1.64
95	1.51	1.55	1.49	1.57	1.47	1.60	1.45	1.62	1.42	1.64
100	1.52	1.56	1.50	1.58	1.48	1.60	1.46	1.63	1.44	1.65

n = number of observations.
k' = number of explanatory variables.
This Table is reproduced from *Biometrika*, vol. 41, p. 175, 1951, with the permission of the Trustees.

Figure A.5   Durbin–Watson statistic (d)—significance points: 1%.

n	$k'=1$ d_L	$k'=1$ d_U	$k'=2$ d_L	$k'=2$ d_U	$k'=3$ d_L	$k'=3$ d_U	$k'=4$ d_L	$k'=4$ d_U	$k'=5$ d_L	$k'=5$ d_U
15	1.08	1.36	0.95	1.54	0.82	1.75	0.69	1.97	0.56	2.21
16	1.10	1.37	0.98	1.54	0.86	1.73	0.74	1.93	0.62	2.15
17	1.13	1.38	1.02	1.54	0.90	1.71	0.78	1.90	0.67	2.10
18	1.16	1.39	1.05	1.53	0.93	1.69	0.82	1.87	0.71	2.06
19	1.18	1.40	1.08	1.53	0.97	1.68	0.86	1.85	0.75	2.02
20	1.20	1.41	1.10	1.54	1.00	1.68	0.90	1.83	0.79	1.99
21	1.22	1.42	1.13	1.54	1.03	1.67	0.93	1.81	0.83	1.96
22	1.24	1.43	1.15	1.54	1.05	1.66	0.96	1.80	0.86	1.94
23	1.26	1.44	1.17	1.54	1.08	1.66	0.99	1.79	0.90	1.92
24	1.27	1.45	1.19	1.55	1.10	1.66	1.01	1.78	0.93	1.90
25	1.29	1.45	1.21	1.55	1.12	1.66	1.04	1.77	0.95	1.89
26	1.30	1.46	1.22	1.55	1.14	1.65	1.06	1.76	0.98	1.88
27	1.32	1.47	1.24	1.56	1.16	1.65	1.08	1.76	1.01	1.86
28	1.33	1.48	1.26	1.56	1.18	1.65	1.10	1.75	1.03	1.85
29	1.34	1.48	1.27	1.56	1.20	1.65	1.12	1.74	1.05	1.84
30	1.35	1.49	1.28	1.57	1.21	1.65	1.14	1.74	1.07	1.83
31	1.36	1.50	1.30	1.57	1.23	1.65	1.16	1.74	1.09	1.83
32	1.37	1.50	1.31	1.57	1.24	1.65	1.18	1.73	1.11	1.82

n	$k'=1$ d_L	$k'=1$ d_U	$k'=2$ d_L	$k'=2$ d_U	$k'=3$ d_L	$k'=3$ d_U	$k'=4$ d_L	$k'=4$ d_U	$k'=5$ d_L	$k'=5$ d_U
33	1.38	1.51	1.32	1.58	1.26	1.65	1.19	1.73	1.13	1.81
34	1.39	1.51	1.33	1.58	1.27	1.65	1.21	1.73	1.15	1.81
35	1.40	1.52	1.34	1.58	1.28	1.65	1.22	1.73	1.16	1.80
36	1.41	1.52	1.35	1.59	1.29	1.65	1.24	1.73	1.18	1.80
37	1.42	1.53	1.36	1.59	1.31	1.66	1.25	1.72	1.19	1.80
38	1.43	1.54	1.37	1.59	1.32	1.66	1.26	1.72	1.21	1.79
39	1.43	1.54	1.38	1.60	1.33	1.66	1.27	1.72	1.22	1.79
40	1.44	1.54	1.39	1.60	1.34	1.66	1.29	1.72	1.23	1.79
45	1.48	1.57	1.43	1.62	1.38	1.67	1.34	1.72	1.29	1.78
50	1.50	1.59	1.46	1.63	1.42	1.67	1.38	1.72	1.34	1.77
55	1.53	1.60	1.49	1.64	1.45	1.68	1.41	1.72	1.38	1.77
60	1.55	1.62	1.51	1.65	1.48	1.69	1.44	1.73	1.41	1.77
65	1.57	1.63	1.54	1.66	1.50	1.70	1.47	1.73	1.44	1.77
70	1.58	1.64	1.55	1.67	1.52	1.70	1.49	1.74	1.46	1.77
75	1.60	1.65	1.57	1.68	1.54	1.71	1.51	1.74	1.49	1.77
80	1.61	1.66	1.59	1.69	1.56	1.72	1.53	1.74	1.51	1.77
85	1.62	1.67	1.60	1.70	1.57	1.72	1.55	1.75	1.52	1.77
90	1.63	1.68	1.61	1.70	1.59	1.73	1.57	1.75	1.54	1.78
95	1.64	1.69	1.62	1.71	1.60	1.73	1.58	1.75	1.56	1.78
100	1.65	1.69	1.63	1.72	1.61	1.74	1.59	1.76	1.57	1.78

Source: This table is reproduced from *Biometrika*, vol. 41, p. 173, 1951, with the permission of the Trustees.

n = number of observations.

k' = number of explanatory variables.

Figure A.6 Durbin–Watson statistic (d)—significance points: 5%.

Reliability Factors (R)	0.7	0.8	0.9	1.0	1.1	1.2	1.3	1.4	1.6	2.0	2.3	3.0	4.6
Reliability Levels	50%	55%	59%	63%	66%	69%	72%	75%	80%	86%	90%	95%	99%
Rank of Errors[a]	Precision Adjustment Factors (p) For Reliability Levels Shown Above												
	For Errors of Overstatement[b]												
1	1.01	1.05	1.11	1.15	1.20	1.24	1.28	1.32	1.39	1.51	1.59	1.75	2.04
2	1.01	1.04	1.08	1.12	1.15	1.18	1.21	1.24	1.28	1.38	1.44	1.56	1.77
3	1.00	1.04	1.07	1.10	1.13	1.15	1.17	1.20	1.24	1.31	1.36	1.46	1.64
4	1.00	1.03	1.06	1.09	1.11	1.13	1.15	1.17	1.21	1.27	1.32	1.40	1.56
5	1.00	1.03	1.05	1.08	1.10	1.12	1.14	1.16	1.19	1.25	1.29	1.36	1.50
6	1.00	1.03	1.05	1.07	1.09	1.11	1.13	1.14	1.17	1.23	1.26	1.33	1.46
7	1.00	1.02	1.04	1.07	1.09	1.10	1.12	1.13	1.16	1.21	1.24	1.31	1.43
8	1.00	1.02	1.04	1.06	1.08	1.10	1.11	1.12	1.15	1.20	1.23	1.29	1.40
9	1.00	1.02	1.04	1.06	1.08	1.09	1.10	1.12	1.14	1.19	1.22	1.28	1.38
10	1.00	1.02	1.04	1.06	1.07	1.09	1.10	1.11	1.14	1.18	1.21	1.26	1.36
11	1.00	1.02	1.04	1.05	1.07	1.08	1.10	1.11	1.13	1.17	1.20	1.25	1.35
12	1.00	1.02	1.03	1.05	1.07	1.08	1.09	1.10	1.13	1.16	1.19	1.24	1.34
13	1.00	1.02	1.03	1.05	1.06	1.08	1.09	1.10	1.12	1.16	1.18	1.23	1.33
14	1.00	1.02	1.03	1.05	1.06	1.07	1.08	1.10	1.12	1.15	1.18	1.22	1.32
15–19	1.00	1.02	1.03	1.05	1.06	1.07	1.08	1.09	1.11	1.15	1.17	1.22	1.31
20–24	1.00	1.01	1.03	1.04	1.05	1.06	1.07	1.08	1.10	1.13	1.15	1.19	1.26
25–29	1.00	1.01	1.03	1.04	1.05	1.06	1.06	1.07	1.09	1.11	1.13	1.17	1.24
30–39	1.00	1.01	1.02	1.03	1.04	1.05	1.06	1.06	1.08	1.10	1.12	1.15	1.22
40–49	1.00	1.00	1.02	1.03	1.04	1.05	1.05	1.06	1.07	1.09	1.10	1.13	1.19

For Errors of Understatement[b] (Note 2)

	.67	.58	.49	.45	.40	.35	.31	.28	.22	.14	.10	.05	.00
1	.67	.58	.49	.45	.40	.35	.31	.28	.22	.14	.10	.05	.00
2	.96	.92	.87	.82	.78	.74	.70	.66	.60	.49	.42	.30	.14
3	.99	.95	.91	.88	.84	.81	.78	.76	.71	.62	.57	.46	.29
4	.99	.95	.92	.90	.87	.85	.82	.80	.76	.69	.64	.54	.39
5	.99	.96	.93	.91	.89	.87	.85	.83	.79	.73	.68	.60	.45
6	.99	.96	.94	.92	.90	.88	.86	.84	.81	.75	.71	.64	.51
7	.99	.97	.95	.93	.91	.89	.87	.86	.83	.77	.74	.67	.54
8	.99	.97	.95	.93	.91	.90	.88	.87	.84	.79	.76	.69	.57
9	.99	.97	.95	.94	.92	.90	.89	.88	.85	.80	.77	.71	.60
10	.99	.97	.96	.94	.92	.91	.90	.88	.86	.81	.78	.73	.62
11	1.00	.98	.96	.94	.93	.91	.90	.89	.86	.82	.79	.74	.64
12	1.00	.98	.96	.94	.93	.92	.90	.89	.87	.83	.80	.75	.65
13	1.00	.98	.96	.95	.93	.92	.91	.90	.87	.84	.81	.76	.66
14	1.00	.98	.96	.95	.94	.92	.91	.90	.88	.84	.82	.77	.67
15–19	1.00	.98	.96	.95	.94	.93	.91	.90	.88	.85	.83	.78	.68
20–24	1.00	.98	.96	.96	.94	.94	.93	.92	.90	.87	.85	.81	.73
25–29	1.00	.98	.97	.96	.95	.94	.93	.93	.91	.89	.87	.83	.76
30–39	1.00	.98	.97	.96	.96	.95	.94	.93	.92	.90	.88	.85	.78
40–49	1.00	.99	.98	.97	.96	.95	.95	.94	.93	.91	.90	.87	.80

Figure A.7 Reliability factors and related precision adjustment factors.

[a]This column refers to the rank of the estimated population errors (E_i). Errors of overstatement and of understatement should be ranked separately, and within each group the ranking should be from the largest to the smallest amount of error.
[b]The distinction between errors of overstatement and of understatement should be based on their effect on the recorded amount of the dependent variable.

APPENDIX B

STAR PROGRAM PRINTOUTS

B.1 GAMMA COMPANY PRINTOUT

This application is introduced in Chapter 2. The regression base statistics are discussed in Chapter 3. The audit interface calculations are explained in Chapter 5.

```
************* STAR: Statistical Techniques for Analytical Review *************

Specifications for Model

Variables Specified:
Y     Revenue                                    TEST
X1    Time at Standard                       PREDICTING

Observations Used:
Base, 1 - 36                                       36
Projection, 37 - 48                                12
                                                -----
Total                                              48
                                                =====

Data Profile                                 TIME SERIES
Periods per Year                                   12
Seasonal Adjustment Requested                      NO

Type of Test                                     AUDIT
Monetary Precision (MP)                            600
Reliability Factor (R)                             3.0
Direction of Test                          UNDERSTATEMENT

Report Options:
Scatter Diagrams                                   NO
Mathematical Details                               NO


===============================================================================
Stepwise Multiple Regression Model
                             Input Data              Regression Function
                       -------------------------   -------------------------

                                      Standard     Constant or    Standard
        Description       Mean         Error       Coefficient     Error
  --------------------- ----------   ----------    -----------   ----------
Constant                                             13.78

Predicting Variables
X1    Time at Standard  1,832.00      246.16         1.3582        0.1359

Test Variable
Y     Revenue           2,502.00      387.10
Y'    Expectation                                  2,502.00       197.9557

Coefficient of Correlation (100% = Perfect)          86%


Expectation [Y'(t)] for observation t :
Y'(t) = 13.78 + 1.3582*X1(t)
```

```
==============================================================================
Plot of Residuals

Obs    Recorded     Regression      Residual      Residuals Graphed in Units
No     Amount       Estimate      (Difference)       of One Standard Error
----   -----------  -----------   ------------    --------------------------
                                                  -4 -3 -2 -1  0  1  2  3  4
                                                 -| --+--+--+--  --+--+--+-- |-
 1      2,107         2,152           -45         -        *                -
 2      1,915         2,055          -140         -        *                -
 3      1,873         2,248          -375         -   *                     -
 4      1,978         1,888            90         -            *            -
 5      2,010         2,160          -150         -       *                 -
 6      1,969         2,154          -185         -       *                 -
 7      2,228         2,393          -165         -       *                 -
 8      2,152         2,118            34         -          *              -
 9      2,439         2,258           181         -             *           -
10      2,318         2,255            63         -          *             -
11      2,244         2,046           198         -             *          -
12      2,357         2,283            74         -          *             -
                                                 - --+--+--+--  --+--+--+-- -
13      2,103         2,294          -191         -       *                 -
14      2,457         2,434            23         -           *             -
15      2,606         2,258           348         -               *         -
16      2,493         2,399            94         -           *            -
17      2,264         2,126           138         -           *            -
18      2,058         2,215          -157         -        *                -
19      2,516         2,706          -190         -        *                -
20      2,533         2,798          -265         -      *                  -
21      2,958         2,674           284         -              *          -
22      2,564         2,507            57         -          *              -
23      2,318         2,738          -420         -   *                     -
24      2,928         2,953           -25         -          *             -
                                                 - --+--+--+--  --+--+--+-- -
25      2,754         2,431           323         -               *         -
26      2,678         2,804          -126         -      *                  -
27      3,189         3,090            99         -           *            -
28      3,067         2,889           178         -            *            -
29      2,735         2,669            66         -           *            -
30      3,029         2,810           219         -            *           -
31      2,531         2,810          -279         -      *                  -
32      2,765         2,861           -96         -        *               -
33      3,074         3,003            71         -           *            -
34      2,651         2,752          -101         -        *               -
35      3,056         2,998            58         -           *            -
36      3,155         2,843           312         -              *          -
                                                 - --+--+--+--  --+--+--+-- -
37      2,757         2,832           -75         -        *                -
38      2,869         2,708           161         -             *           -
39      3,168         3,200           -32         -          *             -
40      3,210         3,075           135         -            *            -
41      2,958         2,956             2         -          *             -
42      2,698         2,748           -50         -         *|              -
43      3,412         3,396            16         -          *             -
44      2,872         2,973          -101         -       *                 -
45      3,263         3,063           200         -             *           -
46      3,506         3,430            76         -          *             -
47      3,452         3,259           193         -            *           -
48      2,993         3,259          -266         -      *                  -
                                                 -| --+--+--+--  --+--+--+-- |-
```

===
AUDIT test for UNDERSTATEMENT using MP = 600, R = 3.0

						Optional Test	

Obs	Recorded	Regression	Residual		Excess	Select'n	Sam
No	Amount	Estimate	(Difference)	Threshold	<1>	Interval	ple
37	2,757	2,832	-75				
38	2,869	2,708	161 <2>				
39	3,168	3,200	-32				
40	3,210	3,075	135 <2>				
41	2,958	2,956	2				
42	2,698	2,748	-50				
43	3,412	3,396	16				
44	2,872	2,973	-101				
45	3,263	3,063	200 <2>				
46	3,506	3,430	76				
47	3,452	3,259	193 <2>				
48	2,993	3,259	-266	127	138	407	8

	37,158	36,899	259				8
	========	========	========				===

<1> Significant difference in direction of test. Perform further analysis
and inquiry to obtain and corroborate explanation. Perform optional test
of details only if difference cannot be explained. Computed sample sizes
less than 5 are set to the lesser of 5 and REGRESSION ESTIMATE / (MP/R).

<2> Significant difference in opposite direction to that of test. Seek an
explanation.

==
Variables Used (+), Not Used (-)

Obs#	Y+	X1+
1	2,107	1,574
2	1,915	1,503
3	1,873	1,649
4	1,978	1,380
5	2,010	1,580
6	1,969	1,576
7	2,228	1,752
8	2,152	1,549
9	2,439	1,652
10	2,318	1,650
11	2,244	1,496
12	2,357	1,671
13	2,103	1,679
14	2,457	1,782
15	2,606	1,652
16	2,493	1,756
17	2,264	1,555
18	2,058	1,621
19	2,516	1,982
20	2,533	2,050
21	2,958	1,959
22	2,564	1,836
23	2,318	2,006
24	2,928	2,164
25	2,754	1,780
26	2,678	2,054
27	3,189	2,265
28	3,067	2,117
29	2,735	1,955
30	3,029	2,059
31	2,531	2,059
32	2,765	2,096
33	3,074	2,201
34	2,651	2,016
35	3,056	2,197
36	3,155	2,083
37	2,757	2,075
38	2,869	1,984
39	3,168	2,346
40	3,210	2,254
41	2,958	2,166
42	2,698	2,013
43	3,412	2,490
44	2,872	2,179
45	3,263	2,245
46	3,506	2,515
47	3,452	2,389
48	2,993	2,389
	127,230	92,997

B.2 UNIVERSAL CHEMICALS PRINTOUT

This application is used in Chapter 4 and again in Chapter 8 to explain the tests that the STAR Program applies to test for discontinuity in the base period.

```
************* STAR: Statistical Techniques for Analytical Review ************

Specifications for Model

Variables Specified:
Y     Production Costs                         TEST
X1    Quantity Producd                     PREDICTING

Observations Used:
Base, 1 - 36                                    36
Projection                                       0
                                             -----
Total                                           36
                                             =====

Data Profile                             TIME SERIES
Periods per Year                                12
Seasonal Adjustment Requested                   NO

Type of Test                                  NONE

Report Options:
Scatter Diagrams                                NO
Mathematical Details                            NO


=============================================================================
Stepwise Multiple Regression Model
                          Input Data              Regression Function
                    --------------------------  --------------------------
                                    Standard    Constant or    Standard
      Description       Mean         Error      Coefficient      Error
---------------------  ---------   ----------   -----------   -----------
Constant                                          -68.00

Predicting Variables
X1    Quantity Producd   645.31      168.99         0.9266        0.0657

Test Variable
Y     Production Costs   529.92      169.43
Y'    Expectation                                  529.92       65.6586

Coefficient of Correlation (100% = Perfect)            92%


Expectation [Y'(t)] for observation t :
Y'(t) = -68.00 + 0.9266*X1(t)


THERE IS AN INDICATION OF DISCONTINUITY IN THE BASE PROFILE.  STAR will not
process the data further.  Discontinuity is ordinarily caused by a change in
conditions which affects the relationship between the variables.  Examine the
plot of residuals to identify the cause.  Including an appropriate predicting
variable in the model may eliminate the condition.
```

===

Plot of Residuals

Obs No	Recorded Amount	Regression Estimate	Residual (Difference)
1	312	292	20
2	320	295	25
3	320	323	-3
4	363	390	-27
5	512	600	-88
6	334	367	-33
7	390	457	-67
8	185	176	9
9	528	565	-37
10	395	380	15
11	380	394	-14
12	375	392	-17
13	568	617	-49
14	448	492	-44
15	613	661	-48
16	452	529	-77
17	540	612	-72
18	531	537	-6
19	621	687	-66
20	363	365	-2
21	515	579	-64
22	605	696	-91
23	546	596	-50
24	629	678	-49
25	414	470	-56
26	528	501	27
27	1,010	999	11
28	699	611	88
29	831	781	50
30	638	556	82
31	675	587	88
32	710	627	83
33	711	573	138
34	723	620	103
35	660	561	99
36	633	512	121

Residuals Graphed in Units of One Standard Error

```
     -4 -3 -2 -1  0  1  2  3  4
   -|--+--+--+--|--+--+--+--|-
 1 -                |  *      -
 2 -                |  *      -
 3 -                * |       -
 4 -            *    |        -
 5 -       *         |        -
 6 -          *      |        -
 7 -         *       |        -
 8 -                *|        -
 9 -          *      |        -
10 -                |  *      -
11 -            *    |        -
12 -            *    |        -
   -|--+--+--+--|--+--+--+--|-
13 -            *    |        -
14 -            *    |        -
15 -            *    |        -
16 -       *         |        -
17 -        *        |        -
18 -               * |        -
19 -          *     ||        -
20 -                *|        -
21 -          *      |        -
22 -        *        |        -
23 -           *     |        -
24 -          *      |        -
   -|--+--+--+--|--+--+--+--|-
25 -       *         |        -
26 -                |*        -
27 -                | *       -
28 -                |    *    -
29 -                |  *      -
30 -                |    *    -
31 -                |    *    -
32 -                |    *    -
33 -                |      *  -
34 -                |     *   -
35 -                |     *   -
36 -                |      *  -
   -|--+--+--+--|--+--+--+--|-
```

```
================================================================================
Variables Used (+), Not Used (-)

Obs#      Y+        X1+
----   --------  --------
  1       312      388
  2       320      392
  3       320      422
  4       363      494
  5       512      721
  6       334      470
  7       390      567
  8       185      263
  9       528      683
 10       395      483
 11       380      499
 12       375      496
 13       568      739
 14       448      604
 15       613      787
 16       452      644
 17       540      734
 18       531      653
 19       621      815
 20       363      467
 21       515      698
 22       605      825
 23       546      717
 24       629      805
 25       414      581
 26       528      614
 27     1,010    1,152
 28       699      733
 29       831      916
 30       638      673
 31       675      707
 32       710      750
 33       711      692
 34       723      742
 35       660      679
 36       633      626
       --------  --------
       19,077    23,231
       ========  ========
```

B.3   AUTOCORP, INC. PRINTOUT

This application is used in Chapter 4 and again in Chapter 8 to explain the tests that the STAR Program applies to test for autocorrelation of the residuals.

```
************* STAR: Statistical Techniques for Analytical Review *************

Specifications for Model

Variables Specified:
Y    Wages                                          TEST
X1   Hours                                       PREDICTING


Observations Used:
Base, 1 - 36                                          36
Projection, 37 - 39                                    3
                                                   -----
Total                                                 39
                                                   =====

Data Profile                                   TIME SERIES
Periods per Year                                       12
Seasonal Adjustment Requested                         NO

Type of Test                                        AUDIT
Monetary Precision (MP)                               200
Reliability Factor (R)                                1.0
Direction of Test                          OVERSTATEMENT

Report Options:
Scatter Diagrams                                      NO
Mathematical Details                                 NO
```

```
============================================================================
Stepwise Multiple Regression Model
                            Input Data              Regression Function
                   -----------------------    -----------------------
                                 Standard     Constant or   Standard
      Description       Mean      Error       Coefficient    Error
-------------------   --------   --------     -----------   --------
Constant                                        -68.08

Predicting Variables
X1  Hours              367.67     35.08          2.5554      0.2554

Test Variable
Y   Wages              871.44    103.76
Y'  Expectation                                 871.44      53.0021

Coefficient of Correlation (100% = Perfect)       86%
```

Expectation [Y'(t)] for observation t :
Y'(t) = -68.08 + 2.5554*X1(t)

THERE IS AN INDICATION OF DISCONTINUITY BETWEEN BASE AND PROJECTION PROFILES.
This type of discontinuity does not invalidate the model but it may affect
the differences to be audited. If it is not eliminated, it may result in
invalid models in future years. Examine the plot of residuals to identify
the cause.

ABNORMALITY IN THE BASE PERIOD IS INDICATED BY:
. LEFT SKEWNESS--This may be caused by large negative residuals
. KURTOSIS--This may be caused by both large positive and large negative
  residuals.
Abnormality does not invalidate the model but it may affect the differences
to be audited. Examine the plot of the residuals to identify the outliers
and, if possible, eliminate the abnormality by correcting any errors or
unusual events in those observations.

```
===============================================================================
Plot of Residuals

 Obs    Recorded    Regression    Residual      Residuals Graphed in Units
 No      Amount     Estimate     (Difference)      of One Standard Error
 ----  ------------ ------------ ------------    
                                                -4 -3 -2 -1  0  1  2  3  4
                                              - |--+--+--+--|--+--+--+--| -
   1        649          665          -16       -           *            -
   2        660          706          -46       -        *               -
   3        766          839          -73       -      *                 -
   4        747          819          -72       -      *                 -
   5        804          842          -38       -         *              -
   6        686          696          -10       -           *            -
   7        709          729          -20       -          *             -
   8        745          747           -2       -            *           -
   9        904          877           27       -              *         -
  10        968          913           55       -               *        -
  11        824          806           18       -             *          -
  12        806          770           36       -              *         -
                                              - |--+--+--+--|--+--+--+--| -
  13        928          885           43       -              *         -
  14        884          816           68       -               *        -
  15        881          857           24       -             *          -
  16        901          944          -43       -        *               -
  17        986          982            4       -            *           -
  18        863          816           47       -               *        -
  19        987          936           51       -               *        -
  20        989          895           94       -                *       -
  21        945          926           19       -             *          -
  22        980          957           23       -             *          -
  23        885          860           25       -             *          -
  24        942          929           13       -             *          -
                                              - |--+--+--+--|--+--+--+--| -
  25        986          969           17       -             *          -
  26        887          877           10       -             *          -
  27        989          957           32       -              *         -
  28      1,042        1,018           24       -             *          -
  29        943          939            4       -            *           -
  30        905          911           -6       -            *           -
  31        963          908           55       -              *         -
  32        945        1,003          -58       -       *                -
  33        820          831          -11       -          *             -
  34        862          898          -36       -         *              -
  35        786          852          -66       -       *                -
  36        805          998         -193       - *                      -
                                              - |--+--+--+--|--+--+--+--| -
  37        867        1,061         -194       - *                      -
  38        925        1,164         -239       -*                       -
  39      1,200        1,304         -104       -     *                   -
                                              - |--+--+--+--|--+--+--+--| -

===============================================================================
```

THERE IS AN INDICATION OF AUTOCORRELATION IN THE BASE PROFILE. Generalized
least squares regression will be used to correct for the condition.
Autocorrelation can often be attributed to a missing major factor and is
evidenced by a pronounced pattern in the residuals. Examine the plot of
residuals to identify the missing factor. Including that factor as a
predicting variable may eliminate the condition and reduce the differences
to be audited.

Generalized Expectation [Y'(t)] for observation t :
Y'(1) = 118.85 + 2.0386*X1(1) + SQR(1-0.6209^2)*e(1)
Y'(t) = 118.85 + 2.0386*X1(t) + 0.6209*e(t-1), for t > 1
where,
e(t) = Y(t) - (118.85 + 2.0386*X1(t))

Standard Error (t)   = 39.5844
Coefficient of Autocorrelation = 62%
===

Plot of Residuals--Corrected for Autocorrelation

Obs No	Recorded Amount	Regression Estimate	Residual (Difference)	Residuals Graphed in Units of One Standard Error
				-4 -3 -2 -1 0 1 2 3 4
				--+--+--+-- | --+--+--+--
1	649	661	-12	*
2	660	702	-42	*
3	766	795	-29	*
4	747	779	-32	*
5	804	795	9	*
6	686	703	-17	*
7	709	729	-20	*
8	745	741	4	*
9	904	858	46	*
10	968	921	47	*
11	824	857	-33	*
12	806	792	14	*
				--+--+--+-- --+--+--+--
13	928	891	37	*
14	884	854	30	*
15	881	894	-13	*
16	901	941	-40	*
17	986	941	45	*
18	863	842	21	*
19	987	944	43	*
20	989	929	60	*
21	945	975	-30	*
22	980	957	23	*
23	885	886	-1	*
24	942	930	12	*
				--+--+--+-- --+--+--+--
25	986	964	22	*
26	887	898	-11	*
27	989	945	44	*
28	1,042	1,018	24	*
29	943	957	-14	*
30	905	913	-8	*
31	963	901	62	*
32	945	1,014	-69	*
33	820	819	1	*
34	862	879	-17	*
35	786	836	-50	*
36	805	928	-123	*
				--+--+--+-- --+--+--+--
37	867	918	-51	*
38	925	1,007	-82	*
39	1,200	1,104	96	*
				--+--+--+-- | --+--+--+--

```
================================================================================
AUDIT test for OVERSTATEMENT using MP = 200, R = 1.0
--------------------------------------------------------------------------------
                                                             Optional Test
                                                             -------------
  Obs   Recorded   Regression    Residual                Excess  Select'n Sam
  No     Amount     Estimate    (Difference)  Threshold   <1>    Interval ple
 ----  ----------  ----------   -----------   ---------  ------- --------- ---
  37       867        918           -51
  38       925      1,007           -82      <2>
  39     1,200      1,104            96           79       17      240     5
       ----------  ----------   -----------                              ---
          2,992      3,029           -37                                   5
       ==========  ==========   ===========                             ===
```

<1> Significant difference in direction of test. Perform further analysis
    and inquiry to obtain and corroborate explanation. Perform optional test
    of details only if difference cannot be explained. Computed sample sizes
    less than 5 are set to the lesser of 5 and RECORDED AMOUNT / (MP/R).

<2> Significant difference in opposite direction to that of test. Seek an
    explanation.

```
================================================================================
Variables Used (+), Not Used (-)

Obs#       Y+       X1+
----   --------  --------
   1       649       287
   2       660       303
   3       766       355
   4       747       347
   5       804       356
   6       686       299
   7       709       312
   8       745       319
   9       904       370
  10       968       384
  11       824       342
  12       806       328
  13       928       373
  14       884       346
  15       881       362
  16       901       396
  17       986       411
  18       863       346
  19       987       393
  20       989       377
  21       945       389
  22       980       401
  23       885       363
  24       942       390
  25       986       406
  26       887       370
  27       989       401
  28     1,042       425
  29       943       394
  30       905       383
  31       963       382
  32       945       419
  33       820       352
  34       862       378
  35       786       360
  36       805       417
  37       867       442
  38       925       482
  39     1,200       537
        --------  --------
          34,364    14,697
        ========  ========
```

* * * End of Application AUTOCORP.WAG * * *

B.4   HETEROCO, INC. PRINTOUT

This application is used in Chapter 4 and again in Chapter 8 to explain the tests that the STAR Program applies to test for heteroscedasticity of the residuals. In Chapter 6, this printout is referred to as an example of a cross-sectional application.

```
************* STAR: Statistical Techniques for Analytical Review *************

Specifications for Model

Variables Specified:
Y    Sales                                          TEST
X1   Rent Cost                                 PREDICTING
X2   Floor Area                                PREDICTING

Observations Used:
Base, 1 - 30                                           30
Projection, 31 - 31                                     1
                                                    -----
Total                                                  31
                                                    =====

Data Profile                               CROSS-SECTIONAL


Type of Test                                        AUDIT
Monetary Precision (MP)                             1,000
Reliability Factor (R)                                1.0
Direction of Test                           OVERSTATEMENT

Report Options:
Scatter Diagrams                                       NO
Mathematical Details                                  NO
```

```
==================================================================================
Stepwise Multiple Regression Model
                           Input Data                 Regression Function
                    ---------------------------    ---------------------------
                                    Standard       Constant or    Standard
        Description         Mean     Error         Coefficient     Error
    --------------------  ---------  ----------    -----------    ----------
Constant                                               29.72

Predicting Variables
X1   Rent Cost             370.00    268.90          2.9450        0.0306
X2   Floor Area          1,997.67     84.03          0.8393        0.0979

Test Variable
Y    Sales               2,795.93    794.42
Y'   Expectation                                    2,795.93      44.2877

Coefficient of Correlation (100% = Perfect) Exceeds        99%
```

Expectation [Y'(t)] for observation t :
Y'(t) = 29.72 + 2.9450*X1(t) + 0.8393*X2(t)

THERE IS AN INDICATION OF DISCONTINUITY BETWEEN BASE AND PROJECTION PROFILES.
This type of discontinuity does not invalidate the model but it may affect
the differences to be audited. If it is not eliminated, it may result in
invalid models in future years. Examine the plot of residuals to identify
the cause.

ABNORMALITY IN THE BASE PERIOD IS INDICATED BY:
. RIGHT SKEWNESS--This may be caused by large positive residuals
. KURTOSIS--This may be caused by both large positive and large negative
  residuals.
Abnormality does not invalidate the model but it may affect the differences
to be audited. Examine the plot of the residuals to identify the outliers
and, if possible, eliminate the abnormality by correcting any errors or
unusual events in those observations.

```
=================================================================================
```

Plot of Residuals

Obs No	Recorded Amount	Regression Estimate	Residual (Difference)	Residuals Graphed in Units of One Standard Error
				-4 -3 -2 -1 0 1 2 3 4
				- | --+--+--+-- | --+--+--+-- | -
1	2,787	2,772	15	- * -
2	3,095	3,039	56	- * -
3	3,184	3,184	0	- * -
4	2,084	2,099	-15	- *| -
5	2,287	2,283	4	- * -
6	3,228	3,248	-20	- *| -
7	4,842	4,926	-84	- * -
8	2,210	2,206	4	- * -
9	2,565	2,589	-24	- * -
10	2,494	2,509	-15	- * -
11	2,422	2,443	-21	- * -
12	3,090	3,080	10	- * -
13	2,287	2,298	-11	- * -
14	2,669	2,710	-41	- * -
15	3,204	3,187	17	- * -
16	2,105	2,116	-11	- * -
17	2,440	2,463	-23	- * -
18	3,126	3,094	32	- * -
19	4,776	4,618	158	- * -
20	2,030	2,032	-2	- * -
21	2,070	2,084	-14	- *| -
22	4,949	5,031	-82	- * -
23	2,862	2,874	-12	- * -
24	2,347	2,322	25	- * -
25	2,912	2,876	36	- * -
26	2,259	2,292	-33	- * -
27	2,730	2,716	14	- * -
28	2,106	2,112	-6	- * -
29	2,274	2,270	4	- * -
30	2,444	2,406	38	-| * -
31	2,200	2,592	-392	-* | -
				- | --+--+--+-- | --+--+--+-- | -

```
=================================================================================
```

THERE IS AN INDICATION OF HETEROSCEDASTICITY IN THE BASE PROFILE. Weighted least squares regression will be used to correct for the condition. Heteroscedasticity is evidenced by significant correlation between the size of the residuals and one of the predicting variables, in this case X1. The model may be improved by identifying the cause of the heteroscedasticity and introducing appropriate predicting variables. This may also reduce the differences to be audited.

Weighted Expectation [Y'(t)] for observation t :
$$Y'(t) = -97.52 + 2.9701*X1(t) + 0.8987*X2(t)$$

Standard Error (t) $= 0.0860*|X1(t)|$

```
================================================================================
Plot of Residuals--Corrected for Heteroscedasticity

Obs     Recorded     Regression      Residual      Residuals Graphed in Units
No      Amount       Estimate        (Difference)      of One Standard Error
----   ------------  ------------   ------------   ------------------------------
                                                   -4 -3 -2 -1  0  1  2  3  4
                                                  -|--+--+--+--|--+--+--+--|-
  1      2,787        2,775             12        -            |  *            -
  2      3,095        3,045             50        -            |     *         -
  3      3,184        3,185             -1        -           *|               -
  4      2,084        2,093             -9        -         *  |               -
  5      2,287        2,281              6        -            | *             -
  6      3,228        3,247            -19        -         *  |               -
  7      4,842        4,948           -106        -       *    |               -
  8      2,210        2,197             13        -            |   *           -
  9      2,565        2,592            -27        -        *   |               -
 10      2,494        2,503             -9        -          * |               -
 11      2,422        2,443            -21        -        *   |               -
 12      3,090        3,088              2        -            *               -
 13      2,287        2,289             -2        -           *|               -
 14      2,669        2,718            -49        -     *      |               -
 15      3,204        3,198              6        -           *|               -
 16      2,105        2,105              0        -           *|               -
 17      2,440        2,466            -26        -       *    |               -
 18      3,126        3,096             30        -            |  *            -
 19      4,776        4,632            144        -            |      *        -
 20      2,030        2,028              2        -           *|               -
 21      2,070        2,077             -7        -          * |               -
 22      4,949        5,048            -99        -       *    |               -
 23      2,862        2,880            -18        -          * |               -
 24      2,347        2,323             24        -            |    *          -
 25      2,912        2,879             33        -            |   *           -
 26      2,259        2,283            -24        -       *    |               -
 27      2,730        2,707             23        -            |  *            -
 28      2,106        2,104              2        -            *               -
 29      2,274        2,264             10        -            |  *            -
 30      2,444        2,408             36        -|           |     *         -
 31      2,200        2,591           -391        -*           |               -
                                                  -|--+--+--+--|--+--+--+--|-
================================================================================
AUDIT test for OVERSTATEMENT using MP = 1,000, R = 1.0
--------------------------------------------------------------------------------
                                                              Optional Test
                                                              --------------
Obs     Recorded     Regression      Residual          Excess  Select'n Sam
No      Amount       Estimate        (Difference)  Threshold  <1>  Interval ple
----   ------------  ------------   ------------   ----------  -------- -------- ---
 31      2,200        2,591           -391         <2>
       ------------  ------------   ------------
         2,200        2,591           -391
       ============  ============   ============
```

<1> No significant differences detected in direction of test.

<2> Significant difference in opposite direction to that of test. Seek an explanation.

===
Variables Used (+), Not Used (-)

Obs#	Y+	X1+	X2+
1	2,787	347	2,050
2	3,095	437	2,052
3	3,184	517	1,944
4	2,084	139	1,978
5	2,287	189	2,022
6	3,228	551	1,901
7	4,842	1,076	2,058
8	2,210	194	1,912
9	2,565	276	2,081
10	2,494	297	1,912
11	2,422	241	2,030
12	3,090	444	2,077
13	2,287	229	1,899
14	2,669	297	2,151
15	3,204	467	2,123
16	2,105	171	1,886
17	2,440	229	2,096
18	3,126	479	1,970
19	4,776	1,002	1,951
20	2,030	100	2,035
21	2,070	138	1,963
22	4,949	1,144	1,945
23	2,862	371	2,087
24	2,347	185	2,082
25	2,912	388	2,030
26	2,259	234	1,875
27	2,730	393	1,822
28	2,106	153	1,944
29	2,274	200	1,967
30	2,444	212	2,087
31	2,200	300	2,000
	86,078	11,400	61,930

B.5   PARANORMAL PRODUCTIONS PRINTOUT

This application is used in Chapter 4 and again in Chapter 8 to explain the tests that the STAR Program applies to test for abnormality of the residuals.

************* STAR: Statistical Techniques for Analytical Review ************

Specifications for Model

Variables Specified:
Y	PRODUCTION		TEST
X1	HOURS		PREDICTING

Observations Used:
Base, 1 - 40	40
Projection	0

Total	40
	=====

Data Profile   CROSS-SECTIONAL

Type of Test   NONE

Report Options:
Scatter Diagrams	NO
Mathematical Details	NO

===
Stepwise Multiple Regression Model

Description	Input Data		Regression Function	
	Mean	Standard Error	Constant or Coefficient	Standard Error
Constant			-0.01	
Predicting Variables				
X1 HOURS	69.03	20.91	0.7662	0.0354
Test Variable				
Y PRODUCTION	52.88	16.66		
Y' Expectation			52.88	4.6212
Coefficient of Correlation (100% = Perfect)			96%	

Expectation [Y'(t)] for observation t :
Y'(t) = -0.01 + 0.7662*X1(t)

ABNORMALITY IN THE BASE PERIOD IS INDICATED BY:
. LEFT SKEWNESS--This may be caused by large negative residuals
. KURTOSIS--This may be caused by both large positive and large negative
  residuals.
Abnormality does not invalidate the model but it may affect the differences
to be audited. Examine the plot of the residuals to identify the outliers
and, if possible, eliminate the abnormality by correcting any errors or
unusual events in those observations.

===
Plot of Residuals

Obs No	Recorded Amount	Regression Estimate	Residual (Difference)	Residuals Graphed in Units of One Standard Error
				-4 -3 -2 -1 0 1 2 3 4
				- | --+--+--+-- | --+--+--+-- | -
1	31	30	1	- | * | -
2	32	30	2	- | * | -
3	32	32	0	- | * | -
4	36	38	-2	- | * | -
5	41	55	-14	- | * | -
6	33	36	-3	- | * | -
7	39	44	-5	- | * | -
8	19	20	-1	- | * | -
9	53	52	1	- | * | -
10	40	37	3	- | * | -
11	38	38	0	- | * | -
12	38	38	0	- | * | -
13	56	57	-1	- | * | -
14	45	46	-1	- | * | -
15	62	61	1	- | * | -
16	45	49	-4	- | * | -
17	55	56	-1	- | * | -
18	53	50	3	- | * | -
19	61	63	-2	- | * | -
20	37	36	1	- | * | -
21	52	54	-2	- | * | -
22	51	64	-13	- | * | -
23	55	55	0	- | * | -
24	62	62	0	- | * | -
25	41	44	-3	- | * | -
26	53	47	6	- | * | -
27	100	103	-3	- | * | -
28	70	65	5	- | * | -
29	82	81	1	- | * | -
30	65	61	4	- | * | -
31	67	66	1	- | * | -
32	61	70	-9	- | * | -
33	71	64	7	- | * | -
34	72	70	2	- | * | -
35	66	64	2	- | * | -
36	62	58	4	- | * | -
37	82	74	8	- | * | -
38	60	55	5	- | * | -
39	60	56	4	- | * | -
40	37	36	1	- | * | -
				- | --+--+--+-- | --+--+--+-- | -

266 Star Program Printouts

==
Variables Used (+), Not Used (-)

Obs#	Y+	X1+
1	31	39
2	32	39
3	32	42
4	36	49
5	41	72
6	33	47
7	39	57
8	19	26
9	53	68
10	40	48
11	38	50
12	38	50
13	56	74
14	45	60
15	62	79
16	45	64
17	55	73
18	53	65
19	61	82
20	37	47
21	52	70
22	51	83
23	55	72
24	62	81
25	41	58
26	53	61
27	100	134
28	70	85
29	82	106
30	65	79
31	67	86
32	61	92
33	71	84
34	72	91
35	66	83
36	62	76
37	82	97
38	60	72
39	60	73
40	37	47
	2,115	2,761

B.6   ABC TRADING COMPANY PRINTOUT

This application illustrates how the STAR Program can be applied in an Ending Balance Projection. The application is not specifically dealt with in the text, although a general reference to ending balance projection is contained in Section 6.3.1.

In this application COLLECTIONS was regressed against SALES, and SALES lagged by various periods in order to develop a model that could be used to estimate collections in the period between the date at which receivables were confirmed and the balance sheet date. The estimated collections were then used to project the ending balance of accounts receivable. Notice that the audit interface calculations are related to the ending balance.

```
************* STAR: Statistical Techniques for Analytical Review *************
```

Specifications for Model

Variables Specified:

Y	Collections		TEST
X1	Sales		PREDICTING
X2	Sales -1		PREDICTING
X3	Sales -2		PREDICTING
X4	Sales -3		PREDICTING
X5	Sales -4		PREDICTING

Observations Used:

Base, 5 - 46	42
Projection, 47 - 48	2

Total	44
	=====

Data Profile	TIME SERIES
Periods per Year	12
Seasonal Adjustment Requested	NO

Type of Test	ENDING BALANCE
Monetary Precision (MP)	25
Reliability Factor (R)	1.0
Direction of Test	UNDERSTATEMENT

Report Options:

Scatter Diagrams	NO
Mathematical Details	NO

```
===============================================================================
```
Stepwise Multiple Regression Model

		Input Data		Regression Function	
Description	Mean	Standard Error	Constant or Coefficient	Standard Error
Constant			7.93	
Predicting Variables				
X2 Sales -1	196.69	37.24	0.3010	0.0625
X3 Sales -2	194.12	37.20	0.2244	0.0603
X4 Sales -3	191.40	36.88	0.2447	0.0605
X5 Sales -4	188.74	36.44	0.1908	0.0632
Test Variable				
Y Collections	193.52	31.76		
Y' Expectation			193.52	9.9656

Coefficient of Correlation (100% = Perfect)   95%

Expectation [Y'(t)] for observation t :
Y'(t) = 7.93 + 0.3010*X2(t) + 0.2244*X3(t) + 0.2447*X4(t) + 0.1908*X5(t)

===

Plot of Residuals

Obs No	Recorded Amount	Regression Estimate	Residual (Difference)	Residuals Graphed in Units of One Standard Error
				-4 -3 -2 -1 0 1 2 3 4
5	141	142	-1	
6	152	152	0	
7	164	155	9	
8	157	164	-7	
9	166	163	3	
10	153	157	-4	
11	133	144	-11	
12	147	151	-4	
13	165	159	6	
14	168	160	8	
15	174	184	-10	
16	168	183	-15	
17	171	175	-4	
18	173	181	-8	
19	177	171	6	
20	195	177	18	
21	202	188	14	
22	188	194	-6	
23	186	190	-4	
24	209	193	16	
25	187	180	7	
26	177	173	4	
27	192	198	-6	
28	193	192	1	
29	184	202	-18	
30	203	201	2	
31	182	192	-10	
32	204	209	-5	
33	200	207	-7	
34	225	216	9	
35	223	216	7	
36	213	217	-4	
37	230	218	12	
38	219	224	-5	
39	227	224	3	
40	240	233	7	
41	220	231	-11	
42	262	235	27	
43	235	241	-6	
44	230	241	-11	
45	247	248	-1	
46	246	250	-4	
47	249	254	-5	
48	240	256	-16	

```
==============================================================================
ENDING BALANCE test for OVERSTATEMENT of Receivables.  MP = 25, R = 1.0.
```

Receivables is estimated by adjusting the recorded amount for the
difference between recorded and estimated Y (Collections).

```
UNDERSTATEMENT is the specified direction of test for Y.
Y is a CREDIT component of Receivables which is an ASSET.  Therefore,
OVERSTATEMENT is the implied direction of test for Receivables.
------------------------------------------------------------------------------
```

```
Recorded Receivables                                    300
Estimated Receivables                                   279
                                                 ------------
Residual (Difference)                                    21
Threshold                                                17
                                                 ------------
Excess                                                    5
                                                 ============
Optional Test :
Selection Interval                                       60
Sample Size                                               5
```

Significant difference in direction of test. Perform further analysis
and inquiry to obtain and corroborate explanation. Perform optional test
of details only if difference cannot be explained. Computed sample sizes
less than 5 are set to the lesser of 5 and RECORDED Receivables / (MP/R).

==
Variables Used (+), Not Used (-)

Obs#	Y+	X1-	X2+	X3+	X4+	X5+
5	141	172	136	142	140	140
6	152	161	172	136	142	140
7	164	172	161	172	136	142
8	157	147	172	161	172	136
9	166	144	147	172	161	172
10	153	116	144	147	172	161
11	133	178	116	144	147	172
12	147	184	178	116	144	147
13	165	150	184	178	116	144
14	168	211	150	184	178	116
15	174	185	211	150	184	178
16	168	149	185	211	150	184
17	171	179	149	185	211	150
18	173	171	179	149	185	211
19	177	193	171	179	149	185
20	195	202	193	171	179	149
21	202	201	202	193	171	179
22	188	169	201	202	193	171
23	186	196	169	201	202	193
24	209	161	196	169	201	202
25	187	161	161	196	169	201
26	177	257	161	161	196	169
27	192	187	257	161	161	196
28	193	193	187	257	161	161
29	184	182	193	187	257	161
30	203	202	182	193	187	257
31	182	248	202	182	193	187
32	204	197	248	202	182	193
33	200	214	197	248	202	182
34	225	215	214	197	248	202
35	223	234	215	214	197	248
36	213	213	234	215	214	197
37	230	234	213	234	215	214
38	219	221	234	213	234	215
39	227	258	221	234	213	234
40	240	221	258	221	234	213
41	220	239	221	258	221	234
42	262	252	239	221	258	221
43	235	252	252	239	221	258
44	230	254	252	252	239	221
45	247	250	254	252	252	239
46	246	265	250	254	252	252
47	249	263	265	250	254	252
48	240	270	263	265	250	254
	8,617	8,923	8,789	8,668	8,543	8,433

B.7   GAMMA COMPANY MATHEMATICAL PRINTOUT

One of the reports that the STAR Program can produce is one that details all the mathematical calculations performed by the Program. The printout shown here is a detailed mathematical printout for the Gamma Company application that is used in Chapter 9 to explain stepwise multiple regression.

```
************* STAR: Statistical Techniques for Analytical Review ************

Specifications for Model

Variables Specified:
Y     Revenue                                        TEST
X1    Time at Std                               PREDICTING
X2    Expenses                                  PREDICTING
X3    Cost of Services                          PREDICTING

Observations Used:
Base, 1 - 36                                           36
Projection, 37 - 48                                    12
                                                    -----
Total                                                  48
                                                    =====

Data Profile                                  TIME SERIES
Periods per Year                                       12
Seasonal Adjustment Requested                          NO

Type of Test                                       AUDIT
Monetary Precision (MP)                              600
Reliability Factor (R)                               3.0
Direction of Test                        UNDERSTATEMENT

Report Options:
Scatter Diagrams                                       NO
Mathematical Details                                  YES

Mathematical references to "Stringer & Stewart" refer to the book
"Statistical Techniques for Analytical Review" by Kenneth W. Stringer
and Trevor R. Stewart, New York, Wiley.
```

==

*** Correlation Matrix (Stringer & Stewart Chapter 9) ***

	Y	X1	X2	X3
Y	1.0	8.636878e-01	8.232686e-01	8.693496e-01
X1	8.636878e-01	1.0	6.699487e-01	8.617620e-01
X2	8.232686e-01	6.699487e-01	1.0	8.480435e-01
X3	8.693496e-01	8.617620e-01	8.480435e-01	1.0

*** Test for Admission of X3 (Stringer & Stewart Chapter 9) ***

$$F = Vmax/1 \quad / \quad [(yy - Vmax) / (df-1)]$$
$$= 0.755769/1 \quad / \quad [(1.000000 - 0.755769) / 34]$$
$$= 105.212302$$

Equivalent F confidence level = 100.000000%
Critical F confidence level = 95.000000%
Variable admitted
Target F level becomes   = 95.000000%

*** Matrix Following Admission (Stringer & Stewart Chapter 9) ***

	Y	X1	X2	X3
Y	2.442313e-01	1.145154e-01	8.602229e-02	-8.693496e-01
X1	1.145154e-01	2.573662e-01	-6.086306e-02	-8.617620e-01
X2	8.602229e-02	-6.086306e-02	2.808222e-01	-8.480435e-01
X3	8.693496e-01	8.617620e-01	8.480435e-01	1.0

*** Test for Admission of X1 (Stringer & Stewart Chapter 9) ***

$$F = Vmax/1 \quad / \quad [(yy - Vmax) / (df-1)]$$
$$= 0.050954/1 \quad / \quad [(0.244231 - 0.050954) / 33]$$
$$= 8.699784$$

Equivalent F confidence level = 99.418837%
Critical F confidence level = 95.000000%
Variable admitted
Target F level becomes   = 95.555333%

*** Matrix Following Admission (Stringer & Stewart Chapter 9) ***

	Y	X1	X2	X3
Y	1.932776e-01	-4.449511e-01	1.131034e-01	-4.859077e-01
X1	4.449511e-01	3.885514e+00	-2.364843e-01	-3.348389e+00
X2	1.131034e-01	2.364843e-01	2.664290e-01	-1.051837e+00
X3	4.859077e-01	-3.348389e+00	1.051837e+00	3.885514e+00

*** Test for Admission of X2 (Stringer & Stewart Chapter 9) ***

$$F = Vmax/1 \quad / \quad [(yy - Vmax) / (df-1)]$$
$$= 0.048014/1 \quad / \quad [(0.193278 - 0.048014) / 32]$$
$$= 10.577022$$

Equivalent F confidence level = 99.730058%
Critical F confidence level = 95.555333%
Variable admitted
Target F level becomes   = 95.813974%

*** Matrix Following Admission (Stringer & Stewart Chapter 9) ***

```
       Y              X1             X2             X3
Y     1.452634e-01  -5.453424e-01  -4.245159e-01  -3.938621e-02
X1    5.453424e-01   4.095420e+00   8.876070e-01  -4.282007e+00
X2    4.245159e-01   8.876070e-01   3.753345e+00  -3.947906e+00
X3    3.938621e-02  -4.282007e+00  -3.947906e+00   8.038067e+00
```

*** Test for Elimination of X3 (Stringer & Stewart Chapter 9) ***

$$F = |Vmin|/1 \quad / \quad (yy / df)$$
$$= 0.000193/1 \quad / \quad (0.145263 / 32)$$
$$= 0.042514$$

```
Equivalent F confidence level = 16.205038%
Critical F confidence level   = 95%
F level on admission          = 100.000000%
New target confidence level   = 95.813974%
```

*** Matrix Following Elimination (Stringer & Stewart Chapter 9) ***

```
       Y              X1             X2             X3
Y     1.454564e-01  -5.663241e-01  -4.438605e-01   4.899960e-03
X1    5.663241e-01   1.814326e+00  -1.215505e+00   5.327160e-01
X2    4.438605e-01  -1.215505e+00   1.814326e+00   4.911512e-01
X3    4.899960e-03  -5.327160e-01  -4.911512e-01   1.244080e-01
```

===
Stepwise Multiple Regression Model

	Input Data		Regression Function	
Description	Mean	Standard Error	Constant or Coefficient	Standard Error
Constant			-366.46	
Predicting Variables				
X1 Time at Std	1,832.00	246.16	0.8906	0.1406
X2 Expenses	911.00	126.54	1.3578	0.2736
Test Variable				
Y Revenue	2,502.00	387.10		
Y' Expectation			2,502.00	152.0418
Coefficient of Correlation (100% = Perfect)			92%	

Expectation [Y'(t)] for observation t :
Y'(t) = -366.46 + 0.8906*X1(t) + 1.3578*X2(t)

*** Test for Discontinuity in the Base Period (Stringer & Stewart Chapter 8) ***

$$F = ((sse - (sse\_1 + sse\_2)) / (k+1)) \quad / \quad ((sse\_1 + sse\_2) / (n1+n2-2k-2))$$

$$= \frac{(\;7.628515e+05 - (\;3.161658e+05 + \;3.040342e+05)) / 3}{(\;3.161658e+05 + \;3.040342e+05) / 30}$$

= 2.300089

Tail probability P (F | 3, 30) = 9.742368%

Significance level of test = 1%

*** Test Discontinuity Between Base and Audit Periods ***
***   (Stringer & Stewart Chapter 8)   ***

$$F = ((sse\_A - sse) / (n\_A - n)) \quad / \quad (sse / (n-k-1))$$

= ((1.193811e+006 - 7.628515e+005) / 12) /   (7.628515e+005 / 33)

= 1.553566

Tail probability P (F | 12, 33) = 15.472395%

Significance level of test = 1%

*** Test For Abnormality (Stringer & Stewart Chapter 8) ***

Moments
m2 =   2.119032e+04
m3 =   4.112842e+05
m4 =   9.462075e+08

Cumulants
k2 =   2.185252e+04
k3 =   4.515005e+05
k4 =   -4.001704e+08

Normal 1% percentile = 2.576236

Test for Skewness
Test Statistic = 0.312845
Variance   = 0.836436
Critical Value = 2.576236 * sqrt(0.836436)
               = 2.356145

Test for Kurtosis
Test Statistic = -0.880961
Variance   = 0.702368
Critical Value = 2.576236 * sqrt(0.702368)
               = 2.159076

```
================================================================================
Plot of Residuals

 Obs    Recorded     Regression     Residual      Residuals Graphed in Units
 No      Amount       Estimate     (Difference)      of One Standard Error
----  ------------  ------------  ------------    ----------------------------
                                                  -4 -3 -2 -1  0  1  2  3  4
                                                  -|--+--+--+--|--+--+--+--|-
   1     2,107        2,124           -17          -              *         -
   2     1,915        2,038          -123          -        *               -
   3     1,873        2,064          -191          -     *                  -
   4     1,978        2,008           -30          -           *            -
   5     2,010        2,074           -64          -          *             -
   6     1,969        2,009           -40          -          *            -
   7     2,228        2,177            51          -             *          -
   8     2,152        2,035           117          -              *         -
   9     2,439        2,490           -51          -          *             -
  10     2,318        2,295            23          -            *           -
  11     2,244        2,108           136          -              *         -
  12     2,357        2,344            13          -           *            -
                                                  -|--+--+--+--|--+--+--+--|-
  13     2,103        2,207          -104          -        *               -
  14     2,457        2,406            51          -             *          -
  15     2,606        2,366           240          -                *       -
  16     2,493        2,385           108          -               *        -
  17     2,264        2,096           168          -               *        -
  18     2,058        2,181          -123          -      *                 -
  19     2,516        2,602           -86          -       *                -
  20     2,533        2,699          -166          -      *                 -
  21     2,958        2,722           236          -                *       -
  22     2,564        2,576           -12          -           *            -
  23     2,318        2,581          -263          -   *                    -
  24     2,928        2,997           -69          -         *              -
                                                  -|--+--+--+--|--+--+--+--|-
  25     2,754        2,657            97          -              *         -
  26     2,678        2,774           -96          -       *                -
  27     3,189        2,985           204          -                *       -
  28     3,067        2,817           250          -                 *      -
  29     2,735        2,837          -102          -         *              -
  30     3,029        2,972            57          -              *         -
  31     2,531        2,571           -40          -          *            -
  32     2,765        2,995          -230          -    *                   -
  33     3,074        3,204          -130          -       *                -
  34     2,651        2,912          -261          -    *                   -
  35     3,056        2,832           224          -                *       -
  36     3,155        2,931           224          -                *       -
                                                  -|--+--+--+--|--+--+--+--|-
  37     2,757        2,716            41          -             *          -
  38     2,869        2,757           112          -              *         -
  39     3,168        3,128            40          -             *          -
  40     3,210        2,939           271          -                 *      -
  41     2,958        3,393          -435          - *                      -
  42     2,698        2,997          -299          -   *                    -
  43     3,412        3,167           245          -                  *     -
  44     2,872        3,171          -299          -    *                   -
  45     3,263        3,440          -177          -     *                  -
  46     3,506        3,421            85          -               *        -
  47     3,452        3,590          -138          -      *                 -
  48     2,993        3,335          -342          -  *                     -
                                                  -|--+--+--+--|--+--+--+--|-
```

===

*** Test for Heteroscedasticity (Stringer & Stewart Chapter 8) ***

The absolute residuals are most highly correlated with |X1|
Correlation   =   0.421138
F   =   ((0.421138)^2 / 1)   /   ((1 - (0.421138)^2) / 34)
                 =   7.330209
Tail probability P (F | 1, 34) = 1.053198%
Significance level of test = 1%

*** Test for Autocorrelation (Stringer & Stewart Chapter 8) ***

Durbin-Watson Statistic   = 1.240746e+06 / 7.628515e+05
                                   = 1.626458
Tail probability P (d_U | 2, 36)   = 6.437323%
Significance level of test   = 1%

*** Inverse Matrix ***

	Y	X1	X2	X3
Y	0.0	0.0	0.0	0.0
X1	0.0	8.554995e-07	-1.114892e-06	0.0
X2	0.0	-1.114892e-06	3.237151e-06	0.0
X3	0.0	0.0	0.0	0.0

```
===============================================================================
AUDIT test for UNDERSTATEMENT using MP = 600, R = 3.0
-------------------------------------------------------------------------------
```

					Optional Test

Obs	Recorded	Regression	Residual		Excess	Select'n Sam
No	Amount	Estimate	(Difference)	Threshold	<1>	Interval ple

```
---- ------------ ------------ ------------ ---------- --------- -------- ---
```

OBSERVATION NUMBER 37

*** Standard Error (Stringer & Stewart Chapter 9) ***
SE = s * SQRT (1 + 1/n + c'(X'X)c)
    = 152.041805 * SQRT (1 + 1/36 + 0.051613) = 157.961909

*** Most Averse Spread of Error (MAS) (Stringer & Stewart Chapter 5) ***
MAS   = 4
Most Adverse Risk   = EXP(-R) ^ (1 / MAS)
                         = 0.049787 ^ (1 / 4)
                         = 0.472367

*** Excess to be Investigated (Stringer & Stewart Chapter 5) ***
Threshold   = MP / MAS + SE * t (df = 33, risk = 0.472367)
                         = 600 / 4 + 157.961909 * -0.069674
                         = 138.994101
Residual   = -41.305638
No excess to be investigated

```
   37        2,757        2,716             41
```

OBSERVATION NUMBER 38

*** Standard Error (Stringer & Stewart Chapter 9) ***
SE = s * SQRT (1 + 1/n + c'(X'X)c)
    = 152.041805 * SQRT (1 + 1/36 + 0.015008) = 155.260379

*** Most Averse Spread of Error (MAS) (Stringer & Stewart Chapter 5) ***
MAS   = 4
Most Adverse Risk   = EXP(-R) ^ (1 / MAS)
                         = 0.049787 ^ (1 / 4)
                         = 0.472367

*** Excess to be Investigated (Stringer & Stewart Chapter 5) ***
Threshold   = MP / MAS + SE * t (df = 33, risk = 0.472367)
                         = 600 / 4 + 155.260379 * -0.069674
                         = 139.182329
Residual   = -112.149358
No excess to be investigated

```
   38        2,869        2,757            112
```

OBSERVATION NUMBER 39

*** Standard Error (Stringer & Stewart Chapter 9) ***
SE = s * SQRT (1 + 1/n + c'(X'X)c)
   = 152.041805 * SQRT (1 + 1/36 + 0.133676) = 163.856648

*** Most Averse Spread of Error (MAS) (Stringer & Stewart Chapter 5) ***
MAS   = 4
Most Adverse Risk   = EXP(-R) ^ (1 / MAS)
                       = 0.049787 ^ (1 / 4)
                       = 0.472367

*** Excess to be Investigated (Stringer & Stewart Chapter 5) ***
Threshold   = MP / MAS + SE * t (df = 33, risk = 0.472367)
                       = 600 / 4 + 163.856648 * -0.069674
                       = 138.583389
Residual   = -39.881498
No excess to be investigated

   39   3,168   3,128   40

OBSERVATION NUMBER 40

*** Standard Error (Stringer & Stewart Chapter 9) ***
SE = s * SQRT (1 + 1/n + c'(X'X)c)
   = 152.041805 * SQRT (1 + 1/36 + 0.116562) = 162.644953

*** Most Averse Spread of Error (MAS) (Stringer & Stewart Chapter 5) ***
MAS   = 4
Most Adverse Risk   = EXP(-R) ^ (1 / MAS)
                       = 0.049787 ^ (1 / 4)
                       = 0.472367

*** Excess to be Investigated (Stringer & Stewart Chapter 5) ***
Threshold   = MP / MAS + SE * t (df = 33, risk = 0.472367)
                       = 600 / 4 + 162.644953 * -0.069674
                       = 138.667813
Residual   = -271.077733
No excess to be investigated

   40   3,210   2,939   271 <2>

OBSERVATION NUMBER 41

*** Standard Error (Stringer & Stewart Chapter 9) ***
SE = s * SQRT (1 + 1/n + c'(X'X)c)
   = 152.041805 * SQRT (1 + 1/36 + 0.388177) = 180.920456

*** Most Averse Spread of Error (MAS) (Stringer & Stewart Chapter 5) ***
MAS   = 4
Most Adverse Risk   = EXP(-R) ^ (1 / MAS)
                       = 0.049787 ^ (1 / 4)
                       = 0.472367

*** Excess to be Investigated (Stringer & Stewart Chapter 5) ***
Threshold   = MP / MAS + SE * t (df = 33, risk = 0.472367)
                       = 600 / 4 + 180.920456 * -0.069674
                       = 137.394479
Residual   = 434.794687
Excess   = 297.400208

*** Optional Sample Data (Stringer & Stewart Chapter 5) ***
Effective Risk Point   = (e - MP / MAS) / SE
                       = (434.794687 - 600 / 4) / 180.920456
                       = 1.574143
Effective Risk   = 0.937503
Risk for CMA Sample   = Target Risk / Effective Risk
                       = 0.472367 / 0.937503
                       = 0.503856
Reliability Factor   = 0.685465
Selection Interval Based on (MP / MAS) / R

41	2,958	3,393	-435	137	297	212	16

OBSERVATION NUMBER 42

*** Standard Error (Stringer & Stewart Chapter 9) ***
SE = s * SQRT (1 + 1/n + c'(X'X)c)
   = 152.041805 * SQRT (1 + 1/36 + 0.124643) = 163.218196

*** Most Averse Spread of Error (MAS) (Stringer & Stewart Chapter 5) ***
MAS   = 4
Most Adverse Risk   = EXP(-R) ^ (1 / MAS)
                       = 0.049787 ^ (1 / 4)
                       = 0.472367

*** Excess to be Investigated (Stringer & Stewart Chapter 5) ***
Threshold   = MP / MAS + SE * t (df = 33, risk = 0.472367)
                       = 600 / 4 + 163.218196 * -0.069674
                       = 138.627873
Residual   = 299.203884
Excess   = 160.576011

*** Optional Sample Data (Stringer & Stewart Chapter 5) ***
Effective Risk Point   = (e - MP / MAS) / SE
                       = (299.203884 - 600 / 4) / 163.218196
                       = 0.914138
Effective Risk   = 0.816362
Risk for CMA Sample   = Target Risk / Effective Risk
                       = 0.472367 / 0.816362
                       = 0.578624
Reliability Factor   = 0.547103
Selection Interval Based on (MP / MAS) / R

42	2,698	2,997	-299	139	161	272	11

OBSERVATION NUMBER 43

*** Standard Error (Stringer & Stewart Chapter 9) ***
SE = s * SQRT (1 + 1/n + c'(X'X)c)
    = 152.041805 * SQRT (1 + 1/36 + 0.296193) = 174.945260

*** Most Averse Spread of Error (MAS) (Stringer & Stewart Chapter 5) ***
MAS   = 4
Most Adverse Risk   = EXP(-R) ^ (1 / MAS)
                        = 0.049787 ^ (1 / 4)
                        = 0.472367

*** Excess to be Investigated (Stringer & Stewart Chapter 5) ***
Threshold   = MP / MAS + SE * t (df = 33, risk = 0.472367)
                        = 600 / 4 + 174.945260 * -0.069674
                        = 137.810797
Residual   = -245.250956
No excess to be investigated

    43   3,412   3,167   245 <2>

OBSERVATION NUMBER 44

*** Standard Error (Stringer & Stewart Chapter 9) ***
SE = s * SQRT (1 + 1/n + c'(X'X)c)
    = 152.041805 * SQRT (1 + 1/36 + 0.125299) = 163.264635

*** Most Averse Spread of Error (MAS) (Stringer & Stewart Chapter 5) ***
MAS   = 4
Most Adverse Risk   = EXP(-R) ^ (1 / MAS)
                        = 0.049787 ^ (1 / 4)
                        = 0.472367

*** Excess to be Investigated (Stringer & Stewart Chapter 5) ***
Threshold   = MP / MAS + SE * t (df = 33, risk = 0.472367)
                        = 600 / 4 + 163.264635 * -0.069674
                        = 138.624637
Residual   = 298.836942
Excess   = 160.212305

*** Optional Sample Data (Stringer & Stewart Chapter 5) ***
Effective Risk Point = (e - MP / MAS) / SE
                      = (298.836942 - 600 / 4) / 163.264635
                      = 0.911630
Effective Risk   = 0.815712
Risk for CMA Sample   = Target Risk / Effective Risk
                      = 0.472367 / 0.815712
                      = 0.579085
Reliability Factor   = 0.546307
Selection Interval Based on (MP / MAS) / R

    44   2,872   3,171   -299   139   160   264 12

OBSERVATION NUMBER 45

*** Standard Error (Stringer & Stewart Chapter 9) ***
SE = s * SQRT (1 + 1/n + c'(X'X)c)
    = 152.041805 * SQRT (1 + 1/36 + 0.330177) = 177.176303

*** Most Averse Spread of Error. (MAS) (Stringer & Stewart Chapter 5) ***
MAS   = 4
Most Adverse Risk   = EXP(-R) ^ (1 / MAS)
                        = 0.049787 ^ (1 / 4)
                        = 0.472367

*** Excess to be Investigated (Stringer & Stewart Chapter 5) ***
Threshold   = MP / MAS + SE * t (df = 33, risk = 0.472367)
                        = 600 / 4 + 177.176303 * -0.069674
                        = 137.655350
Residual   = 177.068194
Excess   = 39.412844

*** Optional Sample Data (Stringer & Stewart Chapter 5) ***
Effective Risk Point   = (e - MP / MAS) / SE
                        = (177.068194 - 600 / 4) / 177.176303
                        = 0.152775
Effective Risk   = 0.560247
Risk for CMA Sample   = Target Risk / Effective Risk
                        = 0.472367 / 0.560247
                        = 0.843140
Reliability Factor   = 0.170623
Selection Interval Based on (MP / MAS) / R

45	3,263	3,440	-177	138	39	688	5

OBSERVATION NUMBER 46

*** Standard Error (Stringer & Stewart Chapter 9) ***
SE = s * SQRT (1 + 1/n + c'(X'X)c)
    = 152.041805 * SQRT (1 + 1/36 + 0.220087) = 169.842636

*** Most Averse Spread of Error (MAS) (Stringer & Stewart Chapter 5) ***
MAS   = 4
Most Adverse Risk   = EXP(-R) ^ (1 / MAS)
                        = 0.049787 ^ (1 / 4)
                        = 0.472367

*** Excess to be Investigated (Stringer & Stewart Chapter 5) ***
Threshold   = MP / MAS + SE * t (df = 33, risk = 0.472367)
                        = 600 / 4 + 169.842636 * -0.069674
                        = 138.166319
Residual   = -84.809099
No excess to be investigated

46	3,506	3,421	85

OBSERVATION NUMBER 47

*** Standard Error (Stringer & Stewart Chapter 9) ***
SE = s * SQRT (1 + 1/n + c'(X'X)c)
   = 152.041805 * SQRT (1 + 1/36 + 0.339280) = 177.769157

*** Most Averse Spread of Error (MAS) (Stringer & Stewart Chapter 5) ***
MAS   = 4
Most Adverse Risk   = EXP(-R) ^ (1 / MAS)
                    = 0.049787 ^ (1 / 4)
                    = 0.472367

*** Excess to be Investigated (Stringer & Stewart Chapter 5) ***
Threshold   = MP / MAS + SE * t (df = 33, risk = 0.472367)
                    = 600 / 4 + 177.769157 * -0.069674
                    = 137.614044
Residual   = 138.035299
No excess to be investigated

   47   3,452   3,590   -138

OBSERVATION NUMBER 48

*** Standard Error (Stringer & Stewart Chapter 9) ***
SE = s * SQRT (1 + 1/n + c'(X'X)c)
   = 152.041805 * SQRT (1 + 1/36 + 0.156502) = 165.458923

*** Most Averse Spread of Error (MAS) (Stringer & Stewart Chapter 5) ***
MAS   = 4
Most Adverse Risk   = EXP(-R) ^ (1 / MAS)
                    = 0.049787 ^ (1 / 4)
                    = 0.472367

*** Excess to be Investigated (Stringer & Stewart Chapter 5) ***
Threshold   = MP / MAS + SE * t (df = 33, risk = 0.472367)
                    = 600 / 4 + 165.458923 * -0.069674
                    = 138.471752
Residual   = 341.775863
Excess   = 203.304111

*** Optional Sample Data (Stringer & Stewart Chapter 5) ***
Effective Risk Point = (e - MP / MAS) / SE
                    = (341.775863 - 600 / 4) / 165.458923
                    = 1.159054
Effective Risk   = 0.872624
Risk for CMA Sample = Target Risk / Effective Risk
                    = 0.472367 / 0.872624
                    = 0.541318
Reliability Factor = 0.613749
Selection Interval Based on (MP / MAS) / R

  48   2,993   3,335   -342   138   203   238 14
       ------------ ------------ ------------   ---
          37,158   38,054   -896   58
       ============ ============ ============   ===

<1> Significant difference in direction of test. Perform further analysis
    and inquiry to obtain and corroborate explanation. Perform optional test
    of details only if difference cannot be explained. Computed sample sizes
    less than 5 are set to the lesser of 5 and REGRESSION ESTIMATE / (MP/R).

<2> Significant difference in opposite direction to that of test. Seek an
    explanation.

```
===============================================================================
Variables Used (+), Not Used (-)

Obs#        Y+       X1+       X2+       X3-
----  --------- --------- --------- ---------
  1     2,107     1,574       802     1,527
  2     1,915     1,503       785     1,531
  3     1,873     1,645       711     1,507
  4     1,978     1,380       844     1,681
  5     2,010     1,580       761     1,443
  6     1,969     1,576       716     1,507
  7     2,228     1,752       724     1,545
  8     2,152     1,549       753     1,376
  9     2,439     1,652     1,020     1,870
 10     2,318     1,650       878     1,744
 11     2,244     1,496       841     1,547
 12     2,357     1,671       900     1,864
 13     2,103     1,679       794     1,622
 14     2,457     1,782       873     1,699
 15     2,606     1,652       929     1,683
 16     2,493     1,756       875     1,712
 17     2,264     1,555       794     1,603
 18     2,058     1,621       813     1,550
 19     2,516     1,982       886     1,830
 20     2,533     2,050       913     2,052
 21     2,958     1,959       990     1,855
 22     2,564     1,836       963     1,759
 23     2,318     2,006       855     1,830
 24     2,928     2,164     1,058     2,333
 25     2,754     1,780     1,059     2,005
 26     2,678     2,054       966     2,000
 27     3,189     2,265       983     2,024
 28     3,067     2,117       956     2,182
 29     2,735     1,955     1,077     1,981
 30     3,029     2,059     1,108     2,073
 31     2,531     2,059       813     1,921
 32     2,765     2,096     1,101     2,110
 33     3,074     2,201     1,186     2,120
 34     2,651     2,016     1,092     2,058
 35     3,056     2,197       915     2,039
 36     3,155     2,083     1,062     2,157
 37     2,757     2,075       909     1,979
 38     2,869     1,984       999     2,046
 39     3,168     2,346     1,035     2,072
 40     3,210     2,254       956     1,933
 41     2,958     2,166     1,348     2,433
 42     2,698     2,013     1,157     2,250
 43     3,412     2,490       969     2,224
 44     2,872     2,179     1,176     2,288
 45     3,263     2,245     1,331     2,421
 46     3,506     2,515     1,140     2,447
 47     3,452     2,389     1,347     2,338
 48     2,993     2,389     1,159     2,312
      --------- --------- --------- ---------
      127,230    92,997    46,322    92,083
      ========= ========= ========= =========
```

EXAMPLES OF RELATIONSHIPS

C.1 TYPES OF RELATIONSHIPS

Relationships between data used to develop expectations fall into four types:

1. Prior-year balance modified for changes in the current year
2. Relationship with other financial data
3. Relationship with nonfinancial data
4. Budget modified for expected changes

Examples of the first three types of relationships are included on the following pages, grouped by the type of account for which an expectation is developed. Each expectation is cross referenced to the type of relationship by number.

C.2   EXAMPLES OF RELATIONSHIPS

Sales—Manufacturing and Retail

Expectation (type)	Major predictor	Auxiliary predictors
Sales (1)	Prior-year sales	Changes in sales volumes Changes in prices Unusual (nonrecurring) sales Prior-year unusual (nonrecurring) sales Trade indices
Sales (3)	Store floor area Average sales per square foot	Sales floor area and average sales for each comparable unit Industry indices

Sales (3)	Units shipped
	Unit price or value shipped
		Shipping or dispatch records
		    (e.g., warehouse records)
		Sales tax records of units or
		    value shipped
		Freight shipment records
		Postage records
		Order records of goods sent
		    directly to customers
		Pricing records
		Consumer price index
		Industry indices
		Changes in sales mix
		Receiving records of sales
		    returns

Cost of Sales—Manufacturing and Retail

Expectation (type)	Major predictor	Auxiliary predictors
Cost of sales (1)	Prior-year cost of sales	Changes in sales volumes Changes in costs Unusual (nonrecurring) costs Prior-year unusual (nonrecurring) costs Inflation Trade indices
Cost of sales (2)	Sales	Gross margin percentage Sales price changes Cost changes Sales mix changes Industry statistics Inflation rates

Cost of Sales—Manufacturing and Retail (*Continued*)

Expectation (type)	Major predictor	Auxiliary predictors
Cost of sales (2)	Goods purchased (Predict purchases and adjust for inventory)	Receiving records Order records of goods received Purchase returns Wastage Pilferage Beginning inventory Ending inventory
Cost of sales (3)	Units produced Standard or average cost per unit or Labor usage	Production records Job schedules of completed jobs Order book records of completed orders Inventory records of units received
	Labor hours per unit produced	Incentive wage scheme records (units produced as basis for wage calculations)
	Material usage	Material usage records
	Usage per unit produced or Power/fuel/tool usage	Machine hour records Power/fuel consumption Consumable tool consumption
	Usage per unit produced (Predict production and adjust for inventory)	Cost records Consumer price index Industry indices Product mix Beginning inventory Ending inventory

Sales and Cost of Sales—Services

Expectation (type)	Major predictor	Auxiliary predictors
Secondary sales (e.g., refreshments) (2)	Primary sales (e.g., theater tickets)	Secondary to primary sales ratio
Sales (2)	Contract values	Negotiated fees, % completion
Sales (3)	Uses of physical facilities	Number of users Entry fee Space Time Unit charge Discounts

Sales and Cost of Sales—Services (*Continued*)

Expectation (type)	Major predictor	Auxiliary predictors
Sales (3)	Uses of equipment	Time in use Time charge Distance used Distance charge Weight Unit charge
Sales (3)	Consumption of goods	Number of orders Average sales Number of items repaired Average charge
Revenue (3)	Use of skilled people	Hours worked Time sheets Charge rate Commissions paid Commission records Commission rates
Sales (3)	Number of salespersons	Average sales per salesperson
Cost of sales (3)	Consumption of goods	Number of orders Average cost

Expenses

Expectation (type)	Major predictor	Auxiliary predictors
Sales discounts (2)	Sales revenues	Average discount rate Ineligible sales
Sales returns (2)	Sales revenue	Average rate of returns Management policy
Bad debt expense (2)	Sales revenue	Average % bad debts Aging of receivables

Commissions (1)	Prior-year commission expense	Current-year changes in
		    Commission rates
		    Commission base

Commissions (2)	Sales revenue	Commission rates Noncommission sales
Advertising expense (2)	Revenue	Time lag Management policy

Payroll (1)	Prior-year payroll expense	Current-year changes in
		    Number of employees
		    Pay rates
		    Average hours worked
		    Bonus plan

Expenses (*Continued*)

Expectation (type)	Major predictor	Auxiliary predictors
Payroll (3)	Number of employees	Per employee Average hours worked Average wage rate
Payroll (3)	Number of hours worked	Average wage rate per hour
Payroll tax (2) Employee benefits (2)	Gross payroll expense	Tax rates Benefit rates Management policy
Rent, heat, and electricity expenses (1)	Prior-year expense	Changes in costs Changes in space utilized Changes in production volume of activity Shutdowns Seasonal variation
Maintenance and repair expenses (1)	Prior-year expense	Changes in costs Changes in production volume of activity Shutdowns Age of machinery Postponed maintenance
Freight expense (3)	Sales volume or weight	Average freight charge Freight charge per unit weight
Depreciation expense (2)	Property, plant, and equipment (PPE)	PPE by asset life and depreciation method Depreciation lives Depreciation rates Age of PPE
Insurance expense (1)	Prior-year expense	Changes in asset values Changes in levels of coverage
Insurance expense (2)	Property, plant, and equipment or value of other insurable items	Insurance rates by type of asset
Interest expense (1)	Prior-year interest expense	Changes in debt Changes in interest rates
Interest expense (2)	Average debt balances	Average interest rates on different types of debt

Other Income

Expectation (type)	Major predictor	Auxiliary predictors
Interest income (2)	Average bank balance or Other interest/income bearing investments	Average rates of interest/income on different types of investments
Dividend income (2)	Value of equities	Dividend rates

Balance-Sheet Accounts

Expectation (type)	Major predictor	Auxiliary predictors
Accounts receivable (1)	Prior-year accounts receivable	Current-year changes in Sales Cash receipts Customer credits
Allowance for doubtful accounts (2)	Receivables	Aging of receivables Payment history of large or old receivables Bad debt expense
Inventory (1)	Prior-year inventory	Current-year changes in Cost of sales Purchases Overhead/labor (production costs) Write-offs
Inventory (3)	Units on hand	Average unit cost
Accounts payable (1)	Prior-year payables	Current-year changes in Purchases Cash payments Credit received
Property, plant, and equipment (PPE) (1)	Prior-year balance of PPE	Current year Acquisitions Disposals Write-offs Gain/loss on disposals
Debt (1)	Prior-year debt balances	Current year Principal repayments (scheduled and other) New borrowings Changes in revolving debt

APPENDIX D

STAR WARNING MESSAGES

STAR prints error and warning messages when it detects certain conditions in the regression model. The messages are shown below in bold, followed by expanded explanations and descriptions of what one might do to deal with the conditions identified. It is usually helpful to examine the plot of residuals and the scatter diagrams produced by STAR to assess what problems exist in the data relationships.

NO SIGNIFICANT PREDICTING VARIABLE HAS BEEN FOUND. STAR will not process the data further. Review the base profile and study the relationships analytically to determine why the predicting variable(s) do not have the expected relationships to the test variable.

STAR has determined that none of the predicting variables bears a significant relationship to the test variable. If there are errors in the base profile, correct them and rerun STAR. Otherwise, attempt to identify other variables that will more explicitly represent the expected business relationships. If significant changes have occurred in the relationships during the base period, STAR or other analytical procedures are unlikely to provide effective results.

THERE IS AN INDICATION OF DISCONTINUITY IN THE BASE PROFILE. STAR will not process the data further. Discontinuity is ordinarily caused by a change in conditions, which affects the relationship between the

variables. Examine the plot of residuals to identify the cause. Including an appropriate predicting variable in the model may eliminate the condition.

When any significant shift is detected in the relationships in the data between the most recent base year in a time series application and the previous base years (a discontinuity), STAR will not process the data further. If a discontinuity between base and projection profiles was identified in the prior year, the excesses then identified may assist in finding the cause of the discontinuity. If the reason for the change in relationships is identified, consider the following ways to eliminate the discontinuity.

- Introduce another predicting variable into the model.
- Discard the observations from the first period in the base profile.
- Disaggregate the observations into more homogeneous units.

Discontinuity may also be caused when the business relationship has been disrupted for a short period by, for example, a strike or special discount offer. In these situations, if the effect of the disruption can be quantified, adjust the observations to eliminate the effect (and validate the adjustments by appropriate auditing procedures). If the disruption and its effects are validated but cannot be quantified, introduce a dummy variable to compensate.

THERE IS AN INDICATION OF DISCONTINUITY BETWEEN BASE AND PROJECTION PROFILES. This type of discontinuity does not invalidate the model, but it may affect the differences to be audited. If it is not eliminated, it may result in invalid models in future years. Examine the plot of residuals to identify the cause.

If the relationships that applied in the base profile do not continue to apply in the projection profile, there are likely to be more than usual differences to be audited. Although this type of discontinuity does not invalidate the model (indeed, the reason for the discontinuity may be errors or unusual transactions in the audit period that STAR is intended to detect), one can try to identify the conditions causing the discontinuity and, if appropriate, eliminate them from the model and reprocess STAR.

THERE IS AN INDICATION OF AUTOCORRELATION IN THE BASE PROFILE. Generalized least squares regression will be used to correct for the

condition. Autocorrelation can often be attributed to a missing major factor and is evidenced by a pronounced pattern in the residuals. Examine the plot of residuals to identify the missing factor. Including that factor as a predicting variable may eliminate the condition and reduce the differences to be audited.

Autocorrelation occurs if there is a significant relationship between succeeding values of the residuals, such that the direction or size of the next residual can be predicted based on the preceding residuals. For example, in an inflationary economy, where costs are rising continuously but sales prices are adjusted only periodically, residuals in a model relating sales to cost of sales will tend to show a pronounced cyclical pattern, with runs of positive residuals followed by runs of negative residuals. STAR attempts to compensate for this condition by applying generalized least squares regression (rather than stepwise multiple regression) in which it includes a factor that compensates for the pattern. It is often possible to identify the factor that is the principal cause of the pattern (e.g., inflation) and to include it explicitly as a predicting variable.

FATAL AUTOCORRELATION. This model should not be used for audit purposes.

STAR is unable to compensate for the autocorrelation condition. The model is invalid.

THERE IS AN INDICATION OF HETEROSCEDASTICITY IN THE BASE PROFILE. Weighted least squares regression will be used to correct for the condition. Heteroscedasticity is evidenced by significant correlation between the size of the residuals and one of the predicting variables, in this case X_i. The model may be improved by identifying the cause of the heteroscedasticity and introducing appropriate predicting variables. This may also reduce the differences to be audited.

Heteroscedasticity is not uncommon in cross-sectional analyses in which there is a considerable range in operating system size. For example, in a cross-sectional analysis of a bank's payroll, in which payroll costs are related to factors such as branch headcount, residuals are likely to be larger for the larger branches and smaller for the smaller branches. STAR tests for heteroscedasticity and compensates for it by applying weighted least squares regression in which the significantly correlated predicting variable is used as a weighting factor in the calculations. In some cases (e.g., bank branches) heteroscedasticity can be avoided by stratifying the observations.

ABNORMALITY IN THE BASE PERIOD IS INDICATED BY

- LEFT SKEWNESS. This may be caused by large negative residuals
- RIGHT SKEWNESS. This may be caused by large positive residuals
- KURTOSIS. This may be caused by both large positive and large negative residuals

Abnormality does not invalidate the model, but it may affect the differences to be audited. Examine the plot of the residuals to identify the outliers and, if possible, eliminate the abnormality by correcting any errors or unusual events in those observations.

A basic regression assumption is that the values of the base data test variable will differ from their regression estimates by random factors and that the residuals will be normally distributed in a classic "bell curve." STAR tests this assumption and, if it does not hold up, indicates whether the problem is left skewness, right skewness, or kurtosis. Left skewness indicates that the mean of the distribution lies to the left of the mode (i.e., the peak). It is ordinarily caused by one or more large negative residuals. Right skewness indicates that the mean of the distribution lies to the right of the mode. It is ordinarily caused by one or more large positive residuals. Kurtosis indicates that the distribution is either unusually peaked or unusually flat, often caused by large residuals on both sides of the mean. STAR offsets abnormalities of this nature by adopting a conservative cutoff for the calculation of threshold.

INDEX